A Thoughtful Overview of Gifted Education

JUDY W. EBY
DE PAUL UNIVERSITY

JOAN F. SMUTNY
NATIONAL COLLEGE OF EDUCATION

Longman
New York & London

A Thoughtful Overview of Gifted Education

Longman 95 Church Street, White Plains, N.Y. 10601
A division of Addison-Wesley Publishing Co., Inc.

Associated companies:
Longman Group Ltd., London
Longman Cheshire Pty., Melbourne
Longman Paul Pty., Auckland
Copp Clark Pitman, Toronto

To all the bright, talented children and young people
around the world who deserve rich learning
opportunities in order to grow in thought and experience.

Photos on pages 1, 18, 140, from: Nancy Messman, teacher and
photographer, of Creative Children's Academy, a school for
the creatively talented and academically gifted, Mount Prospect,
Illinois.

Photos on pages 39, 60, 90, 115, 128, 163, 186, 205 from: Doris
Sanford, of Sanford Studios, Inc., Whittier California, Project '87,
Project '88, and Summer Wonders program pictures.

Executive editor: Naomi Silverman
Production editor: Camilla T. K. Palmer
Text design adaptation and cover design: Jill Francis Wood
Text art: K & S Graphics and Susan J. Moore
Production supervisor: Joanne Jay

Library of Congress Cataloging in Publication Data

Eby, Judy W.
    A thoughtful overview of gifted education   /   Judy W. Eby, Joan F.
Smutny.
        p.   cm.
    Bibliography: p.
    Includes index.
    ISBN 0-8013-0132-7
    1. Gifted children—Education. I. Smutny, Joan F. II. Title.
LC3993.E29   1989
371.9—dc19
                                                    89-30296
                                                    CIP

ABCDEFGHIJ-AL-99   98 97 96 95 94 93 92 91 90

Contents

Foreword

The authors of this book are very forthright in their approach. In gifted education texts this is quite unusual. Most such books either embrace a single point of view or take an "either-or" approach, arguing the advantages and disadvantages of two opposing points of view. For so long, we have been afraid of conflict, yet we have much evidence that disagreement improves a group, a school, a curriculum, a family, an aircrew, a discipline.

At or near the beginning of each chapter, we hear parents, teachers, or children expressing divergent opinions about the issues for that chapter. The divergent opinions expressed are real—you find them in every school, every community, every professional group. The authors deal with these differences creatively, citing their rich experiences, information, and research findings until they reach a satisfying conclusion.

Divergent views provide the motivation for creative thinking, and the behavioral variability involved in reactions to divergence provides the possibility of discovering a uniquely useful solution. Creativity may always have its roots in unconscious forces. This seems so contradictory to what we have been taught that we fail to believe that there are potentially positive, creative values in varying views and disagreement.

I stumbled upon my first insights about the creative and productive potentialities of divergent views and disagreement while involved in research dealing with the training of combat aircrews for survival in emergencies and extreme conditions. In decision-making experiments, I found that aircrews that experienced disagreements made superior decisions and excelled in problem solving. These crews also did better jobs of surviving in the realistically simulated situations of survival training. Furthermore, much to everyone's surprise, these crews compiled better combat records on almost every criteria of combat effectiveness than did their more agreeing, harmonious peers.

I think the presentation of conflicts in this book has the following facilitative effects:

1. Such varying approaches create feelings of uncertainty and curiosity. This, in turn, increases the reader's accuracy of observation, problem solving, and creativeness. Doubtless it had the same effect on the authors as they worked through the issues.

2. Posing these divergent opinions at the beginning of each chapter has forced the authors to enlarge their own data base and improve their perspective-taking skills.

3. I marvelled at the effect taking different perspectives had on me. It convinced me anew that this was a powerful strategy for increasing learning.

I agree with the authors when they say that gifted education may be at the crossroads. I join them in challenging the reader to join in the search for meaning and purpose of gifted education. Many gifted, talented, and creative people have contributed many innovative programs, methods, and practices and have tested them. Outside of gifted education these programs and ideas would not have had a chance of adoption and survival. Now that these programs and practices have succeeded, they may be adopted and flourish in the education of all children. All children may have a better chance to grow.

E. Paul Torrance
Athens, Georgia
August 2, 1988

Preface

This book is an attempt to provide an overview of the field of study of gifted education. The authors have been actively involved in the development of gifted programs for both public and private schools. Judy Eby has been a gifted program coordinator and teacher in two Illinois school districts from 1978 to 1985. She is presently an assistant professor of education at De Paul University in Chicago. Joan Smutny, editor of the Illinois Council for the Gifted Journal, teaches graduate courses in gifted education and directs the Center for Gifted at the National College of Education in Evanston, Illinois. She has initiated and directs a number of summer and weekend gifted programs for preprimary through high school students throughout the Chicago metropolitan area.

The point of view held and expressed by the authors can best be described as humanistic. Our educational psychology and philosophy is very closely allied to that of Abraham Maslow, who observed:

> Must we rest content with a definition of intelligence that is derived from what is the case, rather than what should be the case? The whole concept of IQ has nothing to do with wisdom; it is a purely technological concept. For example, Goering had a high IQ but was in a very real sense a stupid man. He was certainly a vicious man. I do not think there is any great harm in separating out the specific concept of high IQ. The only trouble is that in a psychology that limits itself so, the more important subjects—wisdom, knowledge, insight, understanding, common sense, good judgment—are neglected in favor of the IQ because it is technologically more satisfactory. For the humanist, of course, it is a highly irritating concept. (p. 285)[1]

In this book, then, we describe "what is the case": the prevailing notion of gifted education which, in our view, is more technological and mechanistic than humanistic, relying as it does upon definitions of giftedness in terms of IQ or achievement test scores. We then acquaint the reader with our vision of "what could be the case": a more humane and democratic approach to gifted education that defines giftedness in terms of a wide range of talents and gifted behaviors.

It is our aim, in this text, to provide parents, teachers, and administrators with a current knowledge base about this field of study. We also hope to generate diverse responses with provocative questions about the many issues involved in gifted education. We present a wide range of alternative procedures that can be used to establish a new gifted program or to redesign an existing program to meet the unique needs of a specific community. Finally, we present a comprehensive look at ways to evaluate a gifted program so that it continually grows and evolves into a flexible but consistent, and essentially humanistic, educational program for the benefit of its clients.

SPECIAL NOTE TO THE READER REGARDING USE OF THE TERM "GIFTED CHILD"

We have chosen to minimize the use of the term "gifted child" in this book, except in historical contexts or in citations of works written by other authors.

---

[1]Maslow, A. *Motivation and Personality*. Revised ed. New York: Harper & Row, 1970.

Our reason for this is that the term is not well defined and is used by people to mean different things. While some use it to mean a child with a special talent or gift in a wide variety of talent areas, others use it to mean a child with a certain IQ or other standardized test score.

Moreover, we believe that children themselves do not understand this term and are often confused by it. Children who are labeled "gifted" may feel set apart from their peers; they may feel guilt and fear when they don't live up to the label. While their parents may relish the label at first, they may find it difficult to explain to other children in the family. Such a label also causes enormous difficulties in school programs when either a child's performance or the criteria for selection change and the child's eligibility for the program changes. It is difficult to explain to parents why a child who was labeled "gifted" in an earlier grade or in a different school district isn't "gifted" anymore.

Finally, in our view, one effect of labeling a small minority of children "gifted" is that we are also unwittingly labeling the remaining children in the family or school "nongifted." For these reasons, we believe that an important aspect of planning for an appropriately challenging, healthy and supportive academically enriched or accelerated program is to eliminate the use of the label "gifted child." As you will read in this book, we suggest substituting terms which describe the particular talents or achievements of a child, such as "artistically talented" or "a student with unusual ability in math and science."

Judy W. Eby
Joan F. Smutny
July 10, 1988

CHAPTER 1

A Historical Overview of Gifted Education

Near the end of the school year four first grade teachers are meeting with Mrs. Elkin, the district's gifted consultant, to nominate students for the district's gifted program, which begins at the second grade. There are 100 first grade students. The gifted program, partially funded by the state, is designed to serve the top 5 percent of these students. As the discussion proceeds, different opinions are expressed about the nature of giftedness.

TEACHER A: I have brought my list of six nominees for the gifted program. They are all the students in my top reading group.

TEACHER B: Well, you're lucky. I don't have a single gifted child in my room this year. Some may be good in one area, but none of my students are gifted across the board.

TEACHER C: The three students I want to nominate are not necessarily in my top academic groups, but they are very energetic, creative kids with lots of ideas to share.

TEACHER D: Here's my list of 15 names. I think most of my students are gifted in something and deserve a chance to be in the program.

MRS. ELKIN: I'll look at these nominees, but they must all have achievement and ability tests to determine their final eligibility. The recommended students who score above the 95th percentile will be selected for the program.

TEACHER A: My students will do fine on those tests.

TEACHER B: I do have two students in my room with test scores in the 99th percentile, but I would never consider them for the program. They are showoffs and seldom finish the work I give them to do.

TEACHER C: My students will have difficulty scoring high enough on those tests to be in the program. But they ought to be in it. They ask for harder work, and they already write and produce their own plays.

TEACHER D: Those tests are biased and unfair. The kinds of activities you do in the gifted program are suitable for all kids, and I want my class included.

MRS. ELKIN: We have this discussion every year. It makes my job very difficult. I wish we could find a way to settle these issues once and for all.

TEACHER C: What are the district guidelines about selection?

TEACHER D: Yes, what is the district's definition of giftedness?

MRS. ELKIN: The district defines gifted children as those who demonstrate or have the potential to demonstrate above-average performance in academic or creative work.

TEACHER A: Well, my six students demonstrate above-average work in reading.

TEACHER B: And none of mine do, not even the two high scorers.

TEACHER C: Wait a minute, my three students are all way above average in creative work.

TEACHER D: And my 15 students all have the *potential* to demonstrate above-average work. They just need a program that will develop their potential.

These teachers are in conflict over the meaning of the terms ''giftedness'' or ''gifted children.'' Each teacher represents an opinion held by many educators. Some, like Teacher A, believe that gifted children are those who read early and have excellent comprehension skills. Others, like Teacher B, believe that to be gifted, a child must excel in all or many talent areas. Educators represented by Teacher C believe that creative children are gifted despite their average test scores. Still others, like Teacher D, believe that all children are potentially gifted and deserve equal opportunities for enriched programming.

Consider what would happen if these teachers switched classes. If Teacher A had the class assigned to Teacher B, would the top reading group in that class be nominated? Who would be recommended if Teacher C had Teacher B's class?

WHAT DO YOU THINK?

1. Which teacher best represents your point of view on this issue?
2. What are the difficulties faced by Mrs. Elkin?
3. In a school district, who should decide which children are selected for a gifted program?
4. What criteria should be used in the selection process?
5. If you were in Mrs. Elkin's position, what would you do next?

CAN WE DISTINGUISH BETWEEN ''GIFTED'' AND ''NONGIFTED'' CHILDREN?

Most definitions attempt to define or distinguish the ''gifted child'' from all other children. This is easy in some cases. There *are* children who stand out quite clearly from their peers. Some teach themselves to read at age 3, compute equations in their heads before kindergarten, and express such mature and abstract ideas about the nature of the world and human relations that adults are charmed and surprised.

In school, these readily identifiable children devour books and worksheets, asking for more and harder work, while others are just getting started with their assignments. Gifted programs with an academic emphasis were designed for children like these.

Other readily identifiable children amaze us with their prodigious accomplishments in talent areas such as art and music. These children need and deserve special opportunities in their talent fields in order to ensure that their special gifts are fully developed.

The difficulties emerge when schools attempt to identify gifted or talented children who are not quite so readily visible or apparent. It is believed that there are many children who have enormous undiscovered potential to develop valuable talents and gifts. Educators with a concern for their social welfare wish to identify and aid gifted children because of their importance as a national resource. Developmentalists wish to find and assist these children to reach their full potential in order to enhance the child's own quality of life.

Distinguishing potentially gifted children from the rest of the school population causes conflicts as illustrated at the beginning of this chapter. Teachers have differing opinions and values about giftedness. School districts and the communities they serve also have widely disparate values and attitudes about who is gifted. They seek help from state and federal agencies and they look to university researchers with expertise in gifted education to provide clear, usable definitions and procedures for identifying and serving their gifted students. They find, instead, that the policies are incomplete, the principles are conflicting, and that the experts disagree.

In 1972, a federal task force to study gifted education was formed and directed by the then U.S. Commissioner of Education, Sydney Marland, in response to a congressional mandate that gifted and talented children should benefit from federally legislated funds. The document produced by this committee became known as the Marland Report. It included the following definition:

> Gifted and Talented children are those identified by professionally qualified persons who by virtue of outstanding abilities, are capable of high performance. These are children who require differentiated educational programs and/or services beyond those normally provided by the regular school program in order to realize their contribution to self and society.
>
> Children capable of high performance include those with demonstrated achievement and/or potential ability in any of the following areas, singly or in combination:
> 1. general intellectual ability
> 2. specific academic aptitude
> 3. creative or productive thinking
> 4. leadership ability
> 5. visual and performing arts
> 6. psychomotor ability
>
> It can be assumed that utilization of these criteria for identification of the gifted and talented will encompass a minimum of 3 to 5 percent of the school population (Marland 1972, p. x)

In the decade that followed this report, many state offices of education and local educational agencies attempted to use this definition as the basis for identification procedures and program development. As a result, programs were developed with somewhat more uniform goals, but the identification procedures varied widely.

Consider the definition carefully. Each sentence appears to expand the conception of who is gifted and talented. It includes both children with "demonstrated achievement" and those with "potential ability" in any of the six designated categories. This definition clearly states that the population of gifted and talented children is expected to exceed a minimum of 3 to 5 percent of the school population, yet educational agencies around the country tend to interpret 5 percent as a maximum number of students served because of scarce resources.

The U.S. Congress altered the definition in the Marland Report several times in subsequent laws. In 1981, gifted and talented children were defined as:

> Children who give evidence of high performance capability in areas such as intellectual, creative, artistic, leadership capacity, or specific academic fields, and who require services or activities not ordinarily provided by the school in order to fully develop such capabilities. (P.L. 97-35, the Educational Consolidation and Improvement Act, 1981)

This statement is much more general than the Marland Report definition, but includes many of the same components. The category of psychomotor ability has been deleted because it was thought that existing sports programs meet the need for extracurricular offerings to develop such talents. The other five categories are maintained much as originally stated. The discussion of percentages of populations has also been deleted, leaving these decisions to local educational agencies.

THE CURRENT SCENE IN GIFTED EDUCATION

In the mid-1970s, school districts began to implement gifted programs based upon the Marland Report definition. A few attempted to serve children in all six talent categories, but most selected one or two categories as the basis for their programming. The most difficult task they faced was to locate appropriate ways of measuring each of the different abilities. The second most difficult dilemma was faced in terms of the numbers of children to be served. The definition implies that there should be six different strands to the program, each serving a percentage of the school population. But it was not clear whether each strand should include 3 to 5 percent of the school population or whether the total program should aim for that quota.

Local school districts looked to their state education agencies for funding and for guidelines for interpreting the Marland Report definition. The states that mandate or reimburse local districts for gifted programming interpreted the definition to mean that a program should contain a total of 5 percent of the school population. At least, they indicated that the state funding would be held to that level.

Many school districts complied by developing identification procedures that resulted in the selection of approximately 5 percent of their school populations. But there is wide variety in this matter. Some school districts provide substantial funding on their own and include many more than 5 percent of their populations in widely diversified gifted programs, while others limit the numbers to a strict percentage or quota.

After a decade of program initiatives in response to the Marland Report, a nationwide study was undertaken by the Sid W. Richardson Foundation to develop an accurate national picture of what is actually happening nationally in gifted programming. The methods, results, and recommendations of the Richardson Study are fully described in *Educating Able Learners* (Cox, Daniel, and Boston 1985).

Briefly, the Richardson Study discovered that gifted programs differ considerably in quality, in program offerings, in structure, and in identification procedures. Teacher recommendations, achievement tests, and IQ tests were the most frequently used means of identification, but criteria such as tests used and cutoff scores employed varied from school to school. The most typical program offering reported was a "part-time special class" for selected students that meets for part of the school day. But goals and objectives of these part-time special classes were diverse.

A HISTORICAL PERSPECTIVE

Throughout the history of civilization attempts have been made to select the most promising individuals and provide them with appropriately rich and challenging experiences to suit their talents. In historical perspective, the term "gifted" has been applied as an adjective to describe a specific type of talent or ability (e.g., Renoir was considered to be a gifted artist, Mozart a gifted musician, and Brontë a gifted writer). It was in twentieth-century America that the term "gifted" was used in a more general sense to describe "gifted children."

The Nature vs. Nurture Controversy

Events before this century and in other countries have contributed to the evolution of our ideas about the nature of giftedness. The most important and most hotly debated issue has been whether giftedness is a result of nature or of nurture; or, in modern terms, of heredity or environment. As you read the following history, note the interplay between the proponents of each side of the nature vs. nurture debate. Note especially that they all use the term "intelligence" but each defines the term quite differently. Read this material critically and analytically, identifying the ideas and theories that ring true with your own experience and values. Follow up on the references provided in the text to find out more about the specifics on each side of the issue, for this is an unfinished debate, and you may be called upon to add your own opinion to the fray at some point in your career.

Charles Darwin (1859) may have started this long-lasting debate by asserting that some individuals were the "fittest" or most superior of each species. In the late 1800s Darwin's cousin, Sir Francis Galton, focused his own study of intelligence upon similar assumptions and came to the conclusion that intelligence is wholly determined by heredity. Galton described intelligence as a function of sensory acuity because he believed that "the only information that reaches us concerning outward events appears to pass through the avenue of our senses; and the more perceptible our senses are of difference, the larger the field upon which our judgment and intellect can act" (1907, p. 19). He defended his position in his study of the hereditary links among eminent men of his time, which he described in his influential book, *Hereditary Genius* (1972; originally published in 1869). Galton's work was unchallenged for many years and led to a firmly established belief that an individual's intelligence is genetically determined at birth.

A French psychologist, Alfred Binet, offered the first significant counterargument to this view. He believed that intelligence was "educable" (1969). His most significant contribution to the field was a scale or test that he devised to distinguish between normal and "dull" students in Parisian schools. It is important to note that this scale was not developed to identify bright children, but only to identify the dull students in the Parisian school system.

After considering many sorts of measures, Binet inductively established a series of 30 practical tasks and ranked them in order of increasing difficulty. The scale included such tasks as following a lighted match with one's eyes, unwrapping and eating a piece of candy, tying shoe laces, identifying a 4-cm line as longer than a 3-cm line, naming the points of a compass, and recalling digits and sentences. These tasks reflected Binet's conception of intelligence as the use of a variety of mental functions such as attention, memory, and discrimination accompanied by practical judgment or good sense (Fancher 1985, p. 74). On the basis of experimentation (using his own children as part of the norming sample), Binet determined the "mental age" at which most children could accomplish each task. He was then able to compare the responses of an unknown test subject with his scale and determine whether the subject was in the normal or dull range of human intelligence.

Binet believed that with appropriate education or training, an individual could learn to accomplish these tasks and thus raise his or her "mental age." But despite Binet's strongly held view that intelligence is developed as a result of environmental influences, his scale became the basis of the most widely accepted theory of hereditary and fixed intelligence in the twentieth century.

This turnabout occurred after Binet's death and in the following manner. Louis Terman, an American teacher and principal, was interested in studying the differences between bright and dull children. At Clark University in the early 1900s, he studied for his Ph.D. under G. Stanley Hall, who had been a student of Sir Francis Galton. Galton's theory of hereditary genius influenced Terman, who became a strong proponent of this point of view.

After graduating in 1905, Terman went to work at Stanford University. In 1910, he acquired English translations of Binet's scales for research purposes. He adapted and altered the Binet tasks to fit American subjects, and named the new scale the Stanford Revision of the Binet Scale, which soon became known as the Stanford-Binet Intelligence Test.

In 1916, Terman incorporated a new method of calculating the score on the test, by calculating the ratio between the mental and chronological age and multiplying the result by 100 to get rid of decimals. The resulting "Intelligence Quotient" or IQ is represented by the following formula:

$$IQ = \frac{\text{Mental age}}{\text{Chronological age}} \times 100$$

Terman's intelligence test and method of scoring was rapidly and widely accepted as the best measure of intelligence available throughout the United States. It was so well respected that, as other tests were developed, they were validated by correlating them with the Stanford-Binet. Terman was a highly respected and prominent psychologist throughout his long career, and is one of the most highly regarded contributors to the field of gifted education as well.

Studies of Gifted Children

Terman believed that the Stanford-Binet test measures innate, unchanging ability or aptitude, and that youngsters who scored well on his test would become the future leaders of our society. Based on his research and norming studies, he concluded that a score of 130 and above is a mark of "giftedness," while an IQ of 150 and above signifies "genius" (Feldman 1979, p. 660).

To investigate whether intellectually precocious children grow up to be eminent, Terman initiated one of the longest and largest longitudinal studies ever undertaken. In the early 1920s, Terman and his associates tested California schoolchildren to find a sample of 1500 boys and girls with IQs above 140. Background data were collected, and follow-up studies were conducted by Terman himself in 1929, 1950, and 1955, and after his death by his associates in 1960 and 1972.

Ninety percent of the sample entered college and 70 percent graduated. In 1960, at the height of their professional lives, it was determined that *on the average,* the Termites, as they jokingly refer to themselves, have led generally satisfying and successful lives. A high proportion of them achieved distinction in their careers in science, law, banking, and business. The 800 men in the sample had published 67 books, over 1400 scientific journal articles, and over 200 short stories and plays. They had more than 150 patents to their credit. The sample contains one noted science-fiction author, an Oscar-winning motion picture director, and some department heads at universities (Fancher 1985, p. 144).

The women in the study who had careers outside the home achieved more than a chance share of professional citations and awards. The majority of the women, however, became housewives and reported that they suffered acutely from lack of intellectual fulfillment in their lives.

In assessing Terman's work and his contribution to the field of gifted education, Morris Stein (1986) notes that "Terman's motivation, determination, and persistence in following his subjects and the quality of contact he maintained with them is most impressive. In this regard, Terman is a model to be emulated" (p. xxi). But Stein also points out that the samples in the study were not randomly selected, but were all children of middle-class Caucasian families. This significant fact leads to a debate about whether the Stanford-Binet and other similar tests are biased against economically disadvantaged and culturally different children.

Guilford's Structure of the Intellect

The Stanford-Binet Intelligence Test filled a vacuum in the testing of individual differences in ability. A single number, the IQ score, was thought by many to define an individual's intelligence better than any other means available. But in the 1930s, University of Chicago psychologist L. L. Thurstone challenged the single-score concept of intelligence. In his view, the IQ score was useful in predicting verbal academic achievement, but failed to predict success in other, less verbal and less academic endeavors. Thurstone proposed instead that intelligence consists of seven distinct "Primary Mental Abilities," which he called Verbal Comprehension, Word Fluency, Number Facility, Spatial Visualization, Associative Memory, Perceptual Speed, and Reasoning. He believed that each of these factors represents a largely independent aspect of intelligence, and that Terman's IQ score is merely a composite or average (Thurstone 1938; Thurstone and Thurstone 1954).

California psychologist J. P. Guilford expanded upon Thurstone's notion and described a three-dimensional "Structure of the Intellect" model of intelligence that consists of 120 separate elements or basic factors of intelligence. Guilford was motivated to investigate the nature of intelligence by his observation that an individual is uneven in his or her abilities, showing a range of strengths and weaknesses rather than one general ability level in all areas as the single score IQ implies. Using the research method of factor analysis, which was unknown to Terman and Thurstone, he was able to differentiate and classify 80 distinct factors of intelligence, and further predicted that 120 factors could be accounted for by his structure-of-intellect (SOI) theory (1967, p. 35).

Guilford was highly critical of Terman's work because it was not guided by a scientific theory of intelligence, but was simply a practical adaptation of Binet's scale. He believed that the SOI model would allow greater understanding of the nature of individual differences than the more general IQ. Paradoxically, while Guilford criticized Terman's concept of intelligence for being too general, others criticize Guilford's SOI model for being too specific. "These many factors, they argue, made the structure of the intellect meaningless" (Stein 1986, p. xxiv). In practice, the Structure of Intellect Test is very difficult and time consuming to administer, score, and interpret.

The intelligence test that is currently the most widely used in educational and psychological assessments of children is the Wechsler Intelligence Scale for Children—Revised Edition (WISC-R). Developed by psychologist David Wechsler, the WISC-R reports two independent scores of intelligence: one for Verbal Ability (the composite score of six verbal subtests) and the other for Performance Ability (a composite of six performance tasks). While the verbal score on the WISC-R correlates quite highly with the Stanford-Binet IQ, the performance score is designed to measure a different, less verbal, set of abilities that may be useful in the assessment of individuals with cultural or language deficiencies (Wechsler 1974).

Current Views of Intelligence

In the 1980s, two new theories of intelligence were proposed and studied by Howard Gardner at Harvard University and Robert Sternberg at Yale University. These theories are broader in scope than Terman's and Wechsler's, but much more condensed than Guilford's. Gardner (1983) describes several relatively autonomous human intelligences, each of which has its own unique language, symbols, and processes.

In Gardner's view, *linguistic intelligence* involves oral and auditory abilities and results in oral and written expression. *Musical intelligence* is also auditory and results in the composition and performance of music. *Logical-mathematical intelligence* involves the "ability to handle skillfully long chains of reasoning" (p. 139). *Spatial intelligence* demands visual-spatial acuity and results in contributions to art as well as to science in fields that require accurate visual memories or projections. *Bodily-kinesthetic intelligence* requires ability to use action and movement to accomplish a feat of strength and/or grace in sports or the arts.

Gardner also describes two forms of personal intelligence: *intrapersonal intelligence,* which involves a high degree of self-knowledge and understanding, and *interpersonal intelligence,* which connotes an ability to lead, understand, and empathize with others.

In Gardner's view of intelligence, each individual has relative strengths and weaknesses among the various types of intelligence, resulting in a unique profile of these multiple intelligences. While some individuals may show relatively high ability in several intelligences, other individuals may demonstrate high ability in only one area. This theory explains the unique collection of numbers and types of abilities demonstrated by individuals with similar IQ scores.

Sternberg's (1985) triarchic definition of intelligence has grown out of his background and interest in understanding cognition in terms of information processing. He believes that previous theories of intelligence fail to explain the interaction between an individual and the real world. He criticizes earlier theories because they attempt to describe and assess intelligent behavior in terms of a response to an item on a test that is unconnected to the individual's real-life experience. Sternberg proposes that

> intelligent behavior is ultimately behavior that involves adaptation to, selection of, or shaping of people's real-world environments. Adaptation occurs when a person attempts to achieve a "good fit" with the environment he or she is in. Selection occurs when a person decides to find a new environment rather than to adapt to the one he or she is in (such a decision might be motivated by a decision that the present environment is morally reprehensible, or is unsuitable for one's talents or interests, and so on). Shaping of the environment occurs when a person cannot find (select) an environment that seems suitable. In this case, the person makes changes in the environment he or she is in, in order to improve its fit with his or her abilities, interests, values, etc., capitalize on his or her strengths, and compensate for his or her weaknesses. (p. 18)

At present, both Gardner and Sternberg are working to create and validate suitable assessment devices that fit their views of intelligence. It is obvious that traditional testing procedures are unsuitable to either theory. Consider the problems these researchers face. How would you go about creating a test of Gardner's multiple intelligences? What situations would you employ to assess Sternberg's adaptation, selection, and shaping abilities?

Gardner is working with a colleague, David Feldman at Tufts University, to conduct a four-year research project on the assessment of multiple intelligences. Called Project Spectrum, this study is subsidized by the Spencer Foundation. Gardner and Feldman are attempting to devise new means of assessing the "intellectual proclivities of preschool children" by presenting them with "tasks, games and environments whereby these abilities can unobtrusively be assessed" (1986, p. 3). Educational Testing Service (ETS), which publishes the Scholastic Aptitude Test (SAT), is also supporting Gardner's and Feldman's efforts to validate a new means of assessing talents in different domains.

Robert Sternberg, in cooperation with Psychological Corporation, the publisher of the Wechsler IQ test, is also working to develop a new test of practical intelligence.

He is interested in assessing an individual's reactions to novel situations requiring insight such as the following: If you have black socks and brown socks in your drawer, mixed in a 4 to 5 ratio, how many socks must you take out to ensure getting a pair the same color?

The Developmental View of Giftedness

The nature vs. nurture controversy continues to be debated among scientists and educators. While Terman and others of his era held the view that intelligence and giftedness were fixed and innate human traits, developmentalists suggest that the child's environment has a great influence upon the development of his or her talents and abilities.

> Differing from trait views, the developmental view sees each child as proceeding through several sets of stages, each stage succeeding the one before it. . . . Because the developmental framework emphasizes progress within specific fields or domains of knowledge, it leads to selection criteria and program features directly related to particular kinds of excellence. (Feldman 1979, p. 662)

A psychologist specializing in child development, David Feldman has embarked upon a longitudinal study of children known as "prodigies" in several talent fields. He defines a prodigy as a person who performs at a very early age, at or near the level of a professional in a given talent area.

Feldman's study of this group indicates that neither IQ nor ancestry can predict prodigiousness. Instead, he believes that prodigies are developed as a result of a "coincidence" (1984, p. 26). There must be a match or conflux of an unusual talent combined with a nurturing environment and excellent teaching. In support of this view, Feldman points out that the number of prodigies in any one field or talent tend to coincide in one place at one time in history. He cites the great Elizabethan writers and the musical geniuses of eighteenth- and nineteenth-century Vienna. For genius to occur "all of the things that go into it must coincide at exactly the right time, in exactly the right place under exactly the right conditions. There has to be a cultural preparation and an appreciative audience" (MacLeish 1984, p. 78).

Benjamin S. Bloom is another developmentalist who believes that the environment, especially the home environment, is the critical factor in the development of talent. In the early 1980s, Bloom initiated an extensive study of the lives of 120 young adults who had achieved the highest levels of achievement possible in their fields. The subjects of the study included concert pianists, sculptors, research mathematicians, research neurologists, Olympic swimmers, and world-class tennis champions. In all six of these fields, Bloom found that "a long and intensive process of encouragement, nurturance, education and training" was experienced by all subjects (1985, p. 3).

Developmentalists like Feldman and Bloom do not suggest that ability or personality characteristics are not important, but they believe that the environment is the deciding factor in the matter, that an encouraging, nurturing environment is the developmental bridge between potential and actual accomplishment.

Personality Characteristics Associated with Giftedness

The construct of intelligence is an important component of the construct of giftedness, but the two are not synonymous. Terman equated giftedness with high IQ in his earliest writings, but as a result of his longitudinal studies of individuals who had IQs above 140, he concluded that personality factors were extremely important determiners of achievement. The four traits displayed by the highest achievers in his study were labeled (1) persistence in the accomplishment of ends, (2) integration toward goals, (3) self-confidence, and (4) freedom from inferiority feelings (Terman and Oden 1947).

Other researchers have studied the personality traits of highly creative productive adults. Roe (1952) conducted an intensive study of the characteristics of 64 eminent scientists and found that they were all highly autonomous and self-directed. Bloom's (1985) study of individuals who reached the top of their fields in six talent areas in the arts, sports, and cognitive fields led him to conclude that all 150 subjects were characterized by an unusually strong willingness to work and all had made achievement in their talent field a top priority in their lives.

Guilford (1967) and Torrance (1969) believe that creativity is an important component of giftedness. Renzulli (1978) agrees that ability and creativity are essential components of giftedness, but also proposes task commitment as a third essential trait:

> . . . although no single criterion should be used to identify giftedness, persons who have achieved recognition because of their unique accomplishments and creative contributions possess a relatively well-defined set of three interlocking clusters of traits. These clusters consist of above average, though not necessarily superior, general ability, task commitment and creativity. It is important to point out that no single cluster "makes giftedness." Rather it is the interaction among the three clusters that research has shown to be the necessary ingredient for creative/productive accomplishment. (p. 182)

Renzulli's definition of giftedness is graphically represented in Figure 1.1. This definition has been adopted by many gifted specialists who believe that the three traits provide a balanced and defendable basis for selecting students for gifted programming. They use a combination of measurement devices to assess a student's ability, creativity, and task commitment. Renzulli's definition also serves as the basis for decisions regarding planning and selecting programming alternatives. He proposes a Triad Enrichment Model of programming that makes use of and encourages the development of a student's ability, creativity, and task commitment.

While Renzulli's definition of giftedness is comprehensive and useful, there is still work to be done in our field to create an *operational definition* of giftedness. Operational definitions are essential in research because they form the link between theory and practice. "There can be no scientific research without observations, and observations are impossible without clear and specific instructions on what and how to observe" (Kerlinger 1973, p. 32). An operational definition of giftedness would specify the activities or behaviors that can be observed in individuals who are "acting" or "behaving" gifted.

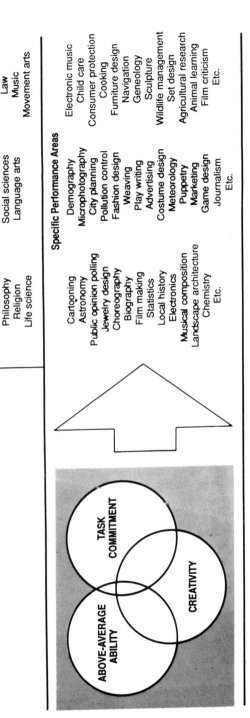

General Performance Areas

Mathematics	Visual arts	Physical sciences
Philosophy	Social sciences	Law
Religion	Language arts	Music
Life science		Movement arts

Specific Performance Areas

Cartooning	Demography	Electronic music
Astronomy	Microphotography	Child care
Public opinion polling	City planning	Consumer protection
Jewelry design	Pollution control	Cooking
Choreography	Fashion design	Furniture design
Biography	Weaving	Navigation
Film making	Play writing	Geneology
Statistics	Advertising	Sculpture
Local history	Costume design	Wildlife management
Electronics	Meteorology	Set design
Musical composition	Puppetry	Agricultural research
Landscape architecture	Marketing	Animal learning
Chemistry	Game design	Film criticism
Etc.	Journalism	Etc.
	Etc.	

ABOVE-AVERAGE ABILITY

TASK COMMITMENT

CREATIVITY

Figure 1.1. A Graphic Representation of Renzulli's Definition of Giftedness (The arrow should be read as "brought to bear upon . . ."). Reprinted with permission of Joseph Renzulli.

Gifted Behavior

Renzulli used the term "gifted behavior" to distinguish between potential and actual productivity. In the preface to *The Revolving Door Identification Model,* he states that ". . . being a good test taker or lesson-learner does not necessarily guarantee that a child will display gifted behavior in the creative and productive sense of the term" (p. xi).

In an effort to create an operational definition of gifted behavior, Judy Eby (1986) reviewed the research done on behaviors and characteristics of individuals who have been unusually creative and productive in their chosen talent fields. She synthesized an operational definition of giftedness in terms of ten observable behaviors employed by these individuals as they initiate, create, evaluate, complete, and disseminate original products or contributions in their talent fields. The ten behaviors are described in Chapter 5. The Eby Gifted Behavior Index, a set of instruments designed to assess the development of these behaviors, is included in Chapter 4.

To validate the instruments and the definition itself, Eby conducted six studies in elementary schools, high schools, and colleges to determine the extent to which these behaviors were exhibited by young people as they worked on original products in writing and art. It was hypothesized that a direct relationship would be found between the extent to which the behaviors were used and the quality and originality of the resulting products. The behaviors were observed and rated by the students' classroom teachers, while the products were independently evaluated by outside judges of art and writing contests who did not know the students or their work.

The results of these studies confirmed the hypothesis. Taken together, the six studies showed a positive correlation of $+.46$ between the demonstration of gifted behaviors and the quality and originality of the resulting products. In other words, these ten "gifted behaviors" explain approximately 25 percent of the variance noted in the quality and originality of the students' products.

Implications of this study suggest that while relatively stable components of general ability and personality characteristics are important determiners of giftedness, alterable behaviors are also important aspects of giftedness.

ARTICULATING A DEFINITION OF GIFTEDNESS

The nature of intelligence and giftedness are enormously complex constructs. Until the twentieth century, researchers described them in rather simple ways, related to sensory inputs or even bumps on the head. Binet and Terman described intelligence as a quotient of correct responses to a series of test items related to mental age. Guilford objected to the notion of a single score describing intelligence. He proposed 120 separate elements or factors of intelligence. Gardner and Feldman are currently describing different domains of intelligence, while Sternberg describes intelligence as a set of practical reactions to one's environment.

Each of these researchers has developed, or is developing, his own test of intelligence to fit his own theory. At present there is no single expert or prevailing theory on which to rely. As you enter the field of gifted education, you must expect ambiguity and diversity of opinions. While you may find the ambiguity to be a difficult and frustrating experience, you may also find that the unsettled questions and problems provide stimuli for creative, innovative responses on your part. If you enter the field with inquisitiveness and a willingness to delve deeply into the controversies, you may find yourself involved in an experience or investigation that contributes greatly to the field.

As you take your role as an educator in gifted education, you will find the number and complexity of choices and decisions overwhelming at times. In order to be able to make sound choices, it is vital to establish a well-clarified definition of giftedness and philosophy of gifted education at the district level. You may adopt a definition created by Guilford, Renzulli, Eby, Sternberg, Gardner, or another researcher in the field, but it is more likely that you will synthesize your own unique definition of giftedness to fit the special needs of the community you serve. In either case, you will find that a clear, unambiguous, operational definition will give you greater confidence in the complex tasks and decisions you will be called upon to make.

Your definition will serve as criteria to select appropriate tests or other assessment procedures for identification. It will also serve as the basis for selecting alternatives in programming, and will provide you with a basis for evaluating the program you develop. When identification, program alternatives, and evaluation procedures are congruent with a well-clarified statement of definition and philosophy, the program goals and accomplishments can be readily communicated to the entire school community.

OPPORTUNITIES FOR DISCUSSION AND ACTION

Opportunities will be presented throughout this text to enable you to clarify and articulate your own philosophy and definitions in gifted education. As a beginning, work with your classmates to brainstorm a list of gifted characteristics and behaviors. You may wish to use the procedure described below.

1.   What is giftedness? Take a few quiet minutes in class for each person to write down on paper the behaviors and characteristics that he or she feels are important determiners of giftedness.
2.   List all these elements (behaviors and characteristics) on the blackboard or on an overhead projector.
3.   Discuss the following questions:
     a.   Which of these elements are easy to spot in children?
     b.   Which are usually hidden?
     c.   Are some elements generally agreed upon by the whole group?
     d.   Does that make them true or valid?
     e.   Which ones are supported by experts' opinions or research?
     f.   Does that make them true or valid?
     g.   What makes a person an expert in gifted education?

    h. How do we account for the fact that the experts disagree?

    i. How can you synthesize your values and observations with those of the experts to create your own district definition?

    j. How many such elements does one need to be gifted?

    k. To what degree is an element needed?

4. After this discussion, each person may write down the elements from the group's list that appear to be most fitting and useful in his or her own district or setting. Try to create some hierarchy or order in the elements you select. Keep this initial list throughout the course. Observe the changes you make in this list of elements as you learn more about the many aspects of giftedness in the next few weeks.

REFERENCES

Binet, A. 1969. The education of intelligence. In *Issues and advances in educational psychology,* ed. P. Torrance and W. White. Itasca, Ill.: F. E. Peacock.

———, and T. Simon. 1973. *The development of intelligence in children (the Binet-Simon Scale).* New York: Arno Press.

Bloom, B., ed. 1985. *Developing talent in young people.* New York: Ballantine.

Cox, J., N. Daniel, and B. Boston. 1985. *Educating able learners.* Austin, Tex.: University of Texas Press.

Darwin, C. 1859. *On the origin of species.* London: Murray.

Eby, J. 1986. *The relationship between gifted behavioral processes observed in students and the quality and originality of the products they created.* Ann Arbor, Mich.: University Microfilms.

———. 1989. *Eby Gifted Behavior Index.* Aurora, N.Y.: D.O.K. Publishers.

Fancher, R. 1985. *The intelligence men: Makers of the IQ controversy.* New York: W. W. Norton.

Feldman, D. 1979. Toward a nonelitist conception of giftedness, *Phi Delta Kappan* 60:660–63.

———. 1984. Giftedness as a developmentalist sees it. In *Conceptions of giftedness,* ed. R. Sternberg and J. Davidson. New York: Cambridge University Press.

Galton, F. 1907. *Inquiries into human faculty and its development.* New York: Dutton.

———. 1972. *Hereditary genius.* Gloucester, Mass.: Peter Smith.

Gardner, H. 1983. *Frames of mind.* New York: Basic Books.

———, and D. Feldman. 1986. *Second annual report to the Spencer Foundation on Project Spectrum.* Cambridge, Mass.: Harvard University Press.

Guilford, J. P. 1967. *The nature of human intelligence.* New York: McGraw-Hill.

Kerlinger, F. 1973. *Foundations of behavioral research,* 2nd ed. New York: Holt, Rinehart & Winston.

MacLeish, R. 1984. Gifted by nature, prodigies are still mysteries to man, *Smithsonian* 14: 70–74.

Marland, S. *Education of the gifted and talented.* Vol. 1. Report to the Congress of the United States by the U.S. Commissioner of Education. Washington, D.C.: U.S. Government Printing Office.

Renzulli, J. 1978. What makes giftedness? *Phi Delta Kappan* 60: 180–84.

———. 1981. *The revolving door identification model.* Mansfield Center, Conn.: Creative Learning Press.

Roe, A. 1952. *The making of a scientist.* New York: Dodd, Mead.

Sharp, E. 1972. *The IQ cult.* New York: Coward, McCann & Geoghegan.

Stein, M. 1986. *Gifted, talented, and creative young people: Studies in excellence.* Vol. 1. New York: Garland.

Sternberg, R. 1984. Toward a triarchic theory of human intelligence, *Behavioral and Brain Sciences* 7: 269–87.

———. 1985. *Human abilities: An information processing approach.* New York: W. H. Freeman.

Terman, L., and M. Oden. 1947. *Genetic studies of genius: The gifted child grows up.* Stanford, Calif.: Stanford University Press.

Thurstone, L. L. 1938. *Primary mental abilities.* Psychometric Monograph No. 1.

———, and T. G. Thurstone. 1954. *SRA primary mental abilities technical supplement.* Chicago: Science Research Associates.

Torrance, E. P. 1969. *Creativity.* Belmont, Calif.: Dimensions.

Wechsler, D. 1974. *Wechsler intelligence scale for children—revised.* New York: Psychological Corporation.

CHAPTER 2

The Physical and Psychosocial Aspects of Giftedness

A group of prospective parents in a childbirth class are discussing a current topic: the intelligence of their unborn children.

PARENT A: Every night for the past few weeks I've been reading aloud to my unborn baby so that he'll be an early reader and do well in school.

PARENT B: That's ridiculous! There's a time for everything, but infants shouldn't be forced to learn how to read. Babies should be babies.

PARENT C: I think the best thing we can do for our babies' development is to eat food that will build healthy brain cells, like protein and minerals.

PARENT D: I don't think we can do anything to change our baby's intelligence now. It was decided at conception. I know that my wife and I both have high IQs, so we can assume that our child will, too.

PARENT A: Well, our family are all high achievers, but we want our child to do even better than we have in school. Our goal is to have the child reading by age 3 and we have already enrolled him in a private school for kindergarten.

PARENT B: Yes, well, your child may end up in a psychiatry ward instead if you put so much pressure on him at such an early age. It's important to encourage a child, but some expectations can be so high that they backfire.

PARENT C: What I think is strange is that you sit there smoking that cigarette while you are pregnant. How can you expect your child to be brilliant if you're killing his brain cells with nicotine?

PARENT D: Cigarettes, reading aloud, none of that matters one bit. Geniuses are born, not made.

WHAT DO YOU THINK?

1. Which parent best expresses your point of view?
2. Do you believe that genetics determines intelligence?
3. How much does prenatal or early childhood nutrition matter?
4. What are the effects of parental expectations on children?
5. What kind of experiences could raise a child's intelligence?

INTRODUCTION

Genetics, brain growth, early experiences, nutrition—how does each contribute to our potential and our actual performance? Foster (1986) notes that at present there are two prevailing explanatory models of giftedness: endowment and development. In the endowment model, "Giftedness is understood to be synonymous with either or both a divine or biological intervention in the form of a qualitative endowment in individual lives," while in the development model, "The qualitatively different individual is defined through the realization of a life of outstanding innovation and production" (p. 15).

The debate over these two models is especially important in the field of gifted education because of its impact on identification procedures and the establishment of programming goals. Those educators who believe that giftedness is genetically determined look for tests and assessment devices that will allow them to discover or "identify" the gifted or talented children among the general population. Their programming goals are usually a combination of acceleration and enrichment designed to serve the special needs of this special population.

Those educators who believe that giftedness is a developmental phenomenon, and therefore greatly influenced by environmental stimulation and expectations, strive to provide enriched opportunities to the entire school population in order to develop the talents and intelligence of as many students as possible. Children who demonstrate great interest, commitment, or ability in a certain talent field are offered special support and encouragement to develop their giftedness in their chosen interest area or domain.

As you enter the field of gifted education, you may find yourself involved in this debate. This chapter will attempt to provide you with information about both views of giftedness. At the end of the chapter, the authors' own point of view will be presented, but you are encouraged to consider the issues in terms of your own experience, philosophy, and values. There is no one right answer to this issue. The thoughtful educator will analyze the arguments carefully and synthesize his or her own point of view on the matter.

GENETICALLY PREDETERMINED ABILITY

The earliest theories and speculations centered on the endowment argument. It has been generally accepted for several centuries that talents are gifts from God. But the first scientific support for this view came when Darwin theorized that favorable inheritable variations in each species were retained over generations while unfavorable variations decreased. In *On the Origin of Species* he proposed that evolution was a result of physical characteristics being transmitted from parent to offspring. Although Darwin's work did not refer to human beings, his English cousin, Francis Galton, inferred from Darwin's work that human intelligence was inheritable too, based upon individual variations in the brain and nervous system.

To provide evidence that intellectual ability is inherited, Galton compared the abilities of various ethnic groups in the late 1800s. He argued that Americans provided evidence of the heritability theory. Despite the fact that Americans were exposed to a more open educational system than the British, Galton concluded that America had failed to produce many people of genuine intellectual distinction and were "largely impervious to environmental or educational manipulation" (quoted in Fancher 1985, p. 30).

Galton is credited with designing the first *statistical* study of the issue. He selected a representative sample of people who had achieved sufficient eminence in their lives to be listed in biographical dictionaries. According to his calculations these subjects represented a proportion of one person in 4000 from the normal population. He then researched the family trees of each subject and discovered that approximately 10 percent of them had at least one other relative who was also listed in the biographical dictionaries, many in the same or similar fields. For example, James and John Stuart Mill were both listed as "literary men," while Galton and his cousin Darwin were both "men of science" (Fancher 1985, p. 31). Galton concluded from this study that particular abilities ran in families or were inherited. His book on the subject, *Hereditary Genius,* published in 1869, was widely respected and influential for the next half century.

Probably the most reliable method of studying genetic endowments is through the comparison of twins. Galton is credited with undertaking the first study of twins to shed light upon the heritability issue. He observed that identical twins shared similar physical and psychological characteristics more than fraternal twins did, which led him to conclude that "There is no escape from the conclusion that nature prevails enormously over nurture . . ." because of the identical twins' remarkable similarities (quoted in Fancher 1985, p. 34).

Galton's endowment viewpoint was supported during the next several decades by Charles Spearman and Cyril Burt. Spearman theorized that there exists a stable general intelligence factor (which he termed the g factor) in every individual. The g factor, if it could be measured, would indicate an individual's innate brain power.

Burt conducted studies of twins and reported IQ correlations of $+.86$ for 62 pairs of twins reared together and $+.77$ for 15 pairs of twins reared apart. Burt interpreted these studies to mean that intelligence was highly heritable and followed ordinary genetic laws. Summarizing from many studies of twins, Burt concluded that 80 percent of one's intelligence was determined by genetic factors. In recent years there have been very serious questions raised about Burt's research methodologies. It now appears that the studies may have been invalid. But for many years Burt's twin studies were held in great esteem.

The most prominent American researcher to be associated with the endowment explanation of ability is Louis Terman, who developed the first widely accepted and used test of intelligence and coined the term "IQ" in the early 1900s. Terman was greatly influenced by Galton's theories of heritability and believed that his Stanford-Binet IQ test measured a constant and innate genetic quality. He undertook a lifelong longitudinal study of over 1000 children with IQs above 140, and published book-length reports of the study entitled *Genetic Studies of Genius.* Terman and his colleagues reported that the subjects of this study had considerable stability of IQ throughout their lives. He also reported that their superiority of intelligence was maintained as well by those subjects who did not attend college as it was by Ph.D. candidates (Stanley 1977, p. 14).

Terman's theories were implemented in education through the widespread use of his individual IQ test, and subsequent group tests of ability normed against the Stanford-Binet. IQ testing makes it possible for educators to identify the intellectually gifted child in ways that are considered to be far superior to teacher nomination. Intelligence tests are also highly regarded by many educators because the relatively objective scores may be used to document selection decisions in gifted programs. When resources are limited and competition is a factor, documentation of identification procedures becomes very important.

A most controversial proponent of the endowment viewpoint is University of

California researcher Arthur Jensen. He argued, as did Spearman, that there must be a general factor of intelligence, and that IQ tests were the best means of measuring this factor. Jensen analyzed the distribution of IQ scores among different racial groups and found that average score for black people was about one standard deviation (15 points) below the white average. Since he believed that genetics rather than environment accounted for this difference among the races, he concluded that compensatory education for racial minorities was misguided because "genetic factors are strongly implicated in the average Negro-white intelligence differences" (Jensen 1969, p. 82).

While Jensen's argument was not intended to be overtly racist, it sparked a significant debate among psychologists and educators as well as among civil rights activists, who challenged the ways in which IQ tests were created and normed. Citing cultural bias as an overlooked but significant factor in IQ test results, opponents of Jensen's ideas raised serious questions about the objectivity of intelligence tests. In hindsight, it now appears that Jensen's argument provoked such a significant counterresponse that the "nurture" viewpoint gained influence and respect among educators and the general public while the "nature" viewpoint lost ground as a result.

ENVIRONMENTAL EXPERIENCES

Alfred Binet, the French psychologist credited with developing the concept of mental age, created a scale and a set of tasks that were used to determine whether young children were mentally fit for schoolwork. Philosophically, Binet believed that the tasks could be learned if the child was given sufficient experience and practice in carrying them out. In other words, Binet was an early proponent of the nurture or developmental point of view. He believed that mental ability was a function of judgment and common sense, both of which could be influenced by educational experiences.

An early proponent of the nurture point of view was Maria Montessori whose educational theory was translated into action by her establishment of preschools with environments rich in stimulation and high expectations. Montessori believed that education begins at birth and that the first few years of life are the most formative. She observed that children are ready and eager for stimulation, but that if the environment is lacking in stimulation, the child becomes apathetic—a condition that may last throughout his lifetime.

Montessori's educational program centers on a stimulating environment full of materials, toys, and objects that children enjoy. The child is given freedom to make guided choices and decisions about what to play or work with, but must complete each task before going on to another activity. In this way, Montessori believed that the child would develop behavior patterns of independence and responsibility at an early age that would subsequently become stable traits of the child's adult personality.

J. McVicker Hunt (1961) reexamined many earlier studies and claims of fixed intelligence. He cited instances in which an individual's IQ changed radically during his or her lifetime depending upon the quality of the home environment, and the effects of schooling. Hunt synthesized the work done by neuropsychologists on the effects of experience on the brain with Piaget's theories of developmental intelligence. Piaget demonstrated that successful development depended upon sufficient experience to encounter and master the perceptual tasks within each stage. Hunt concluded that intelligence varies "with opportunities for perceptual and perhaps even motor experience in which a variety of inputs with appropriate degrees of redundancy are available" (p. 352).

Benjamin Bloom (1964) contributed greatly to the viewpoint that environment influences human development. He summarized almost 1000 previously reported longitudinal studies, and described the typical growth curve for each of several important human characteristics, including intelligence and achievement. He found that the growth curve of a characteristic reveals rapid change in the early years of life. In later years, the curve is far less changeable. This finding was just as true for intelligence and achievement as it was for height and weight.

> . . . it is possible to say, that in terms of intelligence measured at age 17, at least 20% is developed by age 1, 50% by about age 4, 80% by about age 8 and 92% by age 13. Put in terms of intelligence measured at age 17, from conception to age 4, the individual develops 50% of his mature intelligence, from ages 4 to 8 he develops another 30%, and from ages 8 to 17 the remaining 20%. This differentially accelerated growth is very similar to the phenomenon we have noted . . . with regard to height growth.
>
> With this in mind, we would question the notion of an absolutely constant I.Q. Intelligence is a developmental concept, just as is height, weight, or strength. (p. 68)

It is interesting to note that much of the data reviewed by Bloom had been previously analyzed by proponents of an inherited and constant IQ. The difference in findings is due to the difference in the way the investigators framed their questions and hypotheses. Jensen, for example, looked for evidence to support the notion of stable intelligence. He reported that 80 percent of one's IQ was stable from childhood to adulthood in support of his hypotheses. Bloom looked for evidence of growth and change and found it in the early years. Bloom interprets the finding of 80 percent stability differently than earlier researchers. In his view, 80 percent stability also implies an alterability of up to 20 percent in human intelligence. As he points out, this could mean that an individual with an average IQ of 100 could be expected to raise this IQ to 120 if the environment is appropriately supportive and stimulating. Even greater growth can be stimulated at the early ages of development.

In contrast with Jensen, Bloom believed that compensatory social programs could alter the cognitive development of culturally deprived children if the programs were offered to children at an early age. The content of such programs, he believed, should stress general knowledge about the world, verbal skills, and problem-solving activities. In response to Bloom's work, new school and other social programs, such as Head Start, were created in the late 1960s and 1970s to provide early stimulation and challenge for children of all socioeconomic groups.

Parental Influences on Talent Development

School programs are important, but Bloom believes that the home environment is the most critical factor in the development of human intelligence and talent. In 1985, he reported the results of another major study in a book entitled *Developing Talent in Young People*. In the talent development study, Bloom identified 120 young people who had reached the top of their fields in one of six talent fields. The six talent fields selected for the study included two aesthetic fields (internationally renowned pianists and sculptors), two psychomotor fields (Olympic swimmers and world-class tennis players), and two cognitive fields (research mathematicians and neurologists). These are fields of singular accomplishment rather than team endeavors. They are also fields with clearly demarked prizes or ranks, which the investigators were able to use as criteria for the selection of the sample of individuals who had truly reached the top of their fields.

The team of researchers hoped to be able to discover a set of environmental conditions that led to success in each of the six fields. To do so, they conducted extensive interviews with the individuals and with their parents, teachers, and coaches. When the notes of all the researchers were compared, there were a number of generalizations that applied to the individuals in all six talent fields.

Regarding the home environment, it was found that, in most cases, the parents of the talented individuals were genuinely child-oriented and were willing to devote enormous time, energy, and money to furthering the child's training and career opportunities. The parents of the individuals studied placed great importance on achievement and were models of the work ethic themselves. As youngsters, the individuals pursued schedules with much time devoted to practice in the talent area and often had other regular chores as well. The parents expected their children to work or study before playing, to do their work well, and most parents encouraged the children to spend their play time in constructive activities such as model building, sports, and the arts.

Three Teaching Styles Associated with Talent Development

An interesting pattern was also found by the investigators regarding the teachers of the highly talented individuals. Within the selected talent field, individuals typically experienced three distinctly different types of teachers in a very specific order. The earliest teacher was often chosen by the parents simply by proximity. The earliest math or science teacher was in the child's school; the earliest piano or art teachers lived nearby; the earliest swimming or tennis teachers were also local. The critical factor that these early teachers had in common was that they were generally warm, supportive, even playful. They made the learning experience joyful and were generous with positive reinforcements and rewards. During their early training, the individuals enjoyed their lessons and their practice sessions.

After a time, however, the early teacher was replaced by a second or middle teacher with very different teaching methods and goals. In some cases, the early teacher would suggest the change, saying, "I've taught the child all that I know." In other cases, the parents would recognize the need for a different set of expectations and teaching style, if the child was to continue to make progress in the field. Frequently, it was necessary to travel some distance to study with an appropriate second teacher. This middle teacher was known to be a specialist in the field, and took the role of diagnosing and correcting the technique of the young student. Expectations for practice and improvement were more rigorous and demanding. The child was, in part, motivated by prizes and awards during this period of training, but also began to see himself or herself as a professional (i.e., as a pianist, sculptor, mathematician, etc.). In other words, the child developed significant inner motivation based upon early success and excellent support from teachers and parents.

The third teacher found in the study is called a ''master teacher'' by Bloom and his colleagues. The researchers found that in each field, there were only a small number of widely recognized master teachers. It was necessary for the young person to audition to win a place to study with one of these master teachers. This often required great sacrifices on the part of the parents, in terms of finances and travel to study with the teacher. Once accepted by the master teacher, the student was expected to make a total commitment to the field, practicing four to seven hours per day. They were also expected to break new records or work at the frontier or cutting edge of the field in question. The master teacher was essential to the career development of the talented young person because he (or she) knew the field so well that he was able to open doors for his students. Bloom notes that, for example, most Nobel Prize winners studied under Nobel Prize winners. The master teacher supported the young person in making the transition from student to professional by apprising him of the expectations and standards in the field.

In general, Bloom believes that the environment created by the parents and teachers was the critical element in the success of the individuals. He stresses that many individuals may have abilities or ''gifts'' that are comparable to those of the individuals his research team studied, but if they did not have the support, encouragement, expectations, and excellent teaching experienced by these subjects, their potential ''gifts'' and abilities would not become fully developed or realized.

A special note: Bloom cautions that he did not write his book to be used as a ''cookbook'' of how to raise children to become world-class successes. Rather, he found that there were sacrifices in terms of social and family life that were made by these individuals and their families because of their great commitment to the success of the individual. Social isolation, inadequate attention paid to siblings, and tendencies to judge one's self-worth in terms of one's success are all possible by-products of the intense commitment made by the subjects in the study. Bloom advises that parents consider these social implications carefully before following the examples of the 120 subjects in the talent development study.

Developmental Giftedness

A pair of researchers who are breaking new ground in providing explanations of developmental giftedness are Howard Gardner of Harvard University and his research partner David Feldman, a developmental psychologist from Tufts University. Gardner (1983) proposes a theory of ''multiple intelligences'' in which an individual may possess a potential talent or ability in one of several different domains, rather than one general type of intelligence. While the potential may be genetically based, the potential has to be triggered by something in the environment, and it must be nourished.

Feldman concurs with Gardner's view, and proposes that giftedness occurs as a result of a "co-incidence." Feldman has undertaken a study of child prodigies in order to explicate the conditions under which a prodigy develops his or her unusual talent. He describes "co-incidence" as a convergence of a number of elements in a very delicate interplay: "it includes a cultural milieu; the presence of a particular domain which is itself at a particular level of development; the availability of master teachers; family recognition of extreme talent and commitment to support it; large doses of encouragement and understanding; and other features as well" (Feldman 1986, p. 12).

NUTRITION

One important element of the developing child's environment is his or her nutritional intake. Medical doctors and psychobiologists agree that for optimal development of the brain an adequate supply of nutrients during decisive developmental periods is essential. A key question facing researchers in the field today is whether subsequent good nutrition can entirely make up for deficiencies incurred during the first years of life. Restak (1979) reports studies of adopted Korean children placed in American homes as a case in point. In one group the children had been severely malnourished early in life. By age 7 these children were normal in IQ testing. This is heartening, but Restak contrasts this finding with studies of adopted Korean children who had been well nourished during infancy. Their IQ scores are significantly above average. "These observations suggest that malnourished children may never be able to reach their full intellectual potential" (p. 109).

International studies of brain development suggest that the biological effects of nutrition are symbiotic with psychological or affective aspects of development. Restak reports on a study comparing the effects of food supplements among the rural poor in a Mexican community. The most dramatic change involved physical activity. The better-fed children became six to eight times more active than the poorly fed children. While the well-fed children crawled away from their mothers in search of new stimulation, the poorly fed children remained timidly, passively close to their mothers. Better-fed babies, Restak concluded, have more energy and curiosity (p. 111).

A related effect of good nutrition was reported in the changing relationship between the mothers and children. "The better-fed infants were more playful and required more attention and more protection against accidents, thus causing the mothers to feel a greater concern about them," reports the investigator. "The mothers found that they had to talk to their children more often. . . . The better-fed infant . . . requires a greater response on the part of the mother. This sets up a feedback which raises the level of stimuli offered to or perceived by the child" (Restak 1979, p. 111).

BRAIN AND NERVOUS SYSTEM

Although brain functions are still not fully understood, it is known that the brain stores and manipulates vast quantities of constantly changing information that travels from one set of neurons to another. Dendrites can be thought of as nerve cell antennae that pick up impulses sent from other neurons. This movement is what creates the complex behaviors we call memory, thought, and learning. "In many ways the number of dendritic connections is considered even more important than the total number of neurons in the brain, since the density and complexity of dendritic connections probably has greater psychobiological consequences for brain development and human intelligence" (Restak 1979, p. 101).

Brain researchers and neurologists have developed methods to create maps of neural and dendritic connections by electrically stimulating tiny areas of the brain in animals and neurosurgical patients and observing what their subjects moved, spoke, or felt. What they find is that the pathways resemble a complex neighborhood, with thought impulses analogous to traffic traveling on many paths to reach a destination. Some pathways run only a short distance, serving "local traffic," while others tie neighborhood to neighborhood, as long axons connect lobes and hemispheres of the brain.

In most cases, researchers have found that traffic moves two ways as functionally related neurons stimulate each other toward and away from a destination. Traffic can converge, diverge, and move along parallel routes. When roadblocks threaten the smooth flow of traffic, new routes can sometimes be found and used.

To illustrate the impact of experience and environmental stimulation on this physiological model, researchers explain that the pathways between various sites in the brain can be constructed, widened, lengthened, and paved depending upon the traffic using that route. "When a group of neurons is stimulated and used time and again, they will create larger and more efficient pathways; this is called learning" (Dobkin 1986, p. 144).

Growth in the capacity of the human brain occurs in three ways: (1) new brain cells are formed, (2) the size of brain cells increases, and (3) the dendritic spines of the neural cells increase in length and number, allowing greater speed and complexity of the synaptic connections between cells. Brain enzymes serve as chemical transmitters of information across the synapses (Wittrock 1980, p. 381).

Current researchers investigating the human brain and nervous system believe that brain growth depends upon both nutrition and environmental stimulation. Some researchers are looking for evidence of environmental effects upon the physical makeup of the brain itself. In essence, they are asking, is it possible that learning, memory, and perhaps other brain functions are largely dependent upon the quality of environmental stimulation? Two noted researchers in the field report that

> Psychobiologists are reluctant to go quite that far, since early enrichment improves some tasks while exerting little effect on others. All are agreed, however, that enrichment, even in small doses, exerts a measurable effect on brain development. (Restak 1979, p. 105)

In animals at least, well-timed enriched experiences increase neural growth, which in turn increases the possibilities of improved learning and improved ability to learn. The implication for educational psychologists is that we should explore in humans the possibility that well-timed, stimulating instruction influences brain growth, and with it, psychological functions that transcend the behaviors measured on commonly used tests of learning. (Wittrock 1980, p. 379)

One area of brain research that has captured the interest of some educators in gifted education is the difference between the functions and capabilities of the right and left hemispheres of the brain. It is known that the left and right hemispheres hold somewhat separate inventories of knowledge and make separate inferences about the world. Current interpretations of brain functions indicate that the right brain works more from an inductive and holistic point of view, while the left takes a more analytic, less unitary approach and uses more abstract and sequential reasoning. The central corpus callosum bridges the two hemispheres, providing pathways between them so that each hemisphere can provide information to the other about their differing perceptions of the world (Dobkin 1986, p. 145).

Brain functions are only partially understood, and this text has presented only a cursory overview of some recent studies. It is risky to assume too much from the limited information available at this point in time. In 1979 Betty Edwards published a book entitled *Drawing on the Right Side of the Brain* that suggested that some individuals are predominantly governed by one hemisphere or the other. People began to speculate that "right-brained" individuals were more creative, intuitive, and visual-spatially imaginative, while "left-brained" individuals were more logical, analytical, and sequential. Although evidence for these brain-mind generalizations seems scanty, they have served to stimulate thought among gifted educators concerning ways of providing learning experiences that develop both logical/analytical and intuitive/imaginative thought processes.

PSYCHOSOCIAL THEORIES
THAT RELATE TO GIFTEDNESS

From brain research findings it appears likely that early childhood experiences stimulate the brain and nervous system to work more or less efficiently, and to develop strong or weak pathways between neurons in the brain. Presumably the number and strength of the pathways and their supporting tissues has a direct effect on the speed and quantity of thoughts that may be processed by an individual.

Some psychobiologists and most psychologists are interested in a more complex distinction: determining how an individual's environment affects the quality of thoughts and their interrelated emotions. It is generally agreed that the quality of one's experiences and relationships affects the quality of one's thoughts and feelings. It is also assumed that the memory, thoughts, and emotions of an individual can be either positive or negative, accurate or inaccurate, productive or destructive, creative or noncreative, satisfying or unsatisfying, happy or sad. Finally, it is generally well agreed that the most positive states of mind create the best opportunities for learning and achievement.

Psychologists and educators are interested in determining what types of early experiences create the positive thoughts, attitudes, beliefs, and self-confidence needed to use one's potential endowment of gifts and talents to accomplish or produce a fully realized contribution to self or society. In other words, we are searching for patterns of child rearing and educational experiences that allow or encourage children to "act gifted" or use and develop creative, productive patterns of "gifted behavior."

There are many psychological theories of human development, but two seem to explain the relationship between experience and accomplishment especially well: the theories of Maslow and Erikson.

Maslow's Hierarchy of Needs

Maslow was trained to be a traditional Freudian psychotherapist, which meant that explanations of human behavior and motivation were largely explained by studying the neurotic and psychotic tendencies of individuals in search of reasons for their ill health. Maslow broke away from this traditional set and asked an entirely new question. He asked, not what causes people to become mentally unfit, but rather, what are the conditions which create healthy, happy, productive individuals? Being a scientist, he began to collect "healthy people" for his subjects, people whose lives were characterized by warm, intimate relationships, spontaneity, excitement, worthwhile achievement, and creativity.

Maslow's (1970) study of "fully human" individuals led him to explain human development in terms of a Hierarchy of Needs that every individual has. In Maslow's view, an infant has a set of basic physical needs that must be met for survival. If the needs at one level of the hierarchy are satisfied by the infant's environment, the child is then motivated to meet the needs in the next level. If the needs of one level are not satisfied, however, the individual may spend a lifetime "stuck" at that level of need satisfaction. Maslow thus explains the healthy individual as one whose needs are well met at each level, allowing that person to function at higher and higher levels as he or she develops.

Maslow's Hierarchy of Needs is traditionally displayed in a triangle (Figure 2.1) to illustrate two elements of his theory: (1) for optimal development, the needs at the lowest levels must be satisfied to provide the basis for development at higher levels; (2) the number of individuals who reach each successive level of needs satisfaction diminishes due to the increasing difficulty of attaining needs satisfaction from the environment.

The physical needs of a child (level 1) may be met by any caretaker or parent who provides basic food, clothing, and shelter for the infant. In some disparate cultures around the globe, there are parents who are unable to satisfy even these needs. In such cases, the parents and the children are totally involved in getting these needs met, to the exclusion of all other activities. This is clearly seen in the documentaries of people waiting for grain deliveries in the deserts of East Africa. When the needs are satisfied, as they are in most American communities, the child is able to move up to the next level on the hierarchy.

The psychological need for security (level 2) is met by parents and other caretakers who provide emotionally stable conditions. When children are physically or

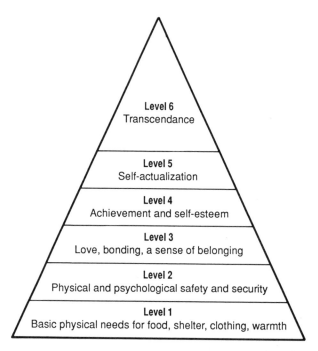

Figure 2.1. A Graphic Representation of Maslow's Hierarchy of Needs and Motivation. Data based on Hierarchy of Needs from *Motivation and Personality,* 2nd ed., by Abraham H. Maslow. Copyright 1954 by Harper & Row, Publishers, copyright © 1970 by Abraham H. Maslow. Reprinted by permission of Harper & Row, Publishers, Inc.

psychologically abused by their caretakers, these needs are thwarted. In such cases, the child may come to expect censure, ridicule, and physical abuse as a steady source of threat. Even when such children leave home as adults, they may be "stuck" at this emotional level, living lives of fear and anxiety, anticipating threats in every new relationship or experience. When the needs at this level are well met, the child perceives the world as a safe place to live. He or she is free to venture to the next level of the hierarchy.

The needs for love and a sense of belonging (level 3) are met primarily by bonding with parents. Even in a safe and secure institutional environment, caretakers cannot meet this need for a child, as it depends on a shared sense of love and caring. In homes where there is an intimate shared experience of love and nurturance, the child feels a sense of self-worth and belonging that allows him or her to progress to the next level of the hierarchy.

The needs for achievement and recognition (level 4) are satisfied primarily by accomplishment in some form of work that receives genuine praise or reward from the environment. Parents and teachers are the prime sources of such reward at early ages. Recognition from peers becomes important as the child grows up. When the rewards are scarce or capriciously withheld, an individual may remain at this stage indefinitely in his or her life, struggling to attain sufficient rewards in the form of money, power, or awards to satisfy this need. In Maslow's view, a great majority of adults in our culture whose earlier needs for security and belonging were insufficiently met may reach this achievement level, but rarely advance beyond it. Instead, they continually seek the next salary raise, material reward, pat on the back, or picture in the paper in an empty and futile effort to fill their belonging needs along with their achievement needs. When the needs at all four stages of the hierarchy are well met, the individual is free to move up to next level.

Self-actualization (level 5) is a very special human condition, in which all of the basic needs have been met. Rather than being motivated to achieve or belong or to gain security or food, the individual is truly free to attain some inner goals. Self-actualized individuals are described by Maslow as "fully human." They are able to fully experience joy and a sense of wonder at the world. They are more able to be spontaneous, creative and productive than others who are struggling to meet needs at a lower order on the hierarchy. The healthy individuals whom Maslow studied were operating at this level. He found that fully functioning individuals are devoted to some cause, search for meaning, or creative endeavor outside of themselves. They are able to concentrate on their chosen endeavor with total absorption, as they do it for their own satisfaction rather than as a means to gain attention and reward from others. Self-actualizing individuals have great courage of conviction and strong sense of honesty. Maslow also reports that self-actualizers have "peak experiences," which he describes as moments of ecstasy in which they are "surprised by joy" (1971, p. 48).

In his later life, Maslow began to describe a sixth level called transcendence, which is analogous to a mystical experience in which one is able to surpass even the greatest goals set for oneself during self-actualization. One is able to do more than one thought one could do, or do it better than ever before. He describes this state as "beyond the merely human," almost a divine state of being (1971, p. 274). His death eclipsed a full description of this stage of development, but it may be best understood as Maslow's description of the very highest level of human consciousness (p. 279).

Erikson's Growth Choices

Erik Erikson (1964) has expanded our understanding of human development beyond the early years of childhood. He charts human development in terms of eight stages from infancy to old age. Each stage of development is seen by Erikson as a time in which the individual makes a growth or a nongrowth choice. Growth choices, according to Erikson, lead to a positive self-concept, productivity, and satisfaction with life. Nongrowth choices, on the other hand, lead to a diminished self-concept, missed opportunities, and despair.

The quality of the child's environment, especially the relationships with the parents and other primary caregivers, determines whether or not the child is able to make the growth or nongrowth choice or decision at each stage. The optimal conditions for human development are a steady pathway of growth choices, but Erikson also believes that with therapeutic intervention an individual whose environment caused him to make nongrowth choices may be able to rethink his or her early choices and make healthier decisions later in life.

Trust vs. Mistrust (The First Year of Life). The degree to which the child comes to trust the world, other people, and himself depends to a considerable extent upon the quality of care he receives during infancy. The infant whose needs are met when they arise, whose discomforts are removed, who is cuddled, played with, and talked to, makes a decision that the world is a safe place to be and that other people are helpful and dependable. If, however, the care is inconsistent, inadequate, or rejecting, the child decides not to trust the world in general and the people in it—especially those particular people who are responsible for the child's care during this and the next few stages of development.

Autonomy vs. Doubt (Ages 2-3). As the child is able to use new motor and mental abilities, she will attempt to walk, climb, open, close, push, pull, hold and let go. If parents recognize and encourage the child's need to try new experiences at her own pace and in her own time, the child will decide that she can control her own muscles, impulses, and thoughts. In other words, she will gain a sense of autonomy. When caretakers are impatient, critical, or overprotective, the child chooses to doubt her own capabilities to control her world and herself. This decision of self-doubt can lead to a lifelong dependence upon others to decide and to do things for her.

Initiative vs. Guilt (Ages 4-5). Children who are given many opportunities to initiate play activities such as running, bike riding, skating, art experiences, word-play, and number-play learn to trust their own initiative. If the child is made to feel that his play choices are bad, inferior, silly, or stupid, he will develop a sense of guilt over self-initiated activities that will persist through later life-stages.

Industry vs. Inferiority (Ages 6-11). This is a period during which the child becomes capable of deductive reasoning, being responsible to follow certain rules, creating products, and of working toward goals. When the child is encouraged to make, do, and build objects, is allowed to finish what she starts and is given appropriate rewards for the results, her sense of industry is enhanced. Parents who treat their child's products as "making a mess," and her efforts to make and do as "mischief," lead the child to decide that her efforts are inferior, so why try.

Identity vs. Role Confusion (Ages 12-18). The adolescent's priority is deciding how to integrate all the things he has learned about his abilities, feelings, desires, and goals into one integrated concept of self that shows continuity with his past and preparation for the future. The influence of the parents at this stage is cumulative rather than direct. If the young person reaches adolescence with a positive sense of trust, autonomy, initiative, and industry, his chances of making a positive decision regarding his identity are greatly enhanced. If the adolescent is unable to integrate a meaningful identity, the resulting role confusion will lead to behavior patterns characterized by inconsistency, lack of goal orientation, and lack of understanding of his own actions and consequences.

Intimacy vs. Isolation (Adolescence to Early Middle Age).   Sometime during early adulthood, the healthy individual with a sense of identity is able to establish intimate relationships with other persons. Intimacy, according to Erikson, means the ability to share with and care about another person without fear of losing oneself in the process. When prior stages of development have been characterized by nongrowth choices, it is virtually impossible for an individual to establish the trusting and sharing bonds of intimacy.

Generativity vs. Self-Absorption (Middle Age).   The growth choice during middle age is one of outreach to society and the world. An individual who actively concerns himself with the welfare of young people and with making the world a better place to live is making the growth choice. In contrast, some individuals become more and more concerned with attaining material possessions and preserving their own youth and beauty. The results of such self-absorption may appear to be marks of success, but may, in fact, contribute to feelings of emptiness and questions of "is that all there is to life?"

As an aside, it is exciting to note here that educators are in an ideal position for making the growth choice at this stage of life. Teachers and other school personnel are able to contribute to the next generation and to the world through their daily actions in schools, whereas people in other careers often have to search for avocations to satisfy this growth choice.

Integrity vs. Despair (Old Age).   Near the end of life, each individual reflects back upon his or her accomplishments and contributions. Those who have made growth choices have a sense of satisfaction and pride that they have lived their lives with integrity. For those whose choices were nongrowth oriented, there is only a sense of despair and regret for all the missed opportunities. At this stage in life there is rarely an opportunity to start again or to redo or relive one's choices.

CAUSES OF UNDERACHIEVEMENT

Joanne Whitmore (1980) describes gifted underachievement and the typically related behavior problems as "expressive symptoms of conflict between internal needs for acceptance, success, and meaningful learning and the external conditions of the classroom environment" (p. 194). She suggests that school programs need to be modified for such children in order to reduce the conflicts and increase the achievement motivation of the child.

In keeping with Whitmore's observation, the developmental theories of Maslow and Erikson can be used to explain some of the causes of underachievement among children with many natural talents and abilities. Even though they may be intellectually gifted or talented in other areas, children whose basic physical or security needs are not being met by their primary caretakers are motivated solely to gain safety and security through any means possible. Their intelligence may allow them to manipulate the environment in complex ways to gain the security they seek, but they are not motivated to achieve academically because that level of functioning, in Maslow's view, is beyond their reach psychologically. Only when their basic needs (levels 1, 2, and 3) are satisfied will they be motivated to achieve (level 4) in school or any other setting.

Erikson's theory of human development gives meaning to the phenomenon of negative and self-defeating behaviors often observed among highly able students. Consider the child whose home environment causes him to distrust rather than trust adults, to feel shame and guilt when he plays or initiates an activity, and to view his work attempts as inferior. Despite an enormous potential, this child will operate at the lower limits of his potential unless the environment is dramatically improved and some form of counseling allows the child to reevaluate these nongrowth decisions, and make new growth choices. When the child learns to trust adults, to feel renewed pride in his play and work activities, and begins to take initiative with confidence, his achievement level and accomplishments will better match his high potential.

For parents or educators who want a set of useful and practical methods for overcoming underachievement in children, Sylvia Rimm has written *Underachievement Syndrome: Causes and Cures.* This book relates the causes of underachievement to an environment in which the child may be allowed to be either too dominant or too dependent by her parents. When this occurs, the child is not allowed much needed opportunities to struggle for achievement in worthwhile learning experiences. The dominant child refuses to do the work and the dependent child gets the parents to do it for her. School programs that are not sufficiently challenging contribute to the problem. But Rimm also cautions against inappropriate interventions in the form of gifted programs that may exacerbate the problem.

> Gifted children's early school experiences are either full of nonlearning, since typical work is not challenging or they find that teachers, principals and parents take action to provide a special individualized program for their needs. The first discourages these children's initiative since the academic environment requires no effort and is indeed boring. The second flatters them into believing that their special talents are extraordinary enough to permit them to change an adult-managed system. This is impressive power for a five or six year old, even one who is known as the "brain" among peers.
>
> In sum, the risk for these gifted children comes from both attention addiction and too much power. They may learn to expect both uninterrupted applause and complete freedom of choice in their education, but neither are possible regardless of their intelligence. (p. 33)

THE EFFECTS OF LABELING ON ACHIEVEMENT

In Rimm's experience as a teacher and psychologist, labeling a child "gifted" may be psychosocially unwise. "Any label that unrealistically narrows prospects for performance by a child may be damaging" (p. 84). Peer pressures or resentments and unrealistic expectations from parents and teachers may result from labeling the child gifted.

Haim Ginott (1965) points out that "Direct praise of personality, like sunlight, is uncomfortable and blinding" (p. 41). June Cox, who led the team that conducted a nationwide survey of gifted programs, known as the Richardson Study, concurs. She and her colleagues recommend using the term "able learners," which is substantially more flexible and less damaging than "gifted children" (Cox, Daniel, and Boston 1985).

SUMMARY

Most of the studies and theories presented in this chapter were initiated in fields outside of gifted education. They are attempts to find meaning and generate understanding of human development and intelligence. The studies reported here were done by scientists, medical doctors, psychotherapists, and cognitive psychologists. In the field of gifted education, we must learn to select and apply the best of such theories and studies to increase our own understanding of what makes giftedness, and how we can design appropriate gifted programs. The major question we have focused on in this chapter is whether giftedness is endowed or developed. The experts are not in agreement on this matter, so each of us must weigh the evidence and examine the issues with reference to our own experience.

In our view, the best answer to this question is that individuals do have biologically determined *ranges* of a variety of abilities and talents, due in part to their genetic makeup and their prenatal nutrition. But as Bloom's work has demonstrated, the home environment plays a crucial role in the development of a child's abilities and talents. The most supportive and stimulating home environment will cause the child to develop and display a talent at the top of his range. As Maslow and Erikson describe, a safe and nurturing environment will enable the child to put his or her energy into establishing and meeting achievement goals. Taken together, the work of Bloom, Maslow, and Erikson allows us to understand the affective and cognitive environment that supports and encourages talent development in children.

We also concur with Gardner's theory that there are a number of different types of intelligences or domains of talent. For example, one individual may be endowed with a range of musical intelligence that far exceeds the norm, a range of several other intelligences that are near the norm, while her range of visual/spatial intelligence is lower than normal. If this child is raised in an environment that favors musical talent, there is a great possibility that she will develop her musical "gift" or intelligence into a unique and special talent. If she is raised in an environment that rewards visual/spatial talent, her ability may appear to be quite ordinary.

Although the home environment is the most powerful influence on an individual's talent development, we believe that the school has a significant influence as well. We especially recommend that the sequence of three teaching styles (nurturing, technical, and mastery) observed by Bloom be investigated further in terms of its usefulness in talent development in the school setting. In our view, teachers can and do spot talent that parents miss and are capable of planning and implementing interventions that allow a child to develop unnoticed talents and abilities into unique and valuable achievements.

OPPORTUNITIES FOR DISCUSSION AND ACTION

In this chapter, we have shared our biases and our values along with our interpretations of many theories and studies. It is impossible to eliminate bias from a book on anything as value-laden as education, and gifted education may be even more intensely value-ridden than the rest of the field. That is because gifted education is relatively new and still in the process of becoming a specialized field of study. We encourage you to reflect upon the ideas and theories in this chapter and arrive at your own conclusions. Read further about the issues that most interest you. Conduct some of the following informal investigations.

1.   Given a certain range of potential or ability, what are the physical and psychosocial conditions that cause individuals to vary in achievement? To answer this question break into small discussion groups, each taking one of the time periods listed below. List the physical and psychosocial conditions at both ends of the range of achievement. Share the information generated by each small group with the entire class.

Underachievement_____Full Achievement

Prenatal
period

Birth to
24 hours

Birth to
4 years

4 years to
8 years

8 years to
adolescence

2.   How does teaching style affect talent or ability development? Consider the information about the three different types of teachers experienced by the highly successful subjects in Bloom's talent development study. If you were a school administrator, how would you use this information to select and hire teachers for different ages and grades in your school? What type of teacher would you hire for primary grades? For middle grades? For high school and college courses? How can teachers, themselves, use this information to find their own best career placement?

3.   In a journal or notebook, analyze your own stages of development in terms of Maslow's Hierarchy of Needs. What experiences did you have that caused you to reach your level of motivation? Do the same for Erikson's Growth Choices. If you had experiences that caused you to make any non-growth choices, what can you do to reassess these decisions? What do you think is the effect on children of working with adults who have made non-growth choices? What is the effect upon children of working with healthy, self-actualized adults?

4. Gardner describes seven different intelligences. On the following base line, draw a series of peaks of different heights to depict your own relative strengths in each of the different domains. What are the effects of having only one peak or of having many peaks? If you had a profile like this for each of your students, how would you use it?

Profile of Multiple Intelligences

Highly
Superior

Normal

Low

_____

Linguistic Logical-   Musical Spatial Bodily-   Inter-   Intra-
            mathematical   kinesthetic personal personal

REFERENCES

Bloom, B. 1964. *Stability and change in human characteristics.* New York: John Wiley.

———, ed. 1985. *Developing talent in young people.* New York: Ballantine.

Clark, B 1983. *Growing up gifted.* Columbus, Ohio: Chas. E. Merrill.

Cox, J., N. Daniel, and B. Boston. 1985. *Educating able learners.* Austin, Tex.: University of Texas Press.

Darwin, C. 1859. *On the origin of species.* London· Murray.

Dobkin, B. 1986. *Brain matters.* New York: Crown Publishers.

Eby, J. 1983. Gifted behavior: A non-elitist approach, *Educational Leadership* 40 (no. 8): 30–36.

Edwards, B. 1979. *Drawing on the right side of the brain.* New York: Tarcher.

Erikson, E. 1964. *Childhood and society.* New York: W. W. Norton.

Fancher, R. 1985. *The intelligence men: Makers of the IQ controversy.* New York: W. W. Norton.

Feldman, D. 1979. Toward a non-elitist conception of giftedness, *Phi Delta Kappan* 60: 660–63.

———. 1986. *Nature's gambit: Child prodigies and the development of human potential.* New York: Basic Books.

Foster, W. 1986. Giftedness: The mistaken metaphor. In *Critical issues in gifted education,* ed. C. J. Maker. Rockville, Md.: Aspen Systems Corp.

Gardner, H. 1983. *Frames of mind.* New York: Basic Books.

Ginott, H. 1965. *Between parents and child.* New York: Macmillan.

Hunt, J. McV. 1961. *Intelligence and experience.* New York: Ronald Press.

Jensen, A. 1969. How much can we boost IQ and scholastic achievement? In *Environment, heredity and intelligence.* Cambridge, Mass.: Harvard Educational Review.

Maslow, A. 1970. *Motivation and personality.* Rev. ed. New York: Harper & Row.

———. 1971. *The farther reaches of human nature.* New York: Viking.

Restak, R. 1979. *The brain: The last frontier.* Garden City, N.Y.: Doubleday.

Rimm, S. 1986. *Underachievement syndrome: Causes and cures.* Watertown, Wis.: Apple Publishing Company.

Rosenzweig, M. 1966. Environmental complexity, cerebral change and behavior, *American Psychologist* 21: 321–32.

Stanley, J. 1977. *The gifted and the creative: A fifty year perspective.* Baltimore: Johns Hopkins University Press.

Whitmore, J. 1980. *Giftedness, conflict and underachievement.* Boston: Allyn & Bacon.

Wittrock, M. C. 1980. *The brain and psychology.* New York: Academic Press.

CHAPTER 3

Perspectives on the Nature of Creativity

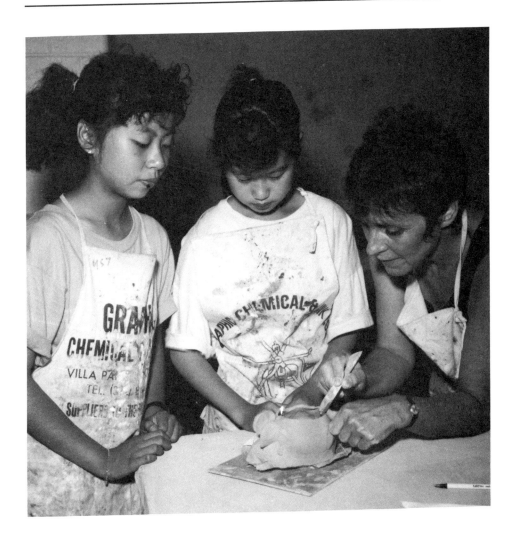

In a Spanish neighborhood in Chicago, a quiet sixth grader begins his next project of graffiti art under the viaduct. His style is unmistakable. Bold, sweeping strokes of blue and red swirl around clenched fists and scowling faces, with a few faint traces of a popular gang symbol suggested in the pattern. Teachers admire his art, but complain about his poor work habits and his rather unrestrained sense of adventure. Trouble follows him everywhere. One day he discovered a passageway from the grating in the auditorium to the roof of the school and explored this during the lunch hour. He was suspended. His test scores show none of the astute intelligence he displays on the street and in his art work. Is this child creative?

A fourth grade girl in a wealthy suburb scribbles on notepaper possible alternatives for solving a word problem in math. The work becomes tedious and even dull, until she finds an aspect to the problem that intrigues her more than the original question. Her growing fascination with this new aspect quickly lures her away from her assigned task. That night at home, she continues to analyze the various parts of her new question until she discovers a solution that satisfies all the conditions. When she shows her work to the teacher excitedly, the teacher scolds her for not dealing directly with the assigned question and sends her home with a note to her mother. Is this child creative?

No one can understand why a little preschooler refuses to listen to stories from children's books. Whenever his mother tries to read to him, he wriggles out of her lap, pulls another book off the shelf, and weaves his own tales from the pictures. In preschool, the teacher tells his mother that he often interrupts story hour by adding elaborate details that he feels she has neglected. When he manages to listen at all, he listens very intently, but he will listen only from behind a desk or under a chair. By now, the teacher has agreed to this arrangement. But she does not appreciate his artistic additions to the school books at all! One morning, to her horror, she found him drawing other characters in the pictures of stories she reads to the children. Is this child creative?

WHAT DO YOU THINK?

1. Who are the creative? Are they solely the art students, the composers, the inventors and playwrights? Can children be called creative if they don't produce paintings or poems?
2. In what ways have the common stereotypes of creativity blinded us to the real thing?
3. The preschool child in the third sketch displays more originality than the studied artist who paints in imitation of others. What do you think will be the long-term effect of his teacher's reactions to his behavior?
4. What is creativity? Can we measure it as we do academic intelligence?
5. Are creatively gifted people also academically gifted or are these separate constructs?

INTRODUCTION

Although years of research and study on creativity have overwhelmed the field with a mass of information, many questions remain unanswered. For example, we still cannot explain why some creative people perform well in many areas, like the girl in the second sketch, while others excel artistically but not academically, like the boy in the first sketch, while others score high in intelligence tests, but prove weak in creative work. To help us explore the many facets of creativity, this chapter has been organized in four sections reflecting four distinct areas of experience: creative feelings, creative thinking, creative processes, and creative products. In the second section, we examine the special role of school and home in fostering creative growth in children and consider the following questions: Why do narrow definitions of creativity persist in spite of evidence disproving such definitions? Why has not research significantly affected how teachers and parents treat their children? Why do those in a position to help, give teachers and parents formulas rather than guidance?

Parents and teachers, charged with the task of providing support, rarely receive support themselves. Crushed under the same system that often squelches creative thinking in children, adults struggle to fulfill their roles as nurturers. As you read, you may want to consider the implications of creativity research on the shaping of our future. As Guilford says, "creativity is the key to education in its fullest sense and to the solution of mankind's most serious problems" (quoted in Parnes 1967, p. iii).

CREATIVE FEELINGS: A WAY OF BEING

For some of us, creativity belongs exclusively to an artistic elite. We classify members of this elite as rarities on the basis of what they accomplish in contrast to the rest of us. They hold a certain mystique—conjuring up unusual creations from nowhere, stumbling upon brilliant ideas in odd places, and ferreting out original solutions with an ease that can be both maddening and admirable. Most research studies on the creative adult or child do what we do—look to the production of visible results to validate that something creative actually happened.

But neither artists nor their prolific productions have a monopoly on creativity. Creative expression is a vast phenomenon, extending beyond narrow, conventional contexts to life itself. We can refer to the creative attitude or the creative experience, for example, without looking for tangible proof of either. Managing an estate, baking bread, or marketing a product may be accomplished with more invention and originality than painting a landscape, even though the latter is executed by the trained hand of an artist (Maslow 1968).

Self-Actualization

Maslow (1968) saw creativity as a way of being, which he called "self-actualization." Self-actualized human beings live lives of spontaneity and freedom. Unhampered by a concern over others' opinions or censorship, they give themselves the license to be original in all that they do. Self-actualized human beings distinguish themselves not by membership in an artistic elite, but by their lack of stale stereotypes and clichés. They have an acute "sense of wonder" about many things (Carson 1965). Puzzling paradoxes intrigue rather than frighten them. They would rather seek the unknown than settle into familiar answers because of some nagging need for security. Their "peak experiences" (Maslow 1968) or "encounters" (May 1975) imply a creative way of being as distinct from either talent or training.

May (1975), Maslow (1968), Carson (1965), and Rogers (1954) noticed several primary characteristics of imaginative people:

> Total immersion in the moment (experiencing a temporary suspension of time, past and present)
>
> Openness to experience as an original event (leaving the past behind and treating the present as new)
>
> Complete self-acceptance (judging one's self independently of others and validating one's own individuality without reservation)

We can see an example of this kind of freedom in the child's simple encounter with nature (Carson 1965). Creating a new relationship with nature every day, the clear-eyed child transcends the level of the adult, who values knowledge over feeling and tries to identify each plant and bird correctly. The child, through imaginative response, often learns more than the classifying adult.

Creativity vs. Technique

Maslow (1968) distinguished raw, creative behavior, which he termed the "primary processes," from technique, which he called the "secondary processes." The two are often confused. The finest artists, of course, have both originality and technique. Yet, the lesser artists manage to produce imitations with a technical brilliance that can masquerade as creativity. Frequently, secondary processes mislead us in this way (i.e., good training is mistaken for creative talent) (May 1975). Impressive imitations can sway even the most critical of us, simply because they evince a technical mastery over something we know and admire, whereas the more original works tend to jolt us where we least like it.

Skill has more status than originality in our society and, what is more, skill can compensate for a lack of creativity. The reverse is not true. Professional people who have acquired a great deal in the way of "secondary processes" do not have to worry about how creative they are. Those who innovate within a prestigious field (i.e., law, physics, the arts) get far more recognition than do the less skillful, but more original craftsmen. Schoolchildren may be more original than many eminent mathematicians, but they lack the accoutrements (training, position, etc.) that distinguish the mathematicians from less sophisticated thinkers. Raw creativeness has become, unfortunately, the servant of superficial judgments.

Yet if every scientist, artist, and performer preserved the unassuming child spirit (his creative self) within, his work would become more original, spontaneous, and imaginative. Even valuing creativity as a natural outcome of imaginative thinking rather than of hard academic labor would bring a healthy new impetus to various fields. Creative self-expression in its most basic element determines how life is experienced, how problems are perceived, how duties are performed, how instruments are played, and how visions are realized. It demands self-acceptance, confidence, openness, and spontaneity, as well as the courage to fend off the unreceptive or antagonistic responses of hard-nosed, narrow-minded thinking.

CREATIVE THINKING: A WAY OF SOLVING PROBLEMS

Creative Attitude

A problem would not really be one unless it required some new behavior for its solution. Creative people often know this. When muddling through a particularly obstinate problem, they think nothing of springing off into the unexplored wilds of the imagination to find new ways of reaching unexpected conclusions. Creative problem solvers are not dissimilar to the free spirits described in the previous section, but they work in a more specific context. The qualities that enable a person to live creatively enable her to think creatively.

Creative problem solving challenges the answer-finding order of traditional academia. Formal schooling in its more authoritarian transmission of knowledge to children often stresses the importance of arriving at *the* answer. Many schoolchildren execute math problems in a formulaic, mindless fashion. They simply crank out predictable outcomes based on reasoning within a prescribed structure of facts. From a limited view of the problem, they apply several rules to a familiar context, analyze the evidence they knew would be there, synthesize the various components (remembered from previous experiments), and evaluate the utility of a solution that proved effective many times before. This, we think, is problem solving.

Solving problems by reasoning alone assumes that there is one logical answer to be had. This has little to do with creative thinking, although it often molds the child's response to problems. To nonconforming thinkers, however, past experiences inform but do not limit the possibility of finding unconventional responses to problems. Charles Kettering once commented that an inventor is "a fellow who doesn't take his education too seriously" (quoted in Guilford 1968, pp. 84–85). Creative people do not let what they know define how they should proceed in a given situation.

Schools frequently place more emphasis on teaching children to retain factual information than on encouraging them to think creatively. Criticism of this tendency crops up continually. At issue is not really the facts children learn, but rather the values unconsciously superimposed on knowledge. Most children have little sense of the process behind the creation of knowledge. All they learn is that facts are ultimate and that knowing them brings success, acceptance, and rewards. For many, the goal of solving a problem becomes the means for solving an even greater problem: getting approval. According to Crutchfield, "The solution of the problem itself becomes of secondary relevance, and his task-involved motivation diminishes" for a student with this outlook (quoted in Parnes 1967, p. 18). The creative thinker, on the other hand, is more interested in questions than answers. The need for acceptance does not drive her to cancel out her curiosity and divergent thinking for hasty answers.

Knowledge Consumption vs. Higher-Level Thinking

Schools and the media often treat creative people as though they disdain the straight facts. Nothing could more misrepresent them, since they often value information more than do most people. But creative thinkers relate to knowledge as an ongoing process, a view that information consumers find both incomprehensible and objectionable. Imaginative individuals are more interested in transforming rather than consuming knowledge—manipulating what they know to new ends (Guilford 1968). As Whitehead put it, "Fools act on imagination without knowledge; pedants act on knowledge without imagination" (quoted in Parnes 1967, p. 7). Knowledge consumers collect and compile data files; inventors question those files, analyze information, probe weak links, and explore and apply innovative ideas. Frequently the old system breaks down in this process, which then allows for creative engineering to take place.

Benjamin Bloom's Taxonomy, a definitive model for the development of higher level thinking, which will be discussed more fully in Chapter 9, demonstrates the relationship between the lower level of knowledge consumerism and the higher processes of thinking: application, analysis, synthesis, and evaluation. The higher levels demand a complete repositioning of thought. From receiving and remembering information, the creative thinker must maneuver these rules and principles along more unpredictable paths. Rising from one rung to the next in the taxonomy, we no longer regard knowledge as an end in itself, but as a means of discovering new ends (which then become means for finding still other ends, etc.).

J. P. Guilford (1968) conducted extensive research on the creative process and included in his Structure of the Intellect Model four major characteristics of creativity: *Fluency* (producing many ideas in response to a problem), *Flexibility* (finding different approaches to the problem and various applications of known facts in new contexts), *Originality* (thinking in an entirely unique and nonconformist fashion), and *Elaboration* (developing and implementing an idea, extending it to uses beyond the conventional). Additional qualities cited by Torrance (1969) and others include sensitivity to problems, visualization, transformation, concentration, suspension of judgment, and intuition. Guided by his conviction that idea generation underlies the work of creative people, Guilford (1968) focused primarily on the quantitative (fluency) and qualitative (flexibility) aspects of the process. His insights have influenced other researchers who, like Guilford, find the creative process something of an enigma. How do artists, inventors and writers discover their ideas? What guides their unconventional meanderings, sudden leaps of faith, and risky experiments? Where do the lines of critical and creative thinking intersect?

Illumination

Creative inspiration rarely occurs during conscious labor. The eminent French mathematician Poincaré noticed that behaviors leading up to discovery typically involve a period of labor, a period of rest, an illumination, followed by additional labor (to solidify illumination). Poincaré's famous story (1913) of his discovery of Fuchsian groups followed this pattern. After many days of working on a solution to his problem, he let the matter rest, drank a cup of black coffee, and then discovered what he termed "Fuchsian functions." Later, Poincaré was stepping into a bus when another idea occurred to him with no conscious effort at all. He realized that the transformations he "had used to define the Fuchsian functions were identical with those of non-Euclidian geometry" (p. 37). He later verified this discovery, which made a significant advance in mathematics.

Other creative thinkers have reported similar experiences. Charles Darwin could not grasp the central theory that he sought in compiling information on the evolution of species. He said, "I can remember the very spot in the road, whilst in my carriage, when to my joy the solution occurred to me" (quoted by Lowes in Kneller 1965, p. 53). What actually happened in that moment? We can trace the process that led up to it, but conscious thought did not originate Darwin's theory of evolution. "Certainly it is plausible to view the creative process as going through the stages of preparation, incubation, inspiration, and verification, but it is also so for the solution of any problem" (Arieti 1976, p. 18). The illumination stage in creative thinking is the only one that actually creates. On the other hand, conscious thought prepares for this magic moment and could claim at least partial credit for the results. It stretches everything known to the outermost limit and then waits. From there, the process eludes us. Helen Parkhurst refers to the "mysterious outcome of processes over which the individual appears to have little or no control—whose end he perhaps cannot even foresee" (quoted in Kneller 1965, p. 54).

It is ironic that the most crucial step in creative production is the one we know least about. Signs of a selective process occurring at the deepest level of thought, however, have challenged the notion of chance as a factor in illumination. Poincaré (1913) noticed that only "good combinations" out of many possible, appeared in his inspired moments. This hints at some organizing principle in the unconscious that takes up the problem where conscious effort stops. How this principle functions, if it exists at all, awaits further exploration.

CREATIVE PROCESSES: A WAY OF BEHAVING

Transformation of Knowledge

The bias of education predisposes most of us to think of solutions even before we examine the problem. This restricts us to the dimensions of a question we have accepted at face value. Most such questions provoke little thought because they include implied answers. In other words, they are founded on a set of knowns. But for imaginative thinkers, both problems and solutions live as ongoing discoveries.

These thinkers probe beyond the surface and ask: What lies outside the context of this problem that would allow for a whole new range of possibilities, and would require the application of something not currently known?

The imaginative person solves problems that others hardly notice. Not content with things as they are, she looks beyond the established limits of academia to question what is missing. Deficiencies in the existing order of knowledge (Torrance 1969), inspire her to question, experiment, and explore until something of an answer appears, but even this appearance lures her on to bigger questions. Renzulli (1981), who linked creativity with ability and task commitment, found creative people to be risk takers, not easily swayed by facile solutions. Given the chance, they would much rather be whisked off on the wings of uncertainty and disorder than know where they are headed.

Creative action begins with formulation of a question or problem. As Ghiselin (1952) understood it, the creative inventor, artist, scientist, or writer discovers the problem in a land of unknowns, rather than in a redefinition of known problems. Sometimes a felt urge or intuition propels the inventor or artist forward, with little sense of direction, an urge "so extremely vague as hardly to identify itself" (p. 14). The formulation that results is much more than the statement of a simple math or science problem, for example, where the thinker redefines a question to perform several known operations.

Getzels and Csikszentmihalyi (1972) in their study of artists' behavior cited formulation of problems as a good predictor of creativity in finished products. The unique problem-solving process indicative of imaginative thinkers could be revealed in the following six questions: (1) Has the problem been formulated before by the problem solver? (2) By anyone else? (3) Is a correct method of solution known to the problem solver? (4) To anyone else? (5) Is correct solution known to the problem solver? (6) To anyone else? Problems never formulated before, those for which no solution or method of finding answers is known, inspire original imaginings that trigger creative responses. When children choose to invent their own problems in painting, sculpting, and drawing rather than accept the ones that are handed to them, they behave in creative ways.

Children learn creative behavior by doing, not by contemplating problems they never tackle themselves. After reworking, analyzing, reshaping, and stretching out an assigned question, they will most likely find a more exciting one. This is half the battle. As Einstein said, "The mere formulation of a problem is far more often essential than its solution, which may be merely a matter of mathematical or experimental skill" (quoted in Parnes 1967, p. 129). So, while narrow, one-answer problem statements require only routine responses, a wide open question demands all the imagination, intuition, hunches, and wildest notions that children can bring to bear upon it.

In a review of highly creative, productive professionals, Eby (1989) noticed ten fundamental behaviors: perceptiveness, active interaction with the environment, reflectiveness, persistence, independence, goal orientation, originality, productivity, self-evaluation, and communication of findings. Teaching that values and encourages these behaviors can enable children to deepen in confidence and daring as they begin to take bold new strides in what is unfamiliar. Though tentative at first, even the uninitiated will begin to seek independent approaches to open-ended problems and to defend positions they have proved. Analyzing the elements of their problem, testing and retesting hypotheses, and synthesizing their findings into a workable solution demands a radical shift from the passivity of authority-based learning. It demands a task commitment that will prevent their best ideas from fizzling out. Higher-level doing keeps higher-level thinking from devolving into an intellectual exercise.

CREATIVE PRODUCTS: A WAY OF ASSESSING OUTCOMES

When the creative process ends, at least temporarily, society passes judgment on the results. Historically, society has devalued creative products (at least initially). Educators tend therefore to avoid evaluating the results of creativity, knowing that "the price of novelty is all too often the skepticism or hostility of one's contemporaries" (Kneller 1965, p. 5). On the other hand, communication is the final stage of the creative process (Stein 1974), which translates a discovery into a tangible form the world can understand and value. Creative products effect change, broaden the scope of thinking, and ensure our survival. The study of them should not be omitted out of sympathy for the ill treatment so many creative minds have endured at the hands of society. On the contrary, more research on this subject of communication could suggest ways to support individuals at this crucial step. As isolated as many creative contributors may appear, their desire to communicate drives them through an arduous process to the completion of their ideas. "The creative act is courage in realizing one's situation, and the reward for it, when there is a reward, is company" (Barron 1975, p. 151).

Novelty

What makes a product creative, according to Rogers (1954), is novelty, and novelty depends more or less on three conditions: openness to experience, an internal locus of evaluation (not judging the work from external standards), and an ability and freedom to toy with many elements and ideas. Novelty means more than elaboration. Ghiselin (1963) could trace in the creative products he studied a complete transformation of an old order into an entirely original one. Flanagan (1963) noticed that novel products uncover principles invisible before, not extensions of or imitations of familiar ones. J. H. McPherson (1963) quotes a German patent officer who, responding to a question about how he recognizes a true invention out of the mass of applications, said: "Very simple. While I look through one drawing after another I feel my attention riveted unexpectedly at times by one of them; from the details lying before me, I see immediately the spark of creative fire—a nervous chill runs along my back; that, then, is an invention" (p. 27).

Yet novelty must also have relevance in order to endure. The public can discover the value of an idea only if it meets a conscious need, and inventions that solve no problems are quickly shelved. Stein (1963) alluded to this requirement when he described creativity as "a process that results in a novel work that is accepted as useful, tenable or satisfying by a significant group of people at some point in time" (p. 218).

Novelty and usefulness must converge to create the impact desired and neither should override the other. Flanagan (1963) in his study of ingenuity in inventors addressed the issue of usefulness to real problems, but concluded that utility should not supersede originality and creativity. He lamented the fate of creative talent, restrained by a system that rewards practicality over invention. No one wants a creative "longhair," he said, to upset the status quo in the field of science.

Communication

Society desires novelty, but clamps the lid over inventions that demand too much change. Creative people who puncture holes in treasured myths are punished for their independence, while the very professions that mete out the punishment continue to complain about the dearth of innovation. Novelty by nature leaves all conventional views behind, and this is its value (though an unwelcome one) to society. Transcending the status quo, novel ideas bring solutions to problems that could not be solved otherwise, while subscription to old standards stifles creativity completely.

Because of this conflict, society often rejects creative ideas or so alters their original form that the inventor no longer recognizes them. Keats' epitaph is telling: "Here lies one whose name was writ in water," a fate met by countless brilliant contributors to our culture. A somewhat dubious fate likewise awaits the "successful" inventor. There is no way to predict how a novel idea will shape an environment or how people will perceive it or use it.

Society's approval, though desirable, quickly converts a new idea into a new limit, a new rule to impress and intimidate future thinkers—a fate never intended or imagined by the author. If the author viewed his work as preciously as society does, he would stop inventing. An imaginative mathematician, for example, confers far less status on either old or new knowledge than does the more conventional lot of mathematicians. Thus, while the field of math or science struggles to surrender old status objects for new ones, the inventor who created the new ones in the first place is already outdating them.

Stein (1974), in his analysis of the communication process that accompanies creativity, proves the need for inventors to have intermediaries (patrons, supporters, professional counselors, etc.) to effectively inform the public and create markets. These intermediaries bridge the gap between the tradition-bound world and the creative individual, who tends to shrink from communicating with those who criticize and label him. They are professionals, friends, family members, teachers, mentors, counselors, or special interest groups who in essence co-create the product as a legitimate innovation. They counsel, nurture, raise funds, offer professional advice, share contacts, and design a marketing plan for the idea they value. Intermediaries know how to see in the raw material of a novel idea the finite marketable thing that will make sense to the product-oriented world. It takes this kind of savvy to lure society out of its narrowness and resistance to change. Many inventors, scientists, or artists have credited their success to the supporters who gave their ideas life in the world.

CONDITIONS THAT ENCOURAGE OR HINDER
THE DEVELOPMENT OF CREATIVITY

Studies of creative people, processes, and products have turned up fresh insights and ideas for adults wondering how they can support the short- and long-term needs of creative children. But they have also raised questions about the effect of adult expectations on creative children, many of whom abandon their gifts at a young age. How do our aspirations for children either enhance or diminish their self-esteem and love of learning? Do we care more for grade point averages than the kind of human beings they are becoming? How superficial or insightful are their judgments of themselves or others? How can we, as parents or teachers, help them reach their potential and set good precedents for lifelong learning and contribution?

School Environment

Clearly, teachers can affect children more by their attitude than by the lessons they design. The most innovative curriculum cannot make up for a restrictive and punitive environment. Children are excited, inspired, and motivated most by teachers who love them and who are themselves enthusiastic learners. Any discussion of creative teaching, therefore, should begin with attitude.

Attitude.   Teaching creatively presumes tolerance of initial failures and mistakes in a new venture, and having a comfort level with the unpredictable. For many, stepping outside the authoritarian structure may be foolhardy and naive. Many teachers, like children and parents, have undergone a disempowering process. Many have learned to succumb to external evaluation, to bow before authority figures, deny their instincts and creative needs, and resign themselves to living inside the obligations of a restrictive educational system. "Teachers are part of a social system and subject to all the pressures in it that may militate against creativity" (Stein 1974, p. 156). If teachers do not receive encouragement for their own creative incentives, they have no reason to reward it in their students.

   While many teachers continue to rejuvenate themselves and their students with new and innovative approaches to curriculum, others have lost the enthusiasm for the classroom that once sustained them. The overwhelming circumstances facing many teachers today practically preclude significant, creative involvement with children. In a study by Torrance (1964), teachers were inclined to credit the progress of their students more to genetically determined development than to their instruction.

   When Torrance and Myers (1967) asked a group of teachers to implement creative teaching ideas in their classrooms, the results of their study clearly unveiled the "forces within teachers which oppose innovation" (p. 161). Most of them proved defensive, authoritarian, driven by time limits, insensitive to the creative and emotional needs of children, lacking energy, preoccupied with channeling information, overly concerned with discipline, and fundamentally unwilling to give of themselves. Torrance and Myers concluded that "when we ask teachers to behave in certain ways we must take their values into consideration" (p. 163).

   Teachers who manage to teach creatively, in spite of all hindrances, know they make a difference and this knowledge sustains them in their more harrying moments

(Torrance 1964). Their students show the difference they make. Nonreaders begin to devour books; estranged students make friends and find ways to contribute; destructive children direct their energies through more constructive channels. Such achievements are possible because the teachers respond sensitively to their students' curiosity needs and make them feel safe from the harshness of academic evaluation. They walk many second miles to help the children take initial steps in a new learning venture, to squelch criticism or judgment by others, and to encourage responsibility and respect in the classroom.

Creative children respond well to this kind of guidance. Every teacher needs to assume at least partial responsibility for the creative child's emotional development, rather than pass the job on to a counselor. Teachers, as well as parents, are the most logical people to help creative young people discover ways to solve their problems (Torrance 1969)—how, for example, to preserve their sense of worth without being defensive; how to accept their own differences and share these qualities with others, rather than seclude themselves; how to persevere when they feel they have failed and continue to risk and experiment in the face of others' opinions. Much talent has needlessly gone to waste because children never learned to handle issues that adults could have helped them solve.

Getting Started.   Students do not automatically jump at the chance to be creative. Traditional schooling may not prepare them for the ambiguities, the unexpected twists and turns of creative work. As most teachers will testify, activities rarely run as smoothly in open-ended learning as they do in the traditional one-answer assignment. Children uninitiated in the ways and means of the unpredictable imagination will not be inclined to commit great leaps of faith when the rewards are not forthcoming. The rewards to be had are intrinsic to a process that children do not yet understand or trust. So teachers need to woo them a little.

Davis (1985) uses creative dramatics to lure children into the creative learning process. Theater activities can snag the curiosity of even the most timid students, especially if the teacher introduces them with a little humor. Through various warm-up exercises, movements, sensory and body awareness activities, pantomime, and playmaking, teachers can shake the seriousness out of a class. A joke or two restores humanness to the learning place and this greatly reassures a frightened or insecure child. Students need this freedom from traditional, academic intensity before they dare diverge from the straight and narrow path.

Experiences that develop visualization, intuition, and imagination help students evolve more original insights. Many teachers of the gifted use copious resources in their writing classes—books, magazines, photographs, posters, records, tapes, and paintings, to name but a few. Children in Smutny's class walk into imaginary castles, meet Mayan Indians at a local Guatemalan vegetable market, experience the sorrow of a wizened old woman feeding birds in the park, and the joy of a child's first jaunt along the beach. Students weave little anecdotes around these visual images and discuss them with each other.

When her students have immersed themselves in the vivid details of castles, landscapes, and people, Smutny will add another medium to expand on their images. Radio programs, music, and sound effects transform first impressions by suggesting more unusual interpretations to the scenes the children are seeing. The sound of laughter and gambling men imposed on a serene Monet landscape, for example, evokes less conventional interpretations than those ordinarily given to impressionist paintings. After having the students write for a short while, Smutny reads their work to the class without mentioning authors' names. This gives the children the joy of hearing their poems and stories read and appreciated after their first attempts. Yet remaining anonymous makes them feel safe while they mold and rework possible submissions for the creative writing magazine.

Unusual catalysts inspire unusual responses. In a class of rather tentative seventh and eighth grade writers, Smutny introduced a poetry section by presenting several lush paintings. She asked the students to close their eyes and place themselves in Monet's soft blue sky, in Toulouse-Lautrec's bold, rusty-red dancing scene, or in the center of O'Keeffe's orange flower. After a minute or so, they jotted down a jumble of words and phrases—whatever came to mind—without any conscious effort to form sentences or make sense. Next, they arranged them into four or five phrases and offered at least two possible interpretations to their writing through dramatic readings. It was in these readings that the students discovered the flexibility of words. Many of them began to experiment. One child read a few lines in a mood that conflicted with the words he wrote, while other children analyzed the dramatic effect of combining disparate images. In this way, an hour of prolific poetry writing began. The furious scribbling of ebullient children had replaced the grim silence of a class staring at blank paper.

A French teacher, in a summer program for talented junior high students, began his class by dramatizing the story of Little Red Riding Hood in humorous vein. As he progressed through the tale, he would pause periodically to make sure the class understood, by asking the students (in French) what happened next. When they told him, he would give them the French translation and ask individual children to repeat. The storytelling gradually transformed into a dialogue, with the students offering little snippets of their French to help him along. Occasionally, when a child responded in English, he would pretend confusion and ask the more fluent speakers to help the others explain what they meant.

Classes that begin with the personal hunch or image engage students' curiosity almost immediately. A math teacher in a class of creative third graders preferred to start the week off with a visualization. One day he asked them to imagine that a man on the twenty-fifth floor of an office building threw his dictionary out the window. They were to place themselves on the outside of the building about half way down and watch the book fall. Did it pick up speed as it fell? They closed their eyes to imagine this. Then the teacher asked for their conclusions and why they suspected the object accelerated or did not accelerate as it fell. He followed this exercise with a simple experiment and validated, to the instant delight of the children, many of their suspicions.

Students love to discover things on their own. Another math teacher started his seventh and eighth grade students building paper models of the Archimedean solids. They cut out orange pentagons, folded the flaps, stapled these together, and found that 12 pentagons fit together nicely to form a three-dimensional object (called a dodecahedron). The teacher then gave them triangles to cut out and fit together into three different regular solids. One of the children suggested putting triangles and pentagons together, which formed a solid called icosadodecahedron. The children took great pleasure in discovering the various solids, which were then hung on the wall and labeled with the name given to them by Archimedes 2000 years ago. Since these solids form the basis for all crystal structures and for the arrangement of atoms in molecules, building them helps children develop the three-dimensional image so necessary in the study of geology or chemistry.

Another math project designed around finding number patterns began with the class looking for patterns that would then enable them to determine the number of straws needed to build a four-dimensional triangle. They built the model out of straws. The students next found that a one-dimensional triangle would need one straw, a two-dimensional triangle three straws, a three-dimensional triangle six straws, and a four-dimensional triangle ten straws. Students quickly saw the pattern and determined that it would take 15 straws to build a five-dimensional triangle and 21 straws to build a six-dimensional triangle. One enterprising child actually constructed on his own a model of a six-dimensional triangle, which the teacher had never seen before.

An art teacher wanted to introduce cubism to her students. So far they had stuck to the more representational mode, and she suspected that the class was beginning to tire. She led them all outside with their sketch pads and asked them to walk up to a nearby tree and study all the intricate shapes in the trunk. Rather than draw the outline of the tree, they simply rendered on paper the designs they saw. Returning to the classroom, they discovered with great surprise the beauty of their patterns and the individuality of each person's rendition. Intuitively the class began to perceive the mazelike internal structure of even the simplest objects and noticed further that the shapes of the space around objects have distinct form and pattern as well. These realizations enlarged their vision and profoundly altered the way they tackled portraits, still lifes, and landscapes.

The first splash into any subject makes a big difference. In a unit on endangered animal species, for example, Eby (1984) designed a "pre-task" activity that had children write a one-page story about an animal. Another one on ancient Egyptian pyramids began with the children's creation of a poster about Egypt and pyramids. A class on aviation and map-making required that children draw a map of their own house and yard, using scale and symbols, while the first session of an architecture unit asked them to draw a scale map of their own room at home, using symbols for furniture. These experiences start with the children's personal lives, whims, interests, and imagination. Beginning with themselves, rather than some external requirement, they evolve original approaches to problems that would normally baffle and frustrate them.

Getting through the Rough Spots. Children soon realize that creative work is a rocky road. Writers, scientists, and performers encounter many potholes and breakdowns, and frequently question their own sanity in prolonging activities that cause so much headache and frustration. The temptation to quit is constant, especially when nothing seems to happen. Children are particularly susceptible to this disillusionment and will prematurely abort their most creative endeavors unless they get support.

There are no easy solutions to this stage of creative work. Teachers have nothing to fall back on but their trust in themselves and the class to work through the problems creatively. This is actually a blessing in disguise, for the worst response, next to no response at all, would be to spew out formulaic directives and suggestions that have little to do with the specific needs or circumstances of the group.

The good news is that children can often find their own answers if properly guided. Smutny consistently found that children can generate many solutions to their own crises. In an early session on creative writing, she noticed six or seven children dawdling with their pens and looking blankly out the window, and saw their need for fresh ideas. She halted the session for a bit of brainstorming. On querying them on their work, she saw that many of the children had unconsciously imposed on themselves narrow and inhibiting ideas of how their poems or stories should turn out. One girl complained that her poem did not hang together well and she kept trying to tackle the problem by changing its structure completely. Smutny asked the class to suggest ideas, even wild and outrageous ones. Their thoughts ranged from reading her poem out loud (to herself), to writing it in one long line on a piece of paper taped to the wall, to jotting each line down on separate pieces of paper to experiment with the order or the lines, to going for a walk and reciting the poem to a nearby tree, to writing the poem backwards. The girl actually used some of these ideas and finished her poem without destroying its unique structure.

The class also requested a change of environment to spur them on: different kinds of music for conjuring up new images, walks outside for clearing out cluttered thoughts, comfy chairs for meditative lounging, and small group activities for sharing ideas on each other's pieces. Several students felt that it would help them to have professional writers come and talk to them, perhaps even work with them on their poetry and stories. Smutny arranged for an arts critic from Nairobi, Kenya, to come and discuss her work and how she handles some of the writing snags that arise before she is able to submit her articles for publication. Children felt reassured by the knowledge that professionals struggle with common writing issues. The African journalist helped the class to be specific about what stopped their work, which automatically suggested a number of things they could do to push themselves over this hump.

Getting Tangible Results.   When students complete their projects, they experience the value of their work immediately. The final evening of Project '86 and '87 had this effect. Children in the performance classes exhibited their choreography and theater pieces, while on several floors in a nearby building, student inventors, artists, and mathematicians explained to parents and peers the discoveries they had made. A video of students doing commercials in French sent gales of laughter across another room where many parents watched with amazement as their timid, barely fluent children rattled off French constructions in a sales pitch for Wheaties or Scott tissues. These displays showed how intently the children had persevered in bringing their projects to completion. The 200-page creative writing magazine, the display of art work and inventions, and the performances expressed three weeks of inspiration, exasperation, energy, curiosity, struggle, perseverance, and determination.

What parents found striking in their children's products was the radical departure from the usual and expected. In the course of the program, children often confront the questions: What do I expect the outcome to be? Am I holding a mental image of how this project will turn out? What would be the most unusual solution to this problem that I can imagine?

Close-mindedness has always tried to deny exciting, unexplainable truths. Do children know that the Arctic has a pollution problem? Scientists, until recently, denied such a possibility even though a lone researcher began submitting evidence to support his assertion (Carey 1988). Do children in math classes know that Einstein used mental imagery in his discoveries, or that many of the early mathematicians were mystics? Probably not in traditional math settings.

Teachers of problem-solving students should encourage the use of open-ended questions, the suspension of judgment, and demonstrate the value of new and unusual solutions, rather than the old, hackneyed response. As these children begin to exchange the narrow values learned in traditional schooling for values that support individuality, intuition, and imagination, they will enjoy finding unexpected answers, and sharing these to benefit others.

Home Environment

Creative learning begins at home. From parents, children learn what to value, how to see themselves and others, and where the limits of possibility lie. Parents who trudge through an evergreen forest with their children and climb over craggy rocks by the sea share the thrill of nature's wilds. It is the same thrill children feel thumbing through a book they have experienced hundreds of times through a family member's dramatic reading. Enthusiasm for all things great and small and in between is catching, and parents can either preserve their children's "sense of wonder" or snuff it out. A child's home has a lot to do with what he or she eventually becomes: a contributor or a criminal; a bold and original thinker or a discipline problem. Although we cannot lay the entire burden of a child's future at the family's door, home is the first and most powerful educator.

Factors That Hinder Creativity.   Many parents fret a great deal over their children's external successes. For the early American pioneers who hacked their way through the wilderness, acquisition and production always seemed more reasonable than imagination or invention (Arieti 1976). This orientation to life persists. Today it is still more important to be practical and materially successful than to think creatively.

Preoccupation with material goals ignores the "curiosity needs" of children (Torrance 1969)—their love of adventure, exploration, and fantasy. Without imagination, a child's creative ability wilts. Yet the adults in his life often persist in caring more about what he acquires than who he is as a person; more about what grades he gets than how he thinks; more about how he compares to others than what he contributes to them. In time, the child's openness to experience gives way to closure;

he becomes one-track, distrustful, and narrow. The ambitions of the adults in his life practically bully the creative spark out of existence.

For too long parents have succumbed to narrow definitions of creativity that revolve around the mystery of the test score or some obscure educational requirements for special programs. The labeling of their children compels them to adopt tactics that intimidate, mystify, and pressure students. Special programs for creative children are not elitist, but labeling is (Eby 1984). The "gifted" label fosters unrealistic and often inhumane expectations, greatly increases emotional stress, and forces superficial values on young people.

Eby (1984) designed a curriculum model that focuses on creative behavior rather than "gifted" children. Parents can serve their children's needs just as effectively, if not more so, by a simple acknowledgment of creative behavior. This takes the heat off the child and allows him to be bold and adventurous. It avoids all the fuss and hubbub over qualifications and test scores that confuse children and drive them mercilessly to live up to a narrow image of excellence. Parents who teach children to share their whimsy and wild imaginings with the rest of the family help them to see that their abilities can inspire joy and interest in others. "Humility about one's gifts combined with the ideal of service to others will prevent snobbery, and it is the home which must take first responsibility in teaching these matters" (Thorne 1967, p. 276).

Factors That Enhance Creativity.   We need only observe the toddler exploring the shelves and cupboards of the kitchen, amusing herself for hours with imaginary games and stories, to know the boundless curiosity of children. Parents can nurture this precious quality without sacrificing good sense and manageability. To do this, parents need to trust their own instincts rather than believe all that "experts" say, value their own capacity for creative expression, recapture their own love of learning, and allow themselves complete freedom to make mistakes. "We as parents and teachers have become overly dependent on outside sources for help when we have access to so many of our own at home or in the classroom" (Khatena 1978, p. 10).

Parents rarely see themselves as primary educators of creative talent. Our society has diminished the value of homemakers in this country. Today, the mothers or fathers of talented children have become as much a neglected resource as have their children. Homemakers often surrender their right to teach because society says that they should stick to recipes and budget matters and leave schooling to schools. "Has it occurred to anyone," asks Thorne (1967, p. 277), "that it might be possible to evolve some suggestions for mothering that would encourage curiosity and learning and creativity among youngsters at home?"

A vibrant, spontaneous, and creative lifestyle is the best gift parents can offer to an imaginative young person. Creativity needs to be organic to daily living, not merely recreational. It begins with relationships. Parents can use creative problem solving to resolve family conflicts, for example. They can transform destructive energy into productive energy, arrange for children to contribute meaningfully to the home and take responsibility for their actions, allow children to experience what it means to have choices and begin to assume ownership of those choices and their results, use children's points of view in a joint family decision-making process, help children see others' points of view without blaming them for not seeing, and involve children in the creation of home rules (Torrance 1969). Creative self-expression does not flourish in a home where children have no voice, never make decisions, never assume responsibility, and never imagine others' feelings or points of view.

Children will continue to love learning if parents do and if the home has plenty of odds and ends to fascinate a curious mind. There is no telling what these might be. As we will see in Chapter 6, for example, creative children in a Nairobi slum converted piles of tin and wire into a rich reserve of building materials for toy automobiles. Resources need not be expensive. "Helping children to love learning involves first, creative materials," advises Thorne (1967, p. 274), whose home was full, not of commercial resources, but of collectible "stuff" ranging from *National Geographic* magazines, charts, maps, and resource books to games, puzzles, art materials, and assorted useful junk. Her children made messes and on one occasion ruined a kitchen knife (under her surveillance) during a science experiment, but they all grew up to be highly creative thinkers who could leap wholeheartedly into projects without fear of ridicule. She also knew how to distinguish the creative mess from the irresponsible junk heap. If children think all messes are "bad," they will never discover that some of the most brilliant ideas come from creative messes.

This kind of creative child-rearing teaches as much as, if not more than, any schooling later in life. In fact, children's activities at school rarely offer enough for creative thinking to deepen and expand. Schools need the special support that parents can lend. Torrance (1969) offers the following suggestions for parents of very young creative children:

> Provide materials that develop imagination
> Provide materials that enrich imagery (e.g., folk tales, myths, fables)
> Permit time for thinking and daydreaming (time to muse and wonder, rather than rush from one activity to the next)
> Encourage children to record their ideas
> Give children's writings some concrete embodiment (frame their pictures or make a book out of their poems)
> Accept the child's natural tendency to take a different look
> Prize rather than punish true individuality
> Be cautious about editing children's writings
> Encourage children to play with words
> Love them and let them know it

Eminent contributors to society have credited home and school for the successful course of their life work. Vibrant, enthusiastic adults (parents or teachers) can be the deciding influence in the life of a creative child. They help her to keep her interests alive when people ridicule her, respect her work and her individuality when she cannot, and support her unique contributions to others when criticism threatens. Unfortunately, creative children who become creative adults are a rarity. Barron (1975) found in the lives of creative people a "solitariness and the need to establish meaning and community" which, he said, were "primary motives in creativity" (p.

155). On some level, creative people in their inventions, poems, songs, and innovations are attempting to establish a connection with the society that outlaws them. The majority of them, however, surrender before this connection is made. Parents and teachers can do much to reverse this tragedy. The love and support of caring adults helps to build in the child a resiliency against narrow assessments and criticisms that would ordinarily dampen her spirits. Research has delved deeply into this subject. What remains is the practice of it.

OPPORTUNITIES FOR DISCUSSION AND ACTION

1. How is creativity most commonly defined? Based on this chapter, how would you broaden this definition?
2. Can you see ways in which creativity could be overlooked? Where would you look for creative ability in your classroom?
3. Is there a difference between teaching creatively and teaching for creativity?
4. Interview a child you think might be creatively talented. Notice your own criteria for determining creative talent. Interview the parent and ask him/her for his/her perception of creativity in the child. What criteria keep emerging in this process?
5. Discover the creative dimensions of so-called noncreative subjects (math, science, etc.). Think of specific ways to ignite children's imaginative or inventive abilities in subject areas that actually rely on creativity for advancement.
6. Confer with people from a wide range of professions and gather as much data as possible on the following: factors that contributed to their professional development; ways in which creativity functions in their work; ways in which they think creativity could be taught more effectively in the schools.

REFERENCES

Arieti, S. 1976. *Creativity: The magic synthesis.* New York: Basic Books.

Barron, F. 1975. The solitariness of self and its imagination. In *Perspectives in creativity,* ed. I. A. Taylor and J. W. Getzels. Chicago: Aldine.

Carey, J. 1988. Peering into the mystery of arctic haze, *International Wildlife,* March–April, pp. 26–28.

Carson, R. 1965. *The sense of wonder.* New York: Harper & Row.

Clark, B. 1988. *Growing up gifted.* 3d ed. Columbus, Ohio: Merrill.

Davis. G. A., and S. B. Rimm. 1985. *Education of the gifted and talented.* Englewood Cliffs, N.J.: Prentice-Hall.

Dettmer, P. 1981. Improving teacher attitudes toward characteristics of the creatively gifted, *Gifted Child Quarterly* 25: 11–16.

Eby, J. W. 1983. Gifted behavior: A non-elitist approach, *Education Leadership,* May, pp. 30–36.

————. 1984. Developing gifted behavior, *Education Leadership,* April, pp. 35–43.

————. 1989. Developing creative productivity. *Illinois Council for the Gifted Journal* 9.

————. (in print) Children as producers rather than consumers of knowledge.

Ellis, J. L. 1985. Creatively gifted children in regular school programs: Their problems and a proposed solution, *B. C. Journal of Special Education* 9: 69–86.

Feldhusen, J. F., and D. J. Treffinger. 1977. *Creative thinking and problem solving in gifted education.* Dubuque, Iowa: Kendall/Hunt Publishing Co.

Firestien, R. L., and D. J. Treffinger. 1983. Creative problem solving: Guidelines and resources for effective facilitation, *G/C/T,* January–February, pp. 2–10.

Flanagan, J. C. 1963. The definition and measurement of ingenuity. In *Scientific creativity: Its recognition and development,* ed. C. W. Taylor and F. Barron. New York: John Wiley.

Gacheru, M. 1986. Children of Nairobi, *Illinois Council for the Gifted* 4: 50.

Getzels, J. W., and M. Csikszentmihalyi. 1972. Concern for discovery in the creative process. In *The creativity question,* ed. A. Rothenberg and C. R. Hausman. Durham, N.C.: Duke University Press.

Ghiselin, B. 1952. *The creative process: A symposium.* Berkeley, Calif.: University of California Press.

————. 1963. Ultimate criteria for two levels of creativity. In *Scientific creativity: Its recognition and development,* ed. C. W. Taylor and F. Barron. New York: John Wiley.

Gowan, J. C. 1965. What makes a gifted child creative?—Four theories. In *Creativity: Its educational implications,* ed. J. C. Gowan, G. D. Demos, and E. P. Torrance. New York: John Wiley.

Gregory, A. 1982. Applying the Purdue Three-Stage Model for gifted education to the development of art education for G/C/T Students, *G/C/T,* November–December, pp. 23–26.

Guilford, J. P. 1968. *Intelligence, creativity and their educational implications.* San Diego: Robert R. Knapp.

Khatena, J. 1978. *The creatively gifted: Suggestions for parents and teachers.* New York: Vantage Press.

Kneller, G. F. 1965. *The art and science of creativity.* New York: Holt, Rinehart & Winston.

McPherson, J. H. 1963. A proposal for establishing ultimate criteria for measuring creative output. In *Scientific creativity: Its recognition and development,* ed. C. W. Taylor and F. Barron. New York: John Wiley.

Maslow, A. H. 1968. *Toward a psychology of being.* 2nd ed. New York: D. Van Nostrand.

————. 1971. *The farther reaches of human nature.* New York: Viking Press.

May, R. 1975. *The courage to create.* New York: W. W. Norton.

Myers, R. E., and E. P. Torrance. 1961. Can teachers encourage creative thinking? In *Creativity: Its educational implications,* ed. J. C. Gowan, G. D. Demos, and E. P. Torrance. New York: John Wiley.

Osborn, A. F. 1963. *Applied imagination: Principles and procedures of creative problem solving.* New York: Scribner's.

Parnes, S. J. 1967. *Creative behavior guidebook.* New York: Scribner's

————. 1975. *Aha! Insights into creative behavior.* Buffalo, N.Y.: D. O. K. Publishers.

————, R. Noller, and A. Biondi. 1977. *Guide to creative action.* New York: Scribner's.

Poincaré, H. 1913. Mathematical creation. In *The Creative Process: A Symposium,* ed. B. Ghiselin. Berkeley: University of California Press, reprinted by New American Library.

Renzulli, J. S., S. M. Reis, and L. H. Smith. 1981. The revolving door models: A new way of identifying the gifted. *Phi Delta Kappan* 62 (no. 9): 648–49.

Rimm, S., G. Davis, and Y. Bien. 1982. Identifying creativity: A characteristic approach. *Gifted Child Quarterly* 26: 165–71.

Rogers, C. 1954. Towards a theory of creativity. In *Creativity: Selected Readings,* ed. P. E. Vernon. Suffolk, England: Richard Clay Ltd.

———. 1969. *Freedom to learn.* Columbus, Ohio: Merrill.

Rubin, L. J. 1963. Creativity and the curriculum. In *Creativity: Its educational implications,* ed. J. C. Gowan, G. D. Demos, and E. P. Torrance. New York: John Wiley.

Stein, M. I. 1963. A transactional approach to creativity. In *Scientific creativity,* ed. C. W. Taylor and F. Barron. New York: John Wiley.

———. 1974. *Stimulating creativity.* New York: Academic Press.

Thorne, A. 1967. Suggestions for mothering the gifted to encourage curiosity, learning, and creativity. In *Creativity: Its educational implications,* ed. J. C. Gowan, G. D. Demos, and E. P. Torrance. New York: John Wiley.

Torrance, E. P. 1962a. Ten ways of helping young children gifted in creative writing and speech. In *Creativity: Its educational implications,* ed. J. C. Gowan, G. D. Demos, and E. P. Torrance. New York: John Wiley.

———. 1962b. Must creative development be left to chance? In *Creativity: Its educational implications,* ed. J. C. Gowan, E. D. Demos, and E. P. Torrance. New York: John Wiley.

———. 1969. *Creativity.* San Rafael, Calif.: Dimensions.

———. 1984. The role of creativity in identification of the gifted and talented. *Gifted Child Quarterly* 28: 153–56.

———. 1986. Who is gifted? *Illinois Council for the Gifted* 4: 2–3.

Toynbee, A. 1964. Is America neglecting her creative minority? In *Widening horizons in creativity,* ed. C. A. Taylor. New York: John Wiley.

CHAPTER 4

Review of Assessment Instruments Used in Gifted Education

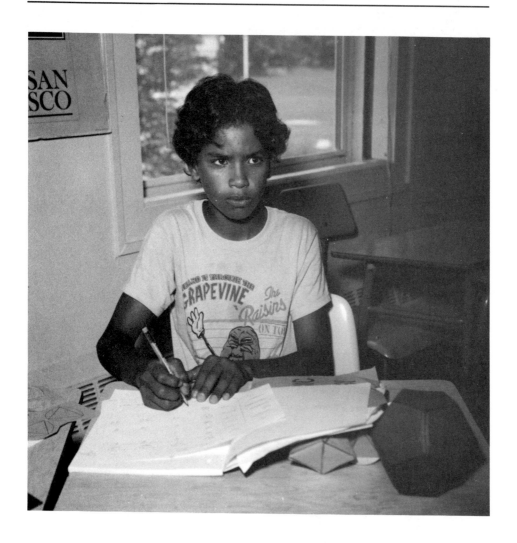

Mr. Duncan, the curriculum director of the school district, has called a meeting to make decisions about the standardized tests used by the district. Part of the discussion centers on the use of standardized test scores for identification of children for the school's gifted program. Mrs. Chong, the gifted coordinator, and Mr. Zenk, the school psychologist, are also attending the meeting.

MR. DUNCAN: We've used the ABC school achievement tests for the last several years, but are considering changing to the XYZ battery. How will this affect your program?

MRS. CHONG: I am very reluctant to change tests. We've been using the ABC scores to select academically gifted students in math, science, and language arts. What are the advantages of the XYZ?

MR. ZENK: The main advantage is that the items on the XYZ test more nearly match our basic curriculum guide than the items on the ABC test did.

MR. DUNCAN: That's right. We think we'll see a general improvement in our schoolwide test results on the XYZ because of the better match.

MRS. CHONG: If children are expected to score higher, I'll have more children qualifying for the gifted program. That will be difficult to manage, as we already serve more than the 5 percent that the state reimburses us for.

MR. DUNCAN: Well, you'll just have to reassess and raise the minimum requirements to keep the numbers in line.

MR. ZENK: I can help you with that. We'll look at the pilot study results and determine how many children would qualify under the old and new tests. Then we'll raise the cutoff scores so that we still get approximately 5 percent of our school population.

MRS. CHONG: I'll have to think about this. It sounds like a new test and new cutoff scores will leave me with a lot of explaining to do. What will I do if the children I have already identified go below the new cutoff scores? What if different children do well on the new test? The parents will have many questions that will be hard to answer.

WHAT DO YOU THINK?

Most identification policies and decisions in U.S. gifted programs attempt to comply with the report issued in 1972 by the U.S. Commissioner of Education, Sydney Marland. This document states that identification of gifted and talented children is to be determined by "professionally qualified persons" including "teachers, administrators, school psychologists, counselors, curriculum specialists, artists, musicians, and others with special training who are also qualified to appraise pupils' special competencies" (Marland 1972, p. 9).

In this scenario, three such professionally qualified persons are grappling with a number of important identification issues that have an impact on gifted programs and the lives of the children they serve. As seen in this scenario, scores on schoolwide achievement tests are often used as a means of identification for gifted programs because they are given to the entire population on a regular basis.

1. What are the advantages of using schoolwide achievement test data as a means of selecting children for gifted programs?
2. What are the disadvantages?
3. What kind of training is needed to ensure that "professionally qualified persons" are capable of "appraising pupils' special competencies"? What kind of training would you want before you made such judgments?
4. How much weight should be given to test scores and how much should be determined by the school or program personnel themselves?
5. What criteria should be used to select tests for identification of children for gifted programs?

INTRODUCTION

One of the best sources of information about tests and other measurement devices in *The Ninth Mental Measurements Yearbook* (Mitchell 1985; abbreviated as *Ninth MMY*) or *Tests in Print* (Mitchell 1983), both published by the University of Nebraska Press. These reference books list thousands of tests of enormous variety, but the Classified Subject Index of the *Mental Measurements Yearbook* lists no tests of giftedness. This illustrates one of the major obstacles to developing a defensible, comprehensive identification system for your own school district's gifted program. Since you cannot, at present, purchase a test for giftedness, it is necessary to adapt or create instruments that fit your own district's definition of giftedness.

In practice, gifted educators employ tests and other assessment instruments that were written to measure constructs that are related to giftedness: tests of intelligence, scholastic aptitude, and achievement, and tests that assess specific aptitudes in mathematics, fine arts, language arts, science, and social studies. But gifted program personnel rarely have sufficient training or experience in understanding and selecting tests and measurement devices, which leads many of them to make naive or uninformed decisions about the selection and use of tests in the identification process. The usual practice is to select tests because they are available, and are already given in the school district for other purposes. A percentage or cutoff score is arbitrarily decided upon for practical reasons. Little or no thought is given to how this practice relates to a theory or definition of giftedness. Yet, the children selected by this process are labeled "gifted children," while other children in the district are unwittingly labeled "nongifted."

A National Conference on Identification was held in New Jersey in 1982 to assess current trends in identification practices. Prior to the conference itself, a survey was sent out to state consultants for the gifted, universities offering training in gifted education, and practitioners and teachers in gifted programs in every state. The survey asked participants to list the categories of giftedness they were identifying and the tests they were using. Analysis of this survey revealed that tests were being inappropriately used to a great extent.

Tests of ability were frequently used for identifying children in the categories of specific academic aptitudes, creativity, arts, and leadership. Achievement test batteries were employed to select children for the categories of general intellectual ability, creativity, and the arts. Measures of creativity were being used to identify students in all categories of the federal definition. Measures of general intellectual ability and specific academic aptitude were used interchangeably. The report of the National Conference concluded that "this analysis of the relation of practices to the categories of the federal definition reveals a manifest lack of direction, uniformity and appropriateness" (Richert et al. 1982, p. 31).

How can you avoid making these misinformed judgments? You must be willing to do two difficult things: (1) create a clear and realistic operational definition of giftedness to fit the needs of your school community, and (2) find or create the assessment devices that best fit your definition.

In Chapter 5 we will work through the entire process of establishing a gifted screening and identification system. Chapter 5 also contains information about creating instruments of your own. The remainder of this chapter will be devoted to an analysis of the published tests and other instruments that are presently available for use in gifted education. We have tried to include the major assessment devices that are presently being used in established gifted programs as well as recently published instruments that may have a value in either gifted screening or identification processes.

Locating Assessment Instruments

As stated above, there are no well-recognized "tests of giftedness" presently available through commercial publishers. There are, however, many very useful tests that may fit the needs of your gifted program philosophy and definition. The gifted coordinator must become familiar with test reviews and the tests themselves in order to make informed decisions regarding the selection of appropriate assessment instruments. The annotated descriptions in this chapter are offered as an aid to help you begin your search for instruments that match or fit your definition of giftedness. Refer to the *Mental Measurements Yearbook* or *Tests in Print* for further information and reviews of each test that seems useful to you. Another useful resource is the *National Report on Identification* (Richert 1982), which provides reviews of a wide variety of tests and makes recommendations about their appropriate use. We hope that you will also examine copies of the tests themselves before making a final decision about their suitability for your program. Our reviews of these materials are necessarily brief, but you may be able to use this section as a place to begin your search for instruments that are congruent with your own definition of giftedness.

ASSESSING INTELLIGENCE

Individual Intelligence Tests

There are two basic categories of tests used to measure intelligence: individual tests and group tests. Individual tests are given by a psychologist or other trained adult to a single child. Most often the adult asks the child a question and notes his or her reply. Group intelligence tests are usually referred to as ability or aptitude tests. They are paper-and-pencil tests administered by a teacher to a classroom of children, who write down their responses on a form that is scored by a computer.

Individual intelligence tests have gained great respect from educators in gifted education. Intelligence is considered by many to be highly correlated with giftedness. Individuals with high IQs are believed to have great potential for high-level thinking, reasoning, and problem solving. They are also expected to perform very well in academic courses. Many gifted programs are designed primarily to serve the highly intelligent student who may be insufficiently challenged in the regular curriculum.

Intelligence tests are also highly regarded because they are usually administered by a trained school psychologist. The IQ score is considered to have valuable diagnostic value in its own right, but the psychologist's report may also contain other information about the child's behavior during the test that can be utilized in understanding the child's individual needs.

The most widely used and respected individual intelligence tests are the Stanford-Binet Intelligence Scale (S-B), and the Wechsler Intelligence Scale for Children—Revised (WISC-R). These tests are so highly regarded that a score in the high 130s or 140s will usually guarantee eligibility in an academic gifted program. With a mean score of 100 and a standard deviation of 16, scores above 132 are statistically quite rare. Approximately 3 percent of the total population would attain such a score. Scores above 140 are attained by only 1 percent of the population.

IQ scores are not, however, infallible. As we discussed in Chapter 1, most present-day educational and psychological researchers believe that an individual's IQ is partially determined by the environmental influences of home and school. This implies that IQ scores should not be interpreted as stable over a long period of time. For example, a child may score very high at one point in time, but if the environment is relatively unstimulating, her score may be near average a few years later. Similarly, a child's score may be quite ordinary at one time, but with a highly stimulating environment, her score may increase into the "gifted" range.

Another thing that must be considered is that every test, including the most highly regarded IQ tests, has a standard error of measurement (SEM), which is reported in the administration manual for the test. Tests are only relatively crude measurements of very complex human traits. Test developers recognize that there are many possible factors that can cause inaccurate estimates. The SEM is calculated to account for such factors as fatigue, difference in examiners, time of day, and health of the individual being tested. Most IQ tests have SEMs of approximately 4 or 5 points. This means that the actual intelligence quotient of a child is the reported score plus or minus 4 points.

Gifted program administrators must take into account the standard error of measurement when using and interpreting test data in identification decisions. This is especially important when students are considered for eligibility on the basis of the single reported score. Often program administrators establish "cutoff scores" that distinguish between eligibility and noneligibility for a program. For example, many programs use a cutoff score of 140. In some programs, a child who receives a score of 138 is considered ineligible for the program, even though the standard error of measurement means that his score of 138 has a literal meaning of a current estimate of intelligence somewhere between 134 and 142.

Intelligence tests are excellent sources of information about children's reasoning abilities and their verbal and quantitative aptitudes. We recognize their importance in defining and substantiating decisions about children's needs for enriched or accelerated programming in school settings. We expect, however, that they should be used intelligently. We recommend that whenever scores are being interpreted, the standard error of measurement should be considered and reported. We also recommend that decisions be made on current data. Test scores more than two years old are no longer accurate reflections of a child's abilities or aptitudes. If possible, retest every two years.

Our annotated list of individual intelligence tests includes old standards, shortened versions, and several relatively new offerings to the field. You will want to look for tests that are suitable for the age of children you wish to evaluate. Then consider carefully the types of items and subtests that make up each test. These tell you how the test authors defined intelligence. Some tests stress verbal skills while others purposely avoid including verbal items. Some tests measure many different components while others include relatively few. Some include previously learned vocabulary or informational tasks, while others use only new, unlearned test items. Some must be administered and interpreted by a school psychologist while others may be given by a classroom teacher.

Each test has its advantages and disadvantages. We have tried to note some of these, but it is your job to examine the tests and other test reviews to learn more about the strengths and weaknesses of each. It's a difficult job, but an important one in the role of gifted coordinator because the decisions you make about the selection, use, and interpretation of these tests could have an enormous impact on the lives of children who are being considered for eligibility in your gifted program.

Individual Intelligence Tests: An Annotated List

The Stanford-Binet Intelligence Scale (S-B), Third Revision

Authors: Lewis M. Terman and M. A. Merrill.
Publisher: Riverside Publishing Co.
Copyright: Third revision, 1973 (initially published in 1916).
Ages: 2 and over.
Administered by: Registered psychologist.
Time for Administration: 30–90 minutes.
Score: A single Intelligence Quotient (IQ) score (m = 100, s.d. = 16).
Assesses: General Intelligence—a composite of verbal ability, math reasoning, memory, visual discrimination, and general information.
Use in Gifted Identification: Used to identify children who are gifted in the category of general intellectual ability.
Advantages: The S-B was the first test of intelligence ever developed and

normed for the general population. It is still widely respected by psychologists and educators as an accurate predictor of school performance.

Disadvantages: The results are reported in one composite score. There is no way to distinguish an individual's strengths and weaknesses. There is also time and expense involved in the individual administration by a psychologist.

Wechsler Intelligence Scale for Children—Revised (WISC-R)

Author: David Wechsler.

Publisher: The Psychological Corporation.

Copyright: 1974.

Ages: 6–16.

Administered by: Registered psychologist.

Time for Administration: 50–75 minutes.

Scores: Verbal, Performance, and Total scores (mean = 100, s.d. = 15).

Assesses: General intelligence.

Sections: Verbal includes information, comprehension, arithmetic, similarities, vocabulary, and digit span. Performance includes picture completion, arrangement, block design, object assembly, coding, and mazes.

Use in Gifted Identification: Used to identify children who are gifted in the category of general intellectual ability.

Advantages: The report provided by the psychologist who administers the WISC-R contains information regarding the subject's general intelligence, and also provides clues to relative strengths and weaknesses of the individual based upon the subtests and the psychologist's observations of the child during testing.

Disadvantages: There is time and expense involved because the test must be administered and interpreted by a psychologist.

WISC-R Split Half Short Form

Author: Kenneth L. Hobby.

Publisher: Western Psychological Services.

Copyright: 1980.

Ages: 6–16.

Administered by: School psychologist.

Time for Administration: half as long as the WISC-R.

Scores: Same as the WISC-R.

Use in Gifted Identification: May appeal to program personnel who use the WISC-R.

Advantages: By using odd numbered items only, this form of the WISC-R takes only half the time to administer.

Disadvantages: Reviewers are cautious because of the lack of research on this shortened version of the WISC-R. Is the time saved worth the lowered validity of the test?

Slosson Intelligence Test (SIT)

Author: Richard L. Slosson.

Publisher: Slosson Educational Publications, Inc.

Copyright: Second edition, 1981.

Ages: 2 weeks and over.

Purpose: General intelligence test designed as a screening measure to correspond to the Stanford-Binet.

Administered by: Teacher or other trained adult.

Time for Administration: 20–40 minutes.

Scores: One composite score.

Assesses: General intelligence as a function of vocabulary, verbal and math reasoning, and memory.

Use in Gifted Identification: Used to screen for general intellectual ability.

Advantages: May be administered by a teacher or gifted coordinator who can observe the child's confidence and speed of responses in the process of administering the test.

Disadvantages: Only one general score is computed. Scores are generally higher than S-B or WISC-R scores. Reviewers in the *Ninth MMY* (Mitchell 1985, pp. 1402–4) suggest that it be used only as a screener because of inconsistent reports of validity and reliability.

Kaufman Assessment Battery for Children (K-ABC)

Authors: Alan and Nadeen L. Kaufman.

Publisher: American Guidance Service.

Copyright: 1983.

Ages: 2.5–12.5.

Administered by: School psychologist.

Time for Administration: 35–85 minutes.

Scores: Two global scores on Mental Processing and Achievement.

Assesses: Intelligence (defined as a function of mental processing) and achievement.

Use in Gifted Identification: The test is relatively new and was not developed with gifted identification in mind, but is described here for its possible application to early primary identification of children with unusually high mental processing abilities.

Advantages: Incorporates recent developments in both psychological theory and statistical methodology. Gives special attention to children with handicaps, learning disabilities, and cultural and linguistic deficiencies.

Disadvantages: The test was developed for primary age children and is therefore not useful for older children.

McCarthy Scales of Children's Abilities (MSCA)

Author: Dorothea McCarthy.

Publisher: The Psychological Corporation.

Copyright: 1970–72.

Ages: 2.5–8.5.

Administered by: School psychologist.

Time for Administration: 45–60 minutes.

Scores: Composite (General Cognitive Index) plus 5 subscores for verbal, perceptual/performance, quantitative, memory, and motor abilities.

Assesses: General cognitive ability.

Use in Gifted Identification: Occasionally used for primary identification.

Advantages: This test has been reviewed positively for its design and its standardization. It provides a diagnostic profile of five separate components of intelligence.

Disadvantages: Designed for primary children, it has a limited ceiling for assessing older children.

Group Intelligence Tests

Group tests are widely used in the identification of children for gifted programs because of their ease of administration and scoring. In most instances these tests are administered to the entire school population periodically as part of a regular standardized testing program. Another significant advantage is that since all children are tested, each child has an equal opportunity of being selected for the special learning opportunities in a gifted program.

Group tests, however, have some very significant disadvantages in their use in gifted identification. The scores look like IQ scores (a mean of 100 and a standard deviation of 16), but they are computed not in terms of an individual's age, but only by his or her grade level, so they are much more generic than an individual score. The ceiling of difficulty of the items on the test is usually much lower than the ceiling on individual tests, so the test cannot discriminate very accurately at the highest levels. Group percentile scores are usually converted to an individual "ability index," but with low ceilings and difficulty levels the scores themselves may be artificially lowered. A correct score of 60 out of 60 possible items may result in a 99th percentile score, which converts to an "index" between 135 and 145. But a score of 59 out of 60 may result in a percentile score in the low 90s or high 80s in a population of high achievers, and a corresponding "index" score in the 120s.

A very important thing to consider is that none of these ability or aptitude tests were designed to be used in identification of children for gifted programs. They were designed to allow educators and parents to compare the general aptitude of a child with his or her present school achievement. For this reason, they are quite limited in their conception of aptitude or intelligence. They were not designed to measure the more complex abstract reasoning abilities that may be related to giftedness.

In our view, gifted program personnel give too much weight to group ability tests. On many of these tests the items are quite similar to achievement test items: a combination of vocabulary and math problem solving with a few figural analogies added. We recommend that you become very familiar with the types and the difficulties of the items on each form. We can understand and accept their use in screening for potentially likely candidates for a gifted program, but we do not agree with their use as final determiners of whether a child is "gifted" or "not gifted." So we hope that you will use them with great caution.

Group Intelligence Tests: An Annotated List

SOI Learning Abilities Test

Authors: Mary and Robert Meeker, adapted from Guilford's work.
Publisher: Western Psychological Services.
Copyright: 1975.
Ages: Grades 2–12.
Administered by: Any teacher or trained adult.
Time for Administration: Untimed, approximately 110 minutes.
Scores: 26 scores on 26 of the factors of intelligence described by Guilford, including cognition, memory, convergent production, divergent production, and evaluation on verbal, figural, and mathematical tasks.
Use in Gifted Identification: Occasionally used in programs that are based upon Guilford's Structure of the Intellect theory.
Advantages: Can be administered in a classroom. Provides very specific profiles of strengths and weaknesses for each child. Prescriptions can then be written to fit each child's needs.
Disadvantages: Assesses factors unique to Guilford's definition of intelligence. It may be difficult to transfer the test results to a program based upon any other definition.

Otis-Lennon School Ability Test (OLSAT)

Authors: Arthur Otis and Roger Lennon.
Publisher: The Psychological Corporation.
Copyright: 1977–82.
Ages: Grades 1–12.
Administered by: Classroom teacher
Time for Administration: 45–60 minutes.
Scores: One composite score called the School Ability Index based upon verbal, numerical, and figural items presented in a spiral order.
Use in Gifted Identification: Frequently used as a measure of general intellectual ability because of its widely accepted use in schools.
Advantages: Ease of administration and scoring. Guilford's Structure of the Intellect view was used in the most recent revision of this test. Items are offered that test cognition, convergent thinking, and evaluation.
Disadvantages: Low ceiling. Verbal-educational orientation may be viewed as a limited conception of giftedness.

Test of Cognitive Skills (TCS)

Publisher: CTB/McGraw-Hill.
Copyright: 1981.

Ages: Grades 2–12.
Administered by: Classroom teacher.
Time for Administration: 50–60 minutes.
Scores: One composite score (Cognitive Skills Index) and four subscores: sequences, analogies, memory, and verbal reasoning.
Use in Gifted Identification: May be used as a measure of general intellectual ability where abstract abilities are highly valued.
Advantages: Ease of administration and scoring. Less emphasis is placed on school-type knowledge than in other group tests. There are no vocabulary or math problem items. Instead, items test abstract reasoning and ability to recall new information (on the memory subtest).
Disadvantages: Group tests have lower ceilings than individual tests. The way they are normed may also contribute to lowering scores for individuals. Reliability and validity information is limited at the present time.

Cognitive Abilities Test (CogAT)

Authors: Robert Thorndike and Elizabeth Hagen.
Publisher: Riverside Publishing Company.
Copyright: 1954–83.
Ages: Grades K–12.
Administered by: Classroom teacher.
Time for Administration: 50–60 minutes.
Scores: Verbal, Quantitative, and Nonverbal scores for grades 3–12. Primary test (K–2nd grade) provides only one composite score.
Use in Gifted Identification: Widely used in both screening and identification of children for gifted programs because it is given as part of the assessment battery that includes the Iowa Test of Basic Skills, a widely used standardized achievement test.
Advantages: The three subtest scores may be useful in screening children for programs with a verbal, quantitative, or nonverbal orientation. The nonverbal subtest may provide valuable information about non-English-speaking children.
Disadvantages: Low ceilings may cause children to score lower than they would on an individual IQ test.

Developing Cognitive Abilities Test (DCAT)

Authors: D. Beggs, J. Mouw, J. Cawley, J. Wick, J. Smith, M. Cherkes, A. Fitzmaurice, and L. Cawley.
Publisher: American Testronics.
Copyright: 1980.
Ages: Grades 2–12.
Administered by: Classroom teacher.
Time for Administration: 50–60 minutes.
Scores: Total score plus three subtest scores: verbal ability, quantitative ability, and spatial ability.

Use in Gifted Identification: There is a growing interest in this test among gifted program personnel because of its orientation to Bloom's Taxonomy.

Advantages: Items have been designed to measure ability in terms of Bloom's Taxonomy of Educational Objectives. Items are designed to measure usual levels of thinking, recall, and comprehension; but some items on this test have also been specifically designed to measure application, analysis, and—to the degree possible on a standardized, computer-scored instrument—synthesis and evaluation.

Disadvantages: The research on the reliability and predictive validity of this new instrument is not as extensive as in other, older assessment devices.

Comments: Gifted program personnel should be aware that the D in DCAT stands for Developing. This means that the items were designed with the developmental viewpoint that cognitive ability can be altered or developed through environmental experiences.

Ross Test of Higher Cognitive Processes

Authors: John and Catherine Ross.
Publisher: Academic Therapy Publications.
Copyright: 1979.
Ages: Grades 4–6.
Administered by: Teacher.
Time for Administration: Timed, 105 minutes.
Scores: Total score and eight subtest scores are provided with norms for gifted and nongifted students. The eight subtests measure deductive reasoning, missing premises, abstract relations, sequential synthesis, questioning strategies, analysis of relevant and irrelevant information, and analysis of attributes.
Use in Gifted Identification: There is a growing interest in this test as a measure of a student's higher-level thinking processes.
Advantages: The test is theoretically based upon Bloom's Taxonomy.
Disadvantages: It is highly verbal and not recommended for populations with English language deficiencies.

Cattell Culture Fair Intelligence Series

Authors: Raymond and A. K. Cattell.
Publisher: Bobbs-Merrill Co., Inc.
Copyright: 1970s.
Ages: 8 to adult.
Administered by: Teacher.
Time for Administration: 25 minutes.
Scores: General Intelligence score as a composite of subtests on classification, series, and matrices.
Use in Gifted Identification: Could be used as a general screener for ability in populations with language or cultural deficiencies, or in program that values abstract reasoning.

Advantage: Culture and language are not being assessed in this scale.
Disadvantages: This brief test may give an incomplete assessment of intelligence.

ASSESSING ACADEMIC ACHIEVEMENT

The two federally recognized categories of giftedness are general intellectual ability and specific academic aptitude. "Aptitude" connotes potential ability while "achievement" connotes demonstrated attainment of school-related learning objectives. Yet, most gifted programs in the public schools are strongly oriented toward recognizing and encouraging academic achievement in the students they serve. Children may be identified on the basis of general intellectual ability alone, but most often they are identified on the basis of a combination of general intellectual ability and academic achievement. In programs with this orientation, identification systems often make use of standardized achievement test scores as one measure of academic achievement. Other measures of academic achievement are grades, teacher recommendations, and evaluation of academic products. Of these, the most frequently used are scores on standardized achievement tests.

In the scenario at the beginning of this chapter, professional educators are choosing between two standardized achievement tests for their school district. As is often the case, their conversation is very practical and pragmatic. The curriculum director would like to see the test changed in order to show improved test scores, which may serve to enhance the status of the school district.

The gifted coordinator has several concerns about making such a change. Since she uses the achievement test data as part of her identification system, much time and effort will have to be given to reassessing the eligibility of children based upon the new test. The eligibility of some children could change. This will cause parents to call and ask her difficult questions about their children's eligibility.

What is missing in this discussion is any mention of whether the tests have validity in the identification of children for gifted programs. Standardized achievement tests were not created or validated for the purpose of identifying children for gifted programs. They measure school achievement on basic skills in school subjects. Their purpose is to provide information about a child's school achievement in the basic school subjects.

Standardized achievement tests do not distinguish individual differences well at either the high or the low end of the population because most of the items on the test are aimed at the middle or average achievement level for each grade. We recommend that you examine the tests given by your school district. Analyze the items for difficulty. On each section of the test, you will probably find one or two easy items, approximately one or two grade levels below the level of the test. You will probably also find one or two relatively difficult items, approximately one or two grade levels above the level of the test. The rest of the items in the section will be at or near grade level. The score for the section is computed by comparing the number correct with the number of items on the section. Percentiles are then computed based upon national and local norms.

On many achievement tests, grade equivalent scores are also reported, and these scores may lead you to unwarranted conclusions about the child's true achievement levels. A child who scores every item or almost every item correct on a given section may be reported to have a grade equivalent score several grade levels above his present grade status. For example, a child in the fifth grade may receive a grade equivalent score of 11.5 on his reading comprehension subtest. This may be interpreted by gifted program personnel to mean that the child is able to read and comprehend passages similar to those given to high school juniors. In actual fact, the test contained no passage of such high difficulty. The score is simply a statistical representation based upon the child's accurate responses to all passages presented on the test, which had a range of difficulty from third to seventh or eighth grade.

Another issue that must be considered is the choice between using nationally or locally normed percentiles in your identification process. Percentiles appear to be quite useful to gifted program personnel who wish to identify the top 2 or 5 percent of the population. It would appear that you can simply choose any child with a score in the 98th or 95th percentile. In actual practice, however, this may result in quite a different quota of children selected. In high socioeconomic school districts, many children may receive high achievement test scores. For example, a score that is in the 95th percentile on the national norms may be only in the 80th percentile on local norms. This is because so many local children do well on the tests that the local norms are depressed. In a low socioeconomic school district, however, the child who scores the highest in his grade level and receives a 99th percentile score on local norms may have a much lower percentile nationally.

Identification systems that employ standardized test data may appear to be very objective, but there are dozens of subjective decisions made by gifted program personnel who can use and manipulate the data to identify certain quotas or numbers of students for the program. The choice between the use of national and local norms is one such decision. Another is the choice of subtest or composite scores that will be used in the identification process. The most manipulative choice of all, however, is the determination of a "cutoff score." Most standardized testing identification systems employ a cutoff score to determine eligibility for the program. Children who score above the cutoff score are eligible for the program while those who score below the cutoff score are ineligible. With eligibility comes the label "gifted child," and all that this label connotes.

While practical decisions are unavoidable and are necessary aspects of establishing a gifted program identification system, it is very important to keep in mind that they are subjective and often quite arbitrary decisions. Do not mislead yourself or others into believing that these scores irrefutably define and identify a population of gifted children that is distinctive and separate from the rest of the student body. They do not! At best, standardized test scores identify the children in your school district who learn somewhat better and more efficiently than the children who score a point or two below them. Given a different test, a different home environment, or a different teacher that year, these students might have obtained quite different scores.

Despite these cautions and limitations, we recognize that standardized tests have a certain expedient value in the assessment process. If a school district does choose to use standardized achievement test scores as part of its identification system, we make the following recommendations:

1. We recommend that they be used only in programs that define giftedness as academic achievement in basic school subjects. If your program is designed for overall academic achievers, use the composite score. If your program is designed for a single academic area, use only the subscores in that area; that is, use math scores for a math-based program; use reading and language usage scores for a literature and writing program.
2. We recommend that the scores gathered in the regular schoolwide standardized testing period be used as a general screener. Any child who scores above the 80th percentile deserves to be considered and tested further for the programs offered in your gifted program.
3. If you wish to use standardized achievement tests for final determinations of eligibility rather than as a general screening device, then use off-level testing so the child will have the opportunity to test his skills on items of greater difficulty. In this case, we recommend giving a child the test that is two grades above his present grade status; that is, give a third grade child the fifth grade level test.
4. If you use percentile scores, we recommend that you choose to use the most *inclusive* of the two in the choice between nationally or locally normed scores; that is, choose the scores that identify the most children rather than the fewest.
5. We recommend using standardized test data only in combination with other measures of ability, achievement, and other gifted attributes.
6. We recommend using two or more years of test data rather than relying upon the scores of a single year's testing.

Standardized Achievement Tests: An Annotated List

Comprehensive Tests of Basic Skills (CTBS)

Publisher: CTB/McGraw-Hill.
Copyright: 1981.
Grades: K–12.
Administered by: Classroom teacher.
Time for Administration: 2½ hours.
Scores: Percentiles, grade equivalents, and scaled scores.
Measures: Basic skills in reading, spelling, math, reference skills, language, science, and social studies.
Comments: Group achievement battery that assesses basic skills only.

Iowa Test of Basic Skills (ITBS)

Publisher: Riverside Publishing Company.
Copyright: 1978.
Grade Levels: Primary Battery, K–2; Multilevel edition, grades 3–9.

Administered by: Classroom teacher.
Time for Administration: 2 hours, 19 minutes.
Scores: Grade and age equivalents, standard scores, and percentile ranks.
Measures: Vocabulary, reading comprehension, spelling, language, reference, math concepts, math problem solving, and math computation.
Comments: Group achievement battery that assesses basic skills only. Off-level testing is easily accomplished with multilevel format. Students may be given tests above their grade level.

Metropolitan Achievement Test (MAT)

Publisher: The Psychological Corporation.
Copyright: 1978.
Grade Levels: 1.5–12.
Administered by: Classroom teacher.
Time for Administration: 85–316 minutes, depending on level.
Scores: Scaled scores, percentile ranks, stanines, and grade equivalents.
Measures: Reading, math, language, science, and social studies.
Comments: Group achievement battery that assesses basic skills only.

Sequential Tests of Educational Progress (STEP)

Publisher: Addison-Wesley Testing Service.
Copyright: 1956–72.
Grade Levels: 3–12.
Administered by: Classroom teacher.
Time for Administration: 40 minutes per test.
Scores: Raw scores, standard scores, percentile bands, and stanines.
Measures: Reading, math, listening, writing skills, science, and social studies.
Comments: Designed for assessment of individual achievement and for program evaluation in the basic skill areas.

Science Research Associates Achievement Test (SRA)

Publisher: Science Research Associates.
Copyright: 1978.
Grade Levels: K–12.
Administered by: Classroom teacher.
Time for Administration: 130–140 minutes plus optional EAS 25–35 minutes.
Scores: Percentile ranks, grade and age equivalents in 11 to 18 achievement test scores depending on level plus three optional Educational Ability Scores.
Measures: Reading (vocabulary, comprehension, total), math (concepts, computation, total), language arts (mechanics, usage, spelling, total), composite plus optional EAS scores (verbal, nonverbal, total).
Comments: Entire battery combines both achievement and group ability tests.

Stanford Achievement Test

Publisher: The Psychological Corporation.
Copyright: 1973.
Grade Levels: 1–10
Administered by: Classroom teacher.
Time for Administration: 190–320 minutes depending on level.
Scores: Percentile ranks, stanines, grade and age equivalents, scaled scores, and total scores.
Measures: Vocabulary, reading, reading comprehension, word study skills, math concepts, math computation, listening, spelling, comprehension, social studies, and science.
Comments: Group achievement battery that assesses basic skills only.

California Achievement Test (CAT)

Publisher: CTB/McGraw-Hill.
Copyright: 1978.
Grade Levels: 1–14.
Administered by: Classroom teacher.
Time for Administration: 89–190 minutes depending on level.
Scores: Percentile ranks, grade placement, stanines, and standard scores.
Measures: Reading vocabulary and comprehension, arithmetic reasoning and fundamentals, English mechanics, spelling, language, and handwriting.
Comments: Group achievement battery that assesses basic skills only.

Educational Development Series (EDS)

Publisher: Scholastic Testing Service.
Copyright: 1984.
Grade Levels: K–12.
Administered by: Classroom teacher.
Time for Administration: 345–365 minutes in three sessions.
Scores: Percentiles, standard scores, stanines, and grade scores.
Measures: Achievement in basic skills plus optional ability test (Cognitive Skills Quotient) and student's interest in school subjects and career plans.
Comments: This series provides information about a student's interests and abilities as well as his or her achievement in basic skill areas.

Other Tests of Specific Academic Aptitudes: An Annotated List

Peabody Individual Achievement Test (PIAT)

Authors: Lloyd Dunna and Frederick Markwardt, Jr.
Publisher: American Guidance Service, Inc.
Copyright: 1970.
Ages: Kindergarten to adult.
Administered by: Classroom teacher.
Time for Administration: Untimed, approximately 30–40 minutes.

Scores: Grade and age equivalents, percentile ranks, and standard scores.

Measures: Achievement in math, reading recognition and comprehension, spelling, and general information.

Comments: This individual achievement test is very useful for retesting a child whose group achievement test is either missing or thought to be inaccurate. For primary children, the ceiling of difficulty on this test is unusually high, allowing for more accurate discrimination at the high ends of the scales. For upper intermediate children, the ceiling is lower. The math and reading comprehension subtests provide usable data about a child's achievement and aptitude in verbal and math skills.

Orleans-Hanna Algebra Prognosis Test

Authors: Joseph Orleans and Gerald Hanna.

Publisher: Harcourt Brace Jovanovich.

Copyright: 1968.

Grade Levels: Upper intermediate and junior high.

Administered by: Classroom teacher.

Time for Administration: Untimed, approximately 30–60 minutes.

Scores: Raw score only.

Comments: The unique format of this test makes it an aptitude test in mathematical reasoning rather than an achievement test of previously learned materials. The student is presented with new information about a math concept, complete with examples. Six items then test his or her understanding of this new concept. A total of 10 prealgebra concepts are tested in this manner.

Meier Art Judgment Test

Author: Norman C. Meier.

Publisher: Stoelting Company.

Copyright: 1967.

Grade Levels: 7 to adult.

Administered by: Classroom teacher.

Time for Administration: Untimed.

Scores: Raw scores with interpretation manual.

Measures: Art judgment and aesthetic perception.

Comments: Provides information about a student's aptitude in art.

Musical Aptitude Profile

Author: Edwin Gordon.

Publisher: Riverside Publishing Company.

Copyright: 1965.

Grade Levels: 4–12.

Administered by: Classroom teacher.

Time for Administration: 110 minutes.

Scores: Standard scores and percentile ranks.

Measures: Aptitudes relating to tonal imagery, rhythm imagery, and musical sensitivity.

Comments: The test battery, including directions, is recorded on tape.

Seashore Measure of Musical Talents

Authors: Carl Seashore, Don Lewis, and Joseph Sactucit.

Publisher: The Psychological Corporation.

Copyright: 1980.

Grade Levels: 4+.

Administered by: Classroom teacher.

Time for Administration: 50 minutes.

Scores: Raw and percentile scores.

Measures: Aptitudes relating to pitch, loudness, rhythm, time, timbre, and tonal memory.

Comments: Musical tones are reproduced on tape. Children's responses give information about basic musical abilities.

ASSESSING CREATIVITY

Creativity is as difficult to assess as it is to define. Over the years a number of creativity tests have been developed based upon a variety of theories or definitions of giftedness. If you wish to include an assessment of creativity in your identification system, it is vital that you understand and concur with the definition of creativity used in the assessment instrument.

At present, the published tests of creativity seem to be highly influenced by Guilford's definition of creativity as a function of fluent, flexible, original, and elaborative thinking abilities. Tests created by Guilford and Torrance use this definition as the basis for the tasks and items on several different tests they have developed. Some tests require verbal responses while others require nonverbal responses.

Another point of view is expressed by the creators of biographical reports of creative behaviors such as curiosity, risk taking, and a wide breadth of interests. These instruments are based upon the assumption that creativity is a function of every-day choices and behaviors rather than a set of responses to a standardized task or problem.

There is an interesting debate about the nature of the testing situation in tests that purport to measure creativity. Recent research suggests that in order to accurately elicit a creative response from a child, the testing situation must be playful and gamelike. Torrance, who has produced the most widely used and highly regarded standardized tests of creativity, offers a test that is quite playful: Thinking Creatively in Action and Movement. In this test, even the examiner is expected to get into the action in order to help evoke a creative response.

Our annotated list of creativity tests includes a wide variety of theories, testing procedures, and interpretations. There is also quite a variety in terms of test quality and the efforts that went into validation. As in other sections of this chapter, we recommend that you read the reviews of these tests in the *Mental Measurements Yearbooks* or in the *National Report on Identification*. You will gain a much more complete understanding of each instrument in these resources than we can provide in this chapter.

Tests of Creativity: An Annotated List

Creativity Assessment Packet (CAP)

Author: Frank Williams.
Publisher: D.O.K. Publishers, Inc.
Copyright: 1986.
Ages: 8–18 years.
Administered by: Classroom teacher.
Time for Administration: Untimed, 20–30 minutes for each test.
Scores: Raw scores and a pupil assessment matrix.
Measures: The Test of Divergent Thinking measures fluency, flexibility, originality, elaboration, and titles. The Test of Divergent Feeling measures curiosity, imagination, complexity, and risk taking. The Williams Scale is a parent or teacher checklist that includes all of the above.
Comments: No standardization of this instrument is reported. Guilford's definition of creative thinking has been employed in the test of divergent thinking, but reviewers in the *Ninth MMY* suggest that CAP needs additions and revisions to live up to its purpose of providing a practical and multiple approach to the assessment of creativity.

Creativity Tests for Children (CTC)

Authors: J. P. Guilford et al.
Publisher: Sheridan Psychological Services.
Copyright: 1976.
Ages: 4+.
Administered by: Classroom teacher.
Time for Administration: 100 minutes.
Scores: 10 scores for 10 subtests.
Measures: Semantic and visual/figural divergent thinking abilities.
Comments: Semantic tests are not recommended for students with English language deficiencies.

Group Inventory for Finding Talent (GIFT)

Author: Sylvia Rimm.
Publisher: Educational Assessment Service, Inc.
Copyright: 1980.
Grades: K–6.
Administered by: Classroom teacher.
Time for Administration: Untimed, 15–30 minutes.
Scores: Percentiles and normal curve equivalent scores.
Measures: Creativity as defined by independence, curiosity, perseverance, flexibility, and breadth of interests.
Comments: The form of this instrument is a student self-report consisting of items that assess biographical information.

Group Inventory for Finding Interests (GIFFI)

Author: Sylvia Rimm.
Publisher: Educational Assessment Service, Inc.
Copyright: 1976.
Grades: Junior and senior high school students.
Administered by: Classroom teacher.
Time for Administration: Untimed, 20–35 minutes.
Scores: Percentiles and normal curve equivalent scores.
Measures: Creativity as defined by independence, curiosity, perseverance, flexibility, breadth of interests, risk taking, and sense of humor.
Comments: Same format as GIFT.

Khatena-Torrance Creative Perception Inventory (KTCPI)

Authors: Joe Khatena and E. P. Torrance.
Publisher: Stoelting Company.
Copyright: 1976.
Ages: 12–20 years.
Administered by: Classroom teacher.
Time for Administration: Untimed, 5–15 minutes per test.
Scores: Creative Perception Index (total score obtained) plus Factor Orientation scores on factors included in the inventory.
Measures: Acceptance of authority, self-confidence, inquisitiveness, awareness of others, disciplined imagination, environmental sensitivity, initiative, self-strength, intellectuality, individuality, and artistry.
Comments: Two separate self-report tests are combined in this inventory: What Kind of a Person Are You? (WKOPAY) and Something About Myself (SAM).

Pennsylvania Assessment of Creative Tendency

Author: Thomas J. Rookey.
Publisher: Educational Improvement Center—Central.
Copyright: 1973.
Grades: 5+.
Administered by: Classroom teacher.
Time for Administration: Untimed.
Scores: Total score and percentile rank.
Measures: Creativity as defined by self-direction, evaluative ability, flexible thinking, original thinking, elaborative thinking, willingness to take risks, ease with complexity, curiosity, and fluent thinking ability.
Comments: PACT was developed on the assumption that creativity is a function of both the affective and cognitive domains.

Test of Creative Potential (TCP)

Authors: Ralph Hoepfner and Judith Hemenway.
Publisher: Monitor.
Copyright: 1973.
Grades: Grade 2 to adult.
Administered by: Classroom teacher.
Time for Administration: approximately 30 minutes.
Scores: Percentile and stanine scores on subtests and total score.
Measures: Creativity factors of fluency, flexibility, originality, and elaboration in three subtests entitled Writing Words, Picture Decoration, and License Plate Words.
Comments: Tasks and factors are related to Guilford's definition of creativity.

Thinking Creatively with Sounds and Words (TCSW)

Authors: E. P. Torrance, Joe Khatena, and Bert Cunnington.
Publisher: Scholastic Testing Service, Inc.
Copyright: 1973.
Ages: 8 years to adult.
Administered by: Classroom teacher.
Time for Administration: Approximately 30 minutes.
Scores: Raw scores with charts for interpretation by grade and sex.
Measures: Verbal originality.
Comments: Auditory stimuli are given in two separate tests, one called Onomatopoeia and one called Sounds and Images.

Thinking Creatively in Action and Movement (TCAM)

Author: E. P. Torrance.
Publisher: Scholastic Testing Service, Inc.
Copyright: 1981
Ages: 3–8 years.
Administered by: Classroom teacher.
Time for Administration: 15 minutes.
Scores: Three raw scores that may be compared to statistical tables of frequency for evaluation.
Measures: Fluency, originality, and imagination through movement and activities.
Comments: In order to encourage appropriate responses, the examiner is encouraged to take part in the activities with the child. Six movement tasks are scored with a Likert-type scale after each task is completed.

Torrance Tests of Creative Thinking (TTCT)

Author: E. P. Torrance.
Publisher: Scholastic Testing Service, Inc.
Copyright: 1966.

Grades: Kindergarten to Graduate school.

Administered by: Classroom teacher.

Time for Administration: 45 minutes.

Scores: Raw scores with table for calculating means and standard deviations for each factor tested.

Measures: Fluency, flexibility, originality, and elaboration.

Comments: There are two different versions of this test: Verbal and Figural forms. The Verbal form has seven tasks (Asking, Guessing Causes, Guessing Consequences, Product Improvement, Unusual Uses, Unusual Questions, and Just Suppose). The Figural form has three subtests (Picture Construction, Picture Completion, and Parallel Lines). Scoring may be subjective on some subtests in which the test administrator judges student responses.

OTHER TESTS USED IN GIFTED IDENTIFICATION

In recent years there has been a growing interest in critical and creative thinking skills within the field of gifted education. There has also been a good deal of experimentation with tests that were not developed for gifted identification, but that some program coordinators have tapped for this use because the tests fill a particular need. The Goodenough-Harris Drawing Test has been used in programs that attempt to identify children at primary and preprimary ages. The Raven's Matrices have been employed in multicultural identification systems because they are nonverbal.

In this section we provide an annotated list of a variety of tests that are used for a variety of purposes in gifted education. There is also a new instrument called SAGES, which was specifically designed and validated for the purpose of identifying gifted children.

Goodenough-Harris Drawing Test

Authors: Florence Goodenough and Dale Harris.

Publisher: The Psychological Corporation.

Copyright: 1963.

Ages: 3–15 years.

Administered by: School or clinical psychologist.

Time for Administration: Untimed, approximately 10 minutes.

Scores: Raw scores, standard scores, and percentile ranks.

Measures: Intellectual maturity, accuracy of observation, and conceptual thinking.

Comments: This widely recognized nonverbal test interprets children's drawings as a measure of mental ability. It was not designed nor standardized as a measure of gifted abilities.

Screening Assessment for Gifted Elementary Students (SAGES)

Authors: Susan Johnson and Ann Corn.

Publisher: Pro-Ed.

Copyright: 1984.

Ages: 7–12 years.

Administered by: Teacher.

Time for Administration: 30–50 minutes.

Scores: Three scores for aptitude, achievement, and divergent thinking.

Measures: Eligibility for gifted programming based upon subtests related to abstract reasoning and aptitude (classification and analogies), school achievement, and divergent thinking.

Comments: This newly published instrument was designed especially for gifted identification. The aptitude subtests include a balance of verbal and nonverbal items. Three different aspects of giftedness are assessed: aptitude, achievement, and creativity.

SOI Gifted Screening Form

Authors: Mary and Robert Meeker.

Publisher: SOI Institute.

Copyright: 1975.

Ages: Grades 2–12.

Administered by: Classroom teacher.

Time for Administration: Untimed, approximately 90 minutes.

Scores: 12 subtests from the SOI Learning Abilities Test (reviewed under Group Intelligence Tests above).

Measures: Creativity, visual and auditory memory, visual perception, and convergent production.

Comments: Shortened administration time. The Meekers have analyzed the complex SOI test and selected subtests for gifted program personnel.

Watson-Glaser Critical Thinking Appraisal

Authors: Goodwin Watson and Edward Glaser.

Publisher: The Psychological Corporation.

Copyright: 1980.

Ages: 9 years to adult.

Administered by: Classroom teacher.

Time for Administration: Approximately 50 minutes.

Scores: Raw score, percentile rank, and stanine rank.

Measures: Inference, recognition of assumptions, deduction, interpretation, and evaluation of arguments.

Comments: Two forms of the test (A and B) can be used as pre- and posttests for individual or program evaluation.

Standard and Advanced Progressive Matrices

Author: J. C. Raven.

Publisher: The Psychological Corporation.

Copyright: 1956, 1962.

Ages: 8–65 years (Standard); adolescents and adults (Advanced).

Administered by: Classroom teacher.

Time for Administration: Untimed, approximately 45 minutes.

Scores: Total score and percentile rank.

Measures: Abstract mental ability through the use of problems using figures and designs.

Comments: A nonverbal test created and normed in Great Britain. It was not designed or normed for identification of gifted students.

ASSESSING GIFTED CHARACTERISTICS AND BEHAVIORS

Standardized tests provide one view of a child's abilities and aptitudes, but the most common form of identification used in school districts is a recommendation made by knowledgeable adults. Primarily teachers, and less frequently parents, are asked to recommend a child for gifted programming. In research conducted in the 1950s and 1960s it was believed that teachers were not good identifiers. Nomination or recommendation forms that describe gifted characteristics or behaviors are one way to educate teachers about giftedness and gather usable information at the same time.

Most school districts have at one time or another created their own nomination or recommendation forms. Gifted program personnel who attend workshops or read widely in the field have seen many dozens of different locally created checklists describing the characteristics of the typical gifted child. Usually, gifted program coordinators will create their own lists of the 20 or so characteristics that seem most reasonable or appropriate in their own setting.

Some researchers, however, are now attempting to provide standardized checklists or recommendation forms based on their own definitions and theories of giftedness. The prepublished forms tend to be moving away from the idea of defining a gifted child in terms of a set of long-term personality characteristics and moving toward the idea of operationally defining a set of behaviors that are related to giftedness.

Rating Scales of Gifted Characteristics and Behaviors: An Annotated List

Eby Elementary Identification Instrument (EEII)

Author: Judy W. Eby.

Publisher: Slosson Educational Publications, Inc.

Copyright: 1984.

Grades: K–9.

Completed by: Teacher.

Time for Completion: 10–20 minutes per student.

Items: 15 items on the Teacher Checklist plus 10 items on a product rating scale entitled the Unit Selection Matrix.

Scores: Raw score is calculated on each form.

Measures: Based upon Renzulli's definition of giftedness as a combination of above-average ability, creativity, and task commitment; the items are grouped into these categories.

Comments: The Teacher Checklist is a standard recommendation form. The Unit Selection Matrix attempts to gather data on the basis of assessing children's original products or "pre-tasks" as part of an identification process. A General Selection Matrix is also provided, which allows scores to be weighed with tests and other data.

Eby Gifted Behavior Index (GBI)

Author: Judy W. Eby.

Publisher: D.O.K. Publishers, Inc.

Copyright: 1989.

Grades: Elementary and secondary.

Completed by: Teacher.

Time for Completion: 10–20 minutes per student.

Items: Seven different forms are provided, each of which consists of 20 items. The teacher may choose the appropriate form(s) to fill out for a child based upon the child's talent areas.

Scores: Raw scores are calculated for each form.

Measures: Ten gifted behaviors are assessed on a general form or on one of six talent area–specific forms: verbal, visual/spatial, math/science/problem solving, musical, social/leadership, and mechanical/inventiveness.

Comments: The GBI was validated by correlating the ratings on the forms with independent, outside judgments of the quality of the children's products in their talent area.

Gifted and Talented Screening Form (GTSF)

Author: David Johnson.

Publisher: The Stoelting Company.

Copyright: 1980.

Grades: K–9.

Number of Items: 24.

Completed by: Self-report.

Time for Completion: 10–20 minutes per student.

Scores: Total score of six talent areas.

Measures: Talent in academics, intelligence, creativity, leadership, visual arts, performing arts, psychomotor athletics, and psychomotor mechanics.

Comments: No standardization or validation procedures reported. The author does not report a rationale or definition of giftedness.

Multi-Dimensional Screening Device (MDSD)

Author: Bella Kranz.

Publisher: Moorhead State University.

Copyright: 1978.

Ages: School-age children.
Completed by: Classroom teacher.
Time for Completion: Untimed.
Scores: Each talent is scored on a scale of 1 to 7.
Measures: Ten talent areas including visual arts, performing arts, creative thinking, specific academic ability, general intellectual ability, leadership, psychomotor, and abstract and spatial thinking.
Comments: The MDSD package contains a videotape and print material. The videotape is used to educate teachers to become better identifiers. This is followed by use of the nomination instruments provided in the package.

Preschool Talent Checklists

Authors: Merle Karnes and Associates.
Publisher: Institute for Child Behavior and Development, University of Illinois.
Copyright: 1978.
Ages: 3–6 years.
Completed by: Parents and teachers.
Time for Completion: 10–20 minutes per student.
Items: Nine checklists.
Scores: Raw score totals for each checklist are graphed on an individual profile.
Measures: Intellectual, academic, creative, leadership, visual and performing arts, and psychomotor giftedness.
Comments: This checklist was normed on handicapped preschool children.

Scales for Rating Behavioral Characteristics of Gifted Children

Authors: J. Renzulli, L. Smith, A. White, C. Callahan, and R. Hartman.
Publisher: Creative Learning Press, Inc.
Copyright: 1971.
Grades: Elementary and secondary.
Completed by: Teacher.
Time for Completion: 20–30 minutes per student.
Items: Ten scales with ten items on each scale.
Scores: Ten subscale scores.
Measures: Learning, motivation, creativity, leadership, artistic, musical, dramatics, communication, precision expressiveness, and planning.
Comments: Separate scales provide usable information about different types of giftedness. The authors did not intend that a composite score be calculated as a measure of overall giftedness, but this does occur in some programs.

SUMMARY

In this chapter, we have examined the many prepublished instruments and tests that have been used in gifted identification systems in recent years. The list of possible instruments may seem overwhelming, but there are systematic ways of evaluating their effectiveness and appropriateness for your own program. In the following chapter we will work through a process that will allow you to establish meaningful criteria for selecting tests, and for creating your own instruments. We will also explore ways in which you can combine data from several different identification instruments in order to make a comprehensive decision about the needs of the children you assess.

OPPORTUNITIES FOR DISCUSSION AND ACTION

1. Select a characteristic or type of giftedness that is important to you and review the annotated lists of instruments to find ones that would be useful in evaluating your chosen characteristic. (Suggestion: try leadership, abstract reasoning ability, or originality.)
2. Reread the scenario at the beginning of the chapter. What would you advise Mrs. Chong to do?
3. Obtain copies of your school's standardized achievement test. Look at the items in a section such as reading comprehension or math concepts. Try to assess the difficulty level of each item by comparing it with textbooks at different grade levels. How many items are at grade level? How far above grade level is the most difficult item?

REFERENCES

Beggs, D., et al. 1980. *Developing Cognitive Abilities Test.* Glenview, Ill.: Scott Foresman.

California Achievement Test. 1978. Monterey, Calif.: CTB/McGraw-Hill.

Cattell, R. and A. K. Cattell. 1970. *Cattell Culture Fair Intelligence Series.* Indianapolis: Bobbs-Merrill.

Comprehensive Tests of Basic Skills, Form U. 1981. Monterey, Calif.: CTB/McGraw-Hill.

Dunna, L., and F. Markwardt, Jr. 1970. *Peabody Individual Achievement Test.* Circle Pines, Minn.: American Guidance Service.

Eby, J. 1984. *Eby Elementary Identification Instrument.* East Aurora, N.Y.: Slosson Educational Publications.

———. 1988. *Eby Gifted Behavior Index.* East Aurora, N.Y.: D.O.K. Publishers.

Educational Development Series. 1984. Bensonville, Ill.: Scholastic Testing Service.

Gallagher, J. 1979. *Teaching the gifted child,* 2nd ed. Boston: Allyn & Bacon.

Goodenough, F., and D. Harris. 1963. *Goodenough-Harris Drawing Test.* New York: Psychological Corporation.

Gordon, E. 1965. *Musical Aptitude Profile.* Lombard, Ill.: Riverside Publishing Co.

Guilford, J. et al. 1976. *Creativity Tests for Children.* Orange, Calif.: Sheridan Psychological Services.

Hobby, K. 1980. *WISC-R Split Half Short Form.* Los Angeles: Western Psychological Services.

Hoepfner, R., and J. Hemenway. 1973. *Test of Creative Potential.* Hollywood, Calif.: Monitor Press.

Iowa Test of Basic Skills, Form 7 & 8. 1978. Lombard, Ill.: Riverside Publishing Co.

Johnson, D. 1980. *Gifted and Talented Screening Form.* Chicago: Stoelting Co.

Johnson, S., and A. Corn. 1984. *Screening Assessment for Gifted Elementary Students.* Austin, Tex.: Pro-Ed.

Karnes, M. 1978. *Preschool Talent Checklists.* Urbana, Ill.: Institute for Child Behavior and Development, University of Illinois.

Kaufman, A., and N. Kaufman. 1983. *Kaufman Assessment Battery for Children. (K-ABC).* Circle Pines, Minn.: American Guidance Service.

Khatena, J., and E. P. Torrance. 1976. *Khatena-Torrance Creative Perception Inventory.* Chicago: Stoelting Co.

Kranz, B. 1978. *Multi-Dimensional Screening Device.* Moorhead, Minn.: Moorhead State University.

McCarthy, D. 1972. *McCarthy Scales of Children's Abilities.* New York: Psychological Corporation.

Marland, S. 1972. *Education of the gifted and talented.* Vol. 1, Report to the Congress of the United States by the U.S. Commissioner of Education. Washington, D.C.: U.S. Government Printing Office.

Meeker, M., and R. Meeker. 1975. *SOI Gifted Screening Form.* El Segundo, Calif.: SOI Institute.

———. 1975. *SOI Learning Abilities Test.* Los Angeles: Western Psychological Services.

Meier, N. 1967. *Meier Art Judgment Test.* Chicago: Stoelting Co.

Metropolitan Achievement Test: Survey Battery. 1978. New York: Psychological Corporation.

Mitchell, J., ed. 1983. *Tests in print.* Lincoln, Neb.: University of Nebraska Press.

———. 1985. *The ninth mental measurements yearbook.* Lincoln, Neb.: University of Nebraska Press.

Orleans, J., and G. Hanna. 1968. *Orleans-Hanna Algebra Prognosis Test.* New York: Psychological Corporation.

Otis, A. and R. Lennon. 1982. *Otis-Lennon School Ability Test.* New York: Psychological Corporation.

Raven, J. 1956. *Standard progressive matrices.* New York: Psychological Corporation.

———. 1962. *Advance progressive matrices.* New York: Psychological Corporation.

Renzulli, J., R. Hartman, et al. 1976. *Renzulli-Hartman Scales for rating the behavioral characteristics of superior students.* Mansfield Center, Conn. Creative Learning Press.

Renzulli, J., et al. 1971. *Scales for rating behavioral characteristics of gifted children.* Mansfield Center, Conn.: Creative Learning Press.

Richert, E. S., et al. 1982. *National report on identification.* Sewell, N.J.: Educational Improvement Center—South.

Rimm, S. 1980. *Group Inventory for Finding Interests.* Watertown, Wis.: Educational Assessment Services.

———. 1980. *Group Inventory for Finding Talent.* Watertown, Wis.: Educational Assessment Services.

Rookey, T. 1973. *Pennsylvania Assessment of Creative Tendency.* Princeton, N.J.: Education Improvement Center.

Ross, J., and C. Ross. 1979. *Ross Test of Higher Cognitive Processes.* Novato, Calif.: Academic Therapy Publications.

Science Research Associates Achievement Test. 1978. Chicago: Science Research Associates.

Seashore, C., D. Lewis, and I. Sactucit. *Seashore Measure of Musical Talents.* New York: Psychological Corporation.

Sequential Tests of Educational Progress. 1956–72. Menlo Park, Calif.: Addison-Wesley Testing Service.

Slosson, R. 1981. *Slosson Intelligence Test,* 2nd ed. East Aurora, N.Y.: Slosson Educational Publications.

Stanford Achievement Test. 1973. New York: Psychological Corporation.

Terman, L., and M. Merrill. 1972. *Stanford-Binet Intelligence Scale, Form L-M, Third Revision.* Lombard, Ill.: Riverside Publishing Co.

Test of Cognitive Skills. 1981. Monterey, Calif.: CTB/McGraw-Hill.

Thorndike, R., and E. Hagen. 1983. *Cognitive Abilities Test.* Lombard, Ill.: Riverside Publishing Co.

Torrance, E. P. 1966. *Torrance Tests of Creative Thinking, Verbal and Figural Forms.* Bensonville, Ill.: Scholastic Testing Service.

———. 1981. *Thinking Creatively in Action and Movement.* Bensonville, Ill.: Scholastic Testing Service.

———, et al. 1973. *Thinking Creatively with Sounds and Words.* Bensonville, Ill.: Scholastic Testing Service.

Watson, G., and E. Glaser. 1980. *Watson-Glaser Critical Thinking Appraisal.* New York: Psychological Corporation.

Wechsler, D. 1974. *Wechsler Intelligence Scale for Children—Revised.* New York: Psychological Corporation.

Williams, F. 1986. *Creativity Assessment Package.* East Aurora, N.Y.: D.O.K. Publishers.

CHAPTER 5

Developing a Viable Identification System for Your District

IDENTIFICATION SIMULATION

Divide the class into several small groups, each representing the gifted task force for a separate school district. Have each group consider the data in Table 5.1 as described below. After 15 or 20 minutes, ask each group to report on their selections. Tally the number of times each child was selected by a school district.

In this simulation each of you is a member of the gifted task force for your school district. The program follows the state guidelines, which call for identifica-

TABLE 5.1. School District XYZ Fourth Grade Identification Data

| Name, Age, Grade | WISC-R | | Ability Test | | | Ach. Test | | Tchr |
	Perf	Verb	Verb	Quan	NonV	Rdg	Math	Rec?
John, 9.5, 4th	128	116	114	118	130	89%	94%	Yes
	—	—	108	124	125	84%	92%	No
Comments: very creative, inventive, makes wonderful projects								
*Sara, 8.9, 4th	No WISC-R		135	110	119	92%	88%	Yes
	Binet 146		131	92	108	99%	90%	(new)?
Comments: new in district, was in gifted program in smaller district								
Pam, 10.2, 4th	142	108	111	108	135	95%	94%	Yes
	138	116	120	104	131	92%	89%	Yes
Comments: repeated 2nd grade, class leader, helps teacher, likes work								
*Ned, 9.1, 4th	—	—	—	—	—	99%	98%	Yes
	120	152	123	141	119	95%	92%	(new)?
Comments: racial minority, was in gifted program in larger district								
Jose, 9.9, 4th	129	128	125	126	128	92%	93%	No
	—	—	134	136	132	94%	98%	Yes
Comments: bilingual child, is doing very well in school this year								
Joan, 8.2, 4th	144	146	137	133	138	99%	99%	Yes
	—	—	132	133	130	97%	99%	Yes
Comments: skipped a grade, has been in gifted program for two years								
Gail, 9.2, 4th	122	118	138	136	129	99%	99%	No
	—	—	141	139	132	99%	99%	??
Comments: works very hard, teachers think she may be an overachiever								
Bill, 9.2, 4th	144	141	132	129	122	94%	97%	No
	136	133	124	108	109	86%	75%	No
Comments: no interest in school, does the minimum, reads constantly								
Dawn, 9.0, 4th	124	145	122	120	129	93%	91%	No
	128	148	123	124	138	98%	94%	Yes
Comments: average worker last year, top performer this year								
Sally, 9.1, 4th	119	123	118	124	122	96%	97%	Yes
	—	—	121	126	128	94%	93%	??
Comments: mother on the board, very supportive of gifted program, wants her child in it								

*New to district.

tion of "those children who consistently excel or show the potential to be consistently superior in General Intellectual Ability or a Specific Aptitude or Talent."

Out of 100 children at the fourth grade level, the ten children listed in Table 5.1 have passed the initial screening for the district's gifted program. Now you must select five for this year's program, which consists of math and language arts enrichment, with extra activities planned for other subjects from time to time as well. The program is well known among both parents and students. It is considered a very positive and desirable program.

There are two lines of data for each child: the top line is for last year; the bottom line is for this year.

Using your own personal value system, try to persuade the group to choose the children who best fit your notion of giftedness. As a group, you must reach consensus on which of the five children you will select. At the end of the discussion period, report your group's selection to the class, giving your rationale for your choices if possible.

WHAT DO YOU THINK?

1. What criteria did you personally use for selecting children for the program?
2. How did your criteria compare with the rest of your group?
3. How were decisions made in a group when different opinions were expressed?
4. Which data were given the most weight—test scores, teacher recommendations, or other comments?
5. Which children were selected by every group? Which children were not selected by any group?

In this simulation, you are presented with a great deal of data, in the form of "objective" test scores and "subjective" teacher recommendations and comments. When the above simulation is done by several small groups the results often vary widely. As in real life, there are one or two children who are selected by almost every simulated school district. There are others who almost never make the final cut. But the most interesting group is the middle group of children who are selected by many groups and eliminated by others.

This simulation illustrates that numbers and test scores are not as objective as one would like to believe. Tests do not identify children for gifted programs . . . people do, and people have values and biases that are applied to the interpretation of test data in a variety of ways.

Since biases can lead to unfair or unsupported discrimination, it is important to be very honest with yourself and your colleagues about the values that each of you has regarding the nature of giftedness. You will undoubtedly work with others in establishing or modifying your identification system. Openly discussing and debating your values, biases, and beliefs, as a group, is the first step toward creating your own operational definition of giftedness. You may want to use this simulation with your planning team as a means of initiating such a discussion.

CREATING A DISTRICT DEFINITION OF GIFTEDNESS

To be most effective, a district definition of giftedness should be jointly written by the gifted program administrators and faculty with input from the community. Many people have a stake in the identification process and want to be heard. This may be accomplished in a variety of ways. Representatives of the parents, classroom teachers, and other interested members of the school community may be asked to serve on a task force that researches and discusses the issues under consideration from the inception through the implementation and evaluation of the program. Surveys and needs assessment instruments may be developed to gather ideas and opinions from the community.

One of the most difficult tasks the gifted program coordinator will face is sorting out and prioritizing the needs of the community and the values of the program staff. A model of administrative decision making proposed by Hoy and Miskel (1978) provides relatively unambiguous guidelines for administrators in the matter of when and with whom decisions should be shared. In this model, the program administrator conducts a needs assessment to gather opinions and information from all stakeholders (staff, students, parents, and other interested members of the community) who have an interest in the gifted program. But not all stakeholders have expertise in the area; that is, not all have training, education, or experience in gifted education. Those people who have *both interest and expertise* are the only ones who should comprise the decision-making team, reviewing and evaluating the opinions of the other interested stakeholders. The team leader should be the program administrator who has the greatest expertise in the field.

Applying this model to the matter of clarifying and writing a definition of giftedness as the basis for a gifted program, the program coordinator may select members of the staff and community who have both interest and expertise in the field to comprise a gifted task force or committee. Surveys should be conducted of other interested stakeholders. The results of the surveys can be interpreted by the committee, which will generate a written statement of definition and philosophy. The program coordinator should lead the committee through this process, and should serve as the arbitrator and judge when different opinions are expressed.

The key to the success of this process is that the program coordinator must have a genuine expertise in the field. If you are the program coordinator you must be prepared to spend a good deal of time and effort on information gathering by reading the gifted education literature, visiting other programs, and attending gifted conferences. During this phase of program development you are likely to feel overwhelmed by the complexity of the task, and the ambiguous nature of the information and ideas that must be considered. Dealing with complexity and ambiguity are attributes often associated with giftedness. These traits are also essential for an effective gifted program coordinator because of the many complex issues and decisions that must be considered.

Establishing or improving a gifted identification system will never be easy, but the process can be simplified if you create an operational definition of giftedness so that you can then select or create identification instruments that fit your definition.

Let's examine these two tasks and discover ways of clarifying the process. First of all, you will want to carefully consider the federal definition of giftedness in Public Law 97-35, the 1981 Education Consolidation and Improvement Act:

> Children who give evidence of high performance capability in areas such as intellectual, creative, artistic, leadership capacity, or specific academic fields, and who require services or activities not ordinarily provided by the school in order to fully develop such capabilities.

Next, you will need to obtain the definitions or guidelines that apply to gifted identification from your own state office of education. Federal and state guidelines are written in general terms because they do not wish or intend to unnecessarily restrict the power of the local school district in developing its own gifted program. While some people might prefer a uniform set of federal or state regulations detailing the categories of gifts or talents that must be served, the identification procedures that must be followed, and the programs that must be offered, such regulations are not likely to be enacted in the United States. Local control of educational programs is highly prized in our country and the current status of gifted programs illustrates both its positive and negative effects. The responsibility for careful consideration of definitions, goals, procedures, and implementation of school programs rests with you. While this may feel overwhelming at times, the freedom to innovate and the flexibility to meet the particular needs of your local community more than make up for the rigorous planning and decision making involved.

IDENTIFICATION MODELS

There are a variety of general identification models in use today. Some are based on the categories of giftedness in the federal and state definitions, while others are based upon an educator's research or theory. Some of these models are presented in Table 5.2

The Individual Education Plan (IEP) Model in gifted education is similar to special education identification methods. The goal is to provide each child with a highly individualized educational program to meet his or her specific needs. Case studies of children are analyzed to determine specific talents and gifts that are not being nourished in the regular educational program. Children with extremely high intellectual abilities or specific talents are identified as those who need, deserve, and will profit from services not normally provided in the regular curriculum. An individual educational plan is established for each identified child. Each year, the child's case is reassessed and updated.

The General Intellectual Ability Model is probably used more than any other identification model. Typically, children are screened for the gifted program on the

TABLE 5.2. Examples of the Variety of Identification Models in Use Today

Model	Number Selected	Method of Selection	Curriculum Objectives
Individual Educational Plan (IEP)	Very few (2%)	Staffing, case study, IQ tests.	Individualized program meeting specific needs of individual.
General Intellectual Ability	Few (<5%)	IQ and ability tests, checklists of characteristics of gifted.	Highly varied enrichment or acceleration.
Specific Academic Aptitude	Many (5–10% per subject)	Criterion tests in specific subject, achievement tests, teacher recommendations.	Programs match area of strength: enrichment and/or acceleration.
Revolving Door Model (Renzulli)	Many (20% in talent pool)	Varied selection methods employed to get all eligible children possible.	Type 1 & 2 enrichment; Type 3 independent study.
Gifted Behavior Pre-Task (Eby)	Many (unlimited)	Children audition or apply by completing a pretask for each unit.	Every unit develops gifted behavioral objectives.

basis of standardized test scores and/or teacher recommendations. Final selections are usually made on the basis of IQ or group ability tests. Children who exceed a certain IQ score are considered to be generally gifted children who need enriched and/or accelerated programming in order to use their high potential to the fullest extent possible in the school setting. The programming differs from IEP programming in that it is usually offered to groups of children rather than individuals. Once identified, these children are generally provided with services until they leave the school district.

The Specific Academic Aptitude Model is used in school districts that wish to provide accelerated or enriched programs on a subject-by-subject basis. Math is the most frequent program offering, but literature/writing programs, science programs, and music and art programs are also quite likely to be offered. Students are screened and identified on the basis of achievement tests in the subject area. Previously earned grades in that subject and teacher recommendations are also given consideration. Students are usually referred to as "talented" in a certain subject rather than as generally "gifted." Yearly evaluations of student progress and interest determine the length of time a child remains in the program.

Renzulli (1981) has proposed a Revolving Door Identification Model. In this system, any child with relatively high standardized test scores is placed in a "talent pool" made up of likely candidates for gifted programming. Teachers are also trained to spot talent in children in a wide variety of interest areas. When a child in the talent pool demonstrates a creative spark or a strong commitment to any talent area, the child is elevated from the talent pool to a gifted resource program in which the child is allowed to explore her interest for as long as it endures with support and aid from the gifted resource teacher. The numbers of children served in this program are limited only by the resources of the school, but Renzulli recommends that the talent pool should consist of at least 20 percent of the population so that no potentially talented child is missed or passed over.

In the Eby Gifted Behavior Pre-Task Model, selection is determined by an evaluation of a student's products in any of a number of subject or talent areas. This system makes no assumptions about the percentage or quota of children who may be included in a gifted program. Program offerings are designed to stimulate creative talents in a variety of subjects or fields, and students are encouraged to apply for each offering by submitting a sample of his or her work in that talent area. No child is labeled "gifted" or "nongifted" in this model; no child is permanently in or out of the program. Every child has equal access to every program offering.

Creating Your Own Operational Definition

After becoming familiar with identification theories and models and analyzing and comparing your state's definitions with the federal definition, the next step is to write your own. Your district definition may have many similarities to the state and federal definitions, but it will also have additional elements and specifications related to specific conditions that exist in your community. The following four suggestions may be helpful in synthesizing your own operational definition.

First, consider which term or terms you wish to define. Much of the literature in the field uses the term "gifted child" or "gifted children," but it is difficult to define "gifted child" in any specific or operational way, since each child is unique. Many educators and researchers have chosen to define the abstract noun, "giftedness." Eby and Smutny suggest the term "gifted behavior." It may also be useful to consider defining several aptitude-specific terms such as "unusual ability in math," "talent in writing," "musical aptitude," or "artistic talent." Each of these terms can be operationally defined separately with great specificity, leading directly to appropriate identification procedures.

For the remainder of this chapter, choose a general term or a set of specific terms that you would like to define as the basis for a gifted program in your school district.

Second, for each term that you select, brainstorm all the attributes that fit or describe that condition. For example, if you are defining the term:

Gifted child—list the characteristics of gifted children
Giftedness—list the components or elements of giftedness
Gifted behavior—list the behaviors used when a person acts gifted

You may find that all of these terms are too general for your district. Many successful programs begin small and expand in increments. You may choose to serve the needs of children with one or more specific academic aptitudes or talents. In this case you may avoid using the term "gifted" altogether. To define a specific aptitude or talent, simply list the abilities, prerequisites, and behaviors that you would expect students to exhibit in each talent area in order to be successful in and profit from special programming in that subject or field of study. For example:

Talent in math—Criteria for success in accelerated math program
Talent in drama—Criteria for success in dramatic production
Talent in philosophy—Criteria for success in philosophy program

Third, arrange your list of characteristics, attributes, behaviors, or criteria for success in some type of order. You may order your list according to priority, listing the most important elements first, and those of lesser importance later. You may find it useful to make categories, and arrange elements on your list within several general groups. Some lists can be arranged in hierarchical order, assuming that the characteristics are developed in a certain sequence.

Fourth, to make your definition more understandable, consider using a figural representation or model. Renzulli's three-ring definition is easily understood and remembered because of the figural representation of a Venn diagram. Consider how your list of elements can best be represented. In the introductory course on gifted education that we teach, we ask our students to create a figural representation of their definition of giftedness at midterm. The responses are imaginative and usually quite useful, as in the examples shown in Figures 5.1, 5.2, and 5.3.

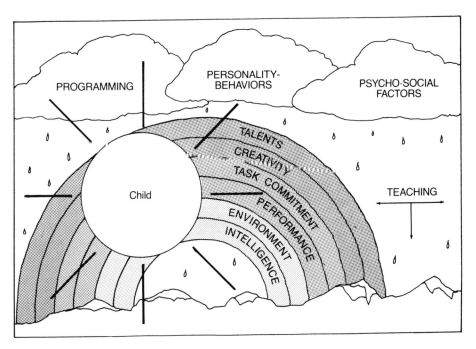

Figure 5.1. Relating Giftedness to a Rainbow.
Reprinted with permission of Sharon Winkelman.

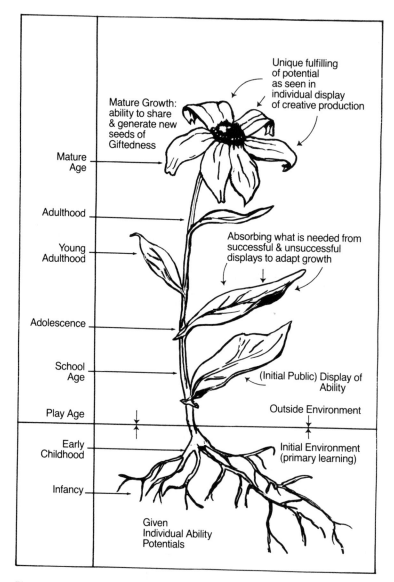

Figure 5.2. Dynamic Eclectic Ecological Model of Gifted.
Reprinted with permission of Yvonne Crammond.

Change and Evolution of Your Definition and Philosophy

We hope that you find this visualization of your definition to be useful and clarifying. As you work with your own, you will surely find that you keep adding to it or revising it to make it ever more accurate and realistic. This is to be expected. In fact, we doubt that you will ever be totally finished with this process of definition. As your knowledge in the field expands and as your own experience working with children in your program grows, your definition will evolve accordingly. Your def-

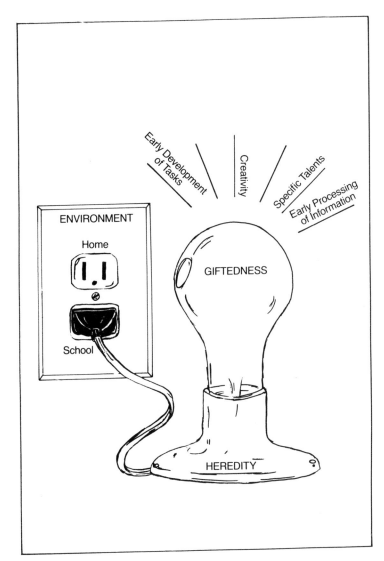

Figure 5.3. Giftedness as a Light Bulb.
Reprinted with permission of Rita Mathias.

inition is meant to provide you with structure and a certain sense of security in making the many decisions that follow, but it is not intended to be restrictive or confining.

Every educational program needs to change over the years. A rigid, uncompromising definition will result in stagnation. But a program with a hastily patched together philosophy and definition will change at the whim of every new educational fad which comes along. A program based on a strong but flexible, clear but evolving operational definition will change in much more positive ways. New initiatives will be added because they are congruent with the existing philosophy and will strengthen an already strong program.

SELECTION OF ASSESSMENT INSTRUMENTS

You have now completed the most difficult task in the development of your gifted program. From now on, every decision you make regarding identification, program alternatives, or evaluation strategies will be made by comparing the alternatives to your definition and selecting the best possible match. To select standardized tests or other instruments for your program, begin by reviewing the assessment instruments described in Chapter 4. Each description indicates the concepts or constructs measured by the test. Look for those that match your definitions. Of course, you still must determine the relative merits and quality of the instruments themselves, but you should now have some confidence in the preliminary selection of instruments.

Write to the publishers for information about the tests that interest you. Ask for specimen tests, if possible, so that you can review them before ordering. Read the reviews of these tests in the *Mental Measurements Yearbook* (Mitchell 1985), which can be found in most university libraries and many community libraries as well. If it is not available in your community, ask your reference library to obtain copies of the reviews of the tests you are considering through an interlibrary loan system.

Creating Your Own Assessment Instruments

Good standardized tests are not available for every definition of giftedness. In this field, theorists studying the nature of intelligence, creativity, and other aspects of giftedness are far ahead of the test makers. We have already seen how Howard Gardner and Robert Sternberg are both working to create tests for their definitions of intelligence because they are not satisfied with the existing lot, and you may have to follow suit. One of the most exciting reasons for choosing gifted education as a specialty in your own career is because it is so unfinished. New ideas are encouraged from practitioners and scholars alike.

So, be creative. Using your criteria, create instruments that exemplify your own definition of giftedness. Frequently, programs use their own teacher recommendation form. Unfortunately, in many instances, the items are selected without a unifying basis. The writer sifts through various lists of "characteristics of the gifted" and chooses the 20 that sound the best. Each item on your recommendation form should be selected because it is consistent with your definition of giftedness.

You may also choose to write your own tests, using specific criteria that match your definition. This is especially true if you are identifying children for any of the specific academic aptitudes. No standardized test can be as specific as your own criterion-referenced test that you have created to measure the extent to which your students have mastered the objectives in the existing regular curriculum and to give evidence that they can achieve mastery of the objectives you are writing into your enriched or accelerated program in that subject.

TRADITIONAL IDENTIFICATION PROCEDURES

The traditional identification process used in school districts today is very time consuming and expensive to do well. Many districts plan to spend the first several weeks or even months on the selection process. Some spend the first several weeks of the school year identifying candidates for the current year. Other districts identify students at the end of the year for the subsequent year. Both must budget for the purchase of tests and for a psychologist's time if they are using individual IQ tests as part of the process.

Most school districts use a two-step identification process that includes an initial *screening* of all students, followed by a plan for determining a *final selection* of eligible students. Standardized achievement and ability tests are frequently used for the screening process because they are given to all students in the school at the same time. Program administrators determine which scores will be used and a bottom line or cutoff score that will be accepted.

In programs based on the General Intellectual Ability Model, composite scores on achievement and group ability tests are used to screen students. In programs based on the Specific Academic Aptitude Model, subscores for math/quantitative are screened for math programs and subscores related to reading/verbal ability are screened for literature and writing programs. The screening cutoff score is usually at the 90th percentile or above, especially in high socioeconomic areas where many children tend to achieve such high scores. In lower socioeconomic areas, the cutoff score may be lower because fewer children score near the top of the scale.

Another screening process that is employed by districts that do not have adequate standardized test data for every student is a nomination process. Classroom teachers and/or parents are asked to nominate likely candidates for the gifted program. Occasionally students are asked to nominate their peers or even themselves.

After a list of candidates for the program is determined by the screening process, further testing is arranged, and a variety of recommendation forms are employed to gather additional information about the candidates. These instruments vary widely from district to district in most states. General Intellectual Ability programs may have each student tested by the school psychologist using an individual IQ test. They may also ask teachers to fill out checklists on each candidate judging the extent to which he or she exhibits the general characteristics of the gifted that were selected by the district to fit their prevailing values.

For programs using the Specific Academic Aptitude Model, initially screened candidates are given a more comprehensive test in their academic area. An excellent example of this identification process is the nationwide Math Talent Search Program. This program is designed to identify sixth and seventh grade students with unusual aptitude in math. Within each region, candidates are screened by cutoff scores on locally administered standardized achievement tests. Students with local achievement test scores at or above the 95th percentile are given the opportunity to take the SAT-Math test, which is employed primarily because of its enormously high test ceiling. The score on the SAT test determines their final eligibility for the program offered in their area. While this is a regional example, a district program can employ a very similar process, using out-of-level achievement tests with a higher ceiling than the original screening test or teacher-made criterion-referenced tests as the second and final step in the process.

For programs with a definition of giftedness that includes leadership, the initial screener is likely to be some form of nomination; further measures of the candidates' leadership abilities are then employed to determine final eligibility. For programs that highlight creativity as an important facet of giftedness, a creativity test and/or an evaluation of the student's creative products are likely to be used to determine the final eligibility of students.

Communication with parents about a student's candidacy is an essential part of an effective identification process. In well-managed traditional programs, parents are kept well informed throughout the entire process. At the outset, letters may be sent to all parents informing them about the program philosophy and goals and outlining the identification process that will be employed. For students who are selected as candidates in the screening process, a second letter goes home informing parents that their child is being considered for the program. Depending upon district policy, the parents may or may not be asked to give permission for the further testing required for final selection. At the conclusion of the final testing, parents of all candidates receive letters that describe the test results and whether the child has been selected for the program or not.

In addition to formal communication, program administrators spend a great deal of time talking with individual parents on the telephone during the identification process. Frequently parents request retesting if they believe that the initial score was an inaccurate reflection of their child's true ability. These calls must be handled diplomatically and nondefensively. We believe that, although these calls may seem to be annoying and time consuming, the information they generate (both ways) is invaluable. Parents do know their children better than any test or any teacher ever can, and are frequently able to point out areas of strength and talent that school personnel miss.

Combining Instruments and Other Procedures to Create a Comprehensive Identification System

Your definition of giftedness may lead you to find many useful identification strategies and instruments. It is then necessary to find ways to combine the information you receive from each assessment procedure to provide a more comprehensive picture of a child's abilities and talents than any one device can provide by itself.

Many districts employ a matrix in order to combine scores from several tests or other instruments. Figure 5.4 shows an example of an identification matrix that combines data related to ability, creativity, and task commitment to provide a more comprehensive view of a child's aptitudes than any one piece of data could do by itself.

School districts find that the use of the weighted matrix provides them with two distinct advantages. The combination of data provides a more realistic, more comprehensive, and probably more accurate picture of a child's giftedness than does a single test score. It also allows for efficient and effective communication with parents about the reasons for eligibility and ineligibility in the gifted program.

EBY ELEMENTARY IDENTIFICATION INSTRUMENT
GENERAL SELECTION MATRIX

Student Name _____ Grade _____ Date _____

Teachers Making Recommendation _____ Avg. Score _____

This Matrix is designed to measure three important components of academic talent: Above Average Ability (*), Task Commitment (**), and Creativity (***).

Enter child's score for each assessment area. Tally and compute score.

ASSESSMENT AREAS	WEIGHTED SCORES				
USE Achievement Test THIS Composite Score (*) Test Used: _____ Norms Used: _____ Date Given: _____	>98%ile	97−94	93−90	89−88	87−85
OR General Intelligence THIS Test (*) Test Used: _____ Date Given: _____	>140	135−139	130−134	125−129	116−124
Grade Point Average (**) 3rd — 8th Grades Only	5.0	4.9−4.8	4.7−4.6	4.5−4.3	4.2−4.0
GIFT or GIFFI Test (***)	>90%ile	89−80	79−70	69−60	59−50
Teacher's Recommendation (*), (**), (***).	60−55	54−49	48−43	42−37	36−30
Column Tally (Number of Entries Per Column)					
Weight	X5	X4	X3	X2	X1
Score					

TOTAL SCORE

_____ ELIGIBLE (_____ or more points)

_____ INELIGIBLE (less than _____ points)

Additional Copies Available From
SLOSSON EDUCATIONAL PUBLICATIONS, INC.
P.O. Box 280, East Aurora, New York 14052

Figure 5.4
Reprinted with permission of Slosson Educational Publications, Inc.

Teacher Recommendations

The earliest method of identifying gifted children was simply teacher nomination. But the question of whether classroom teachers are good identifiers has long been an issue in gifted education. Some studies conducted before 1970 concluded that teachers tended to nominate only "those children who are doing very well in school, much better than their companions" (Gallagher 1979, p. 17). Such a definition would have precluded the identification of Albert Einstein, Thomas Edison, and Winston Churchill.

But teachers do have a unique opportunity to observe students in the process of thinking and doing school-related work. While unguided opinions of teachers may be invalid as identification data, it is our belief that teachers can be adequately informed of the criteria for selection and provide valuable information and insight into the total identification process.

Many program coordinators, therefore, conduct in-services for their classroom teachers to inform them of the philosophy and definitions of giftedness used in their district. Teachers are provided with nomination or recommendation forms that include specific criteria and guidelines. An example of a teacher recommendation form appears in Figure 5.5. This particular form is based upon Renzulli's definition of giftedness. The score on a form such as this can be used as a screening device or included in a final selection matrix.

NONTRADITIONAL IDENTIFICATION STRATEGIES

Critics of traditional identification systems object to the limited nature of giftedness that they usually define. Test validity is frequently questioned, especially for students from a minority group or with any handicap. The labeling and sorting out of children into permanent categories is considered to be ill advised by a growing number of educators in the field. Critics also believe that the traditional identification process consumes too much time, energy, and resources that would be better used in direct services to children. Barbara Clark (1983) suggests that a more natural and humane identification process would simply allow children with talent to "bubble-up" and be served appropriately according to their talents and interests (p. 173). Several researchers have proposed identification systems that do just that.

Calvin Taylor (1986) proposes an identification model based upon his definition of giftedness as outstanding talent in creativity, communication, planning, forecasting, and decision making as well as the more traditional academic talent. Figure 5.6 illustrates his belief that no one child, when compared to his or her peers, is likely to be at the top in all of these talent areas; instead there may be a different child who is the most gifted in each talent area. Taylor believes that teachers should provide learning opportunities in all of these talent areas, and look for children with particular strengths in each area.

Joseph Renzulli (1981) proposes that we modify the traditional identification to fit his definition of giftedness as a combination of ability, creativity, and task commitment brought to bear on a self-selected talent area. Districts that use Renzulli's Revolving Door Identification Model (RDIM) employ a variety of measures

EBY ELEMENTARY IDENTIFICATION INSTRUMENT
TEACHER RECOMMENDATION FORM

Student Name _____ Grade _____ Date _____

Teacher Making Recommendation _____

Recent research has shown that Creative Behavior and/or Academic Talent is a combination of three basic traits: Above Average Ability, Task Commitment, and Creativity. Please circle the number which indicates THIS child's degree of the characteristics described below as compared to other students of the same age.

	HIGHLY SUPERIOR	ABOVE AVERAGE	AVERAGE	BELOW AVERAGE
ABILITY				
1. Learns rapidly, easily, efficiently.	4	3	2	1
2. Reasons things out; uses logic; makes good decisions; organizes tasks well.	4	3	2	1
3. Understands abstract ideas readily; recognizes relationships and implications.	4	3	2	1
4. Uses a large vocabulary with accuracy.	4	3	2	1
5. Academic work is above grade level.	4	3	2	1
TASK COMMITMENT				
1. Is a self-starter; shows initiative.	4	3	2	1
2. Is able to maintain long period of concentration.	4	3	2	1
3. Follows through and completes tasks on time or before.	4	3	2	1
4. Is willing to spend more time than required on subjects which interest him/her.	4	3	2	1
5. Has one or more strong interest; seeks complex and challenging activities.	4	3	2	1
CREATIVITY				
1. Displays great curiosity and imagination.	4	3	2	1
2. Generates many solutions or alternatives.	4	3	2	1
3. Is a risk-taker; shows independence.	4	3	2	1
4. Reveals originality in oral or written work; gives unusual, unique, or clever responses.	4	3	2	1
5. Other students turn to him for ideas and suggestions when something must be decided.	4	3	2	1

TOTAL SCORE

Additional Copies Available From
SLOSSON EDUCATIONAL PUBLICATIONS, INC.
P.O. Box 280, East Aurora, New York 14052

Figure 5.5
Reprinted with permission of Slosson Educational Publications, Inc.

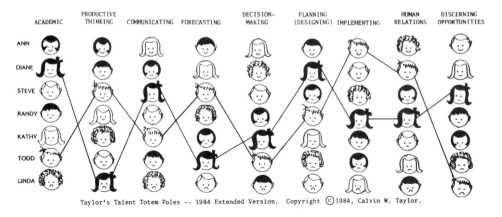

Taylor's Talent Totem Poles -- 1984 Extended Version. Copyright ©1984, Calvin W. Taylor.

Figure 5.6. Taylor's Talent Totem Poles—1984 Extended Version.
Reprinted by permission of *Illinois Council for the Gifted Journal,* Joan Smutny, Editor.

to spot students with talents and abilities, who are all considered to be part of a talent pool. Students in the talent pool are provided with some enrichment experiences, but the goal of the program is to encourage students in the talent pool to select and concentrate upon one interest area. When a student does exhibit a strong interest, Renzulli believes that her "lightbulb has turned on," and that this is the most teachable moment. She is then provided with time and resources from the gifted program personnel to support her interest with a goal of helping her to bring her ability, creativity, and task commitment together to create an original product in her chosen talent area.

The Eby Gifted Behavior Pre-Task Selection Model is based on a definition of giftedness as a series of actions that lead to the creation of a high-quality, original product. But rather than wait for children to turn on their own light bulbs, Eby's program provides a variety of structured learning experiences or curriculum units. She encourages children to apply for a unit of the program that fits their interests and abilities (Eby 1983, 1984).

Consider adult applications for research grants, tryouts for competitive sports teams, auditions for plays or orchestras, and applications for employment with highly regarded companies. What does an editor want to see before awarding a lucrative advance on a book? What does an architect have to do to get a contract? What does an artist show a gallery? Test scores? Hardly.

In real life, the gifted artist is distinguished from his less gifted peers by comparing his paintings with theirs. The musician auditions by playing a sample of his repertoire. The architect provides scale models or drawings to win a contract. The writer provides his editor with a chapter or two of the book she wants to write.

In regard to finding talent, Benjamin Bloom noted that "situational tests in which the examinee attacks real problems are undoubtedly excellent ways of observing and predicting creativity" (1963, p. 260). An educator who specializes in personality and measurement, Fiske believes that "there is no better way of selecting promising applicants than the properly devised and administered work sample" (1971, p.

4). Renzulli describes an identification process in which "activities that are conscientiously and systematically designed to develop task commitment and creativity could be viewed as the situations or occasions whereby we can spot examples of gifted behavior" (1981, p. ix).

We believe that present identification systems can be markedly improved by the use of such situational tests, work samples, and conscientiously and systematically designed activities that allow children to create original products or otherwise demonstrate their gifts and talents. These performance tasks can be used alone or in combination with other assessment devices to aid in the identification process by allowing children to demonstrate their talents and gifts in a meaningful way. They may be especially valuable in the identification of children with language deficiencies or other cultural or physical differences that invalidate their test scores.

One identification strategy that has proved to be very successful is the use of "pre-tasks" as a means of discovering which children in the school can demonstrate ability, creativity, and task commitment in a given subject or topic of study. This strategy is well described in two articles by Eby (1983, 1984). She uses a device called an "Official Entry Form" (see examples in Figures 5.7 and 5.8) to communicate the expectations of a curriculum unit to all children at the appropriate grade level. On the due date, the products are evaluated using the Unit Selection Matrix

OFFICIAL ENTRY FORM

A Study of Leadership

Electing new leaders is one of the privileges of our form of government. The purpose of this unit of study will be to investigate and understand the concept of leadership.

We will research the lives of famous leaders to learn more about their similarities and differences. We will each choose and become an expert on one famous leader and use the information as we practice our own leadership skills in debates, discussions and creative dramatics.

In addition, our group will run an election for the rest of the school. We will be the voter registrars and the election judges. In November, while the adult voters cast their ballots, we will too.

To demonstrate that you have the interest, ability and commitment to take part in this important work, you must complete the following pre-task:

Pretend you are the campaign manager for Abraham Lincoln. Turn in a written report or an oral presentation to convince me to vote for him. You may use any other creative effects you can think of to persuade me, such as color and sound. But please include at least five facts about him that will show what a good leader he will be.

This Pre-task presentation will take place on _____
You must bring this signed entry form with you on that day.

_____   _____
Parent Signature   Student Signature

Figure 5.7. Eby Pre-Task Entry Form for Unit on Leadership.
Created by Judy W. Eby.

OFFICIAL ENTRY FORM

LITERATURE/DRAMA QUARTER

In this unit you will be expected to read a book and work with your classmates to turn all or part of it into a play.

You will become the directors, writers, actors, set designers, and costume makers. You will make all the necessary arrangements to perform your play for your classmates and parents. This will take several different kinds of talent and abilities:

1. Good reading and writing abilities
2. The ability to communicate & cooperate with others
3. Responsibility to do what you say you'll do
4. Lots of CREATIVITY

If you are interested in taking part in this learning unit, you must complete the following pre-task and turn it in by _____.

PRE-TASK

Write a script for a short play. It should include at least 3 characters. Each character should have his or her own unique characteristics. The play should deal with some kind of problem which occurs. Show how the characters each see the problem differently and how they eventually solve it. You may make up your own story and problem or you may re-write a familiar fairy tale or folk tale which is familiar to everyone.

Remember, this pre-task is the minimum required to get into this unit. You are encouraged to be creative and do more than required or find a very original way to present your script. Please turn in your play script and this official entry form on or before the due date.

_____   _____
Parent Signature   Student Signature

Figure 5.8. Eby Pre-Task Entry Form for Literature/Drama Quarter. Created by Judy W. Eby.

(Figure 5.9). In this way, no child is "in" or "out" of the gifted program. All children have equal access and opportunity to take part in activities that match their talents and interests.

Identification for Different Levels and Types of Programming

The most recent trend in school districts is to offer more than one type of gifted program to meet the needs of students with different talents and abilities. A Pyramid Model of programming is proposed by June Cox, director of the Gifted Students' Institute in Fort Worth, Texas, and chairperson of the Richardson Foundation Survey of gifted programs in the early 1980s. The Pyramid concept is based on the premise that there are many children who can benefit from enrichment experiences, a smaller group of children who need special classes that provide challenging, fast-paced learning experiences, and an even smaller number of children who have such unusual talents and abilities that they require special schools or other radically accelerated programs to meet their needs. In Cox's view, many children have need

EBY IDENTIFICATION INSTRUMENT
UNIT SELECTION MATRIX

Student Name _____ Grade _____ Date _____

Unit of Study _____ Evaluated by _____

Description of Pre-task _____

EVALUATION OF PRE-TASK	HIGHLY SUPERIOR	ABOVE AVERAGE	AVERAGE	BELOW AVERAGE
TASK COMMITMENT				
1. Is turned in on time or before	4	3	2	1
2. Shows accuracy and authenticity	4	3	2	1
3. Shows completeness and attention to detail	4	3	2	1
4. Shows care and pride of workmanship	4	3	2	1
5. Goes beyond the minimum required	4	3	2	1
CREATIVITY				
1. Captures attention of reader or viewer	4	3	2	1
2. Shows originality and imagination (unique responses)	4	3	2	1
3. Shows flexibility and independence (re-defines problem or goal)	4	3	2	1
4. Shows complexity of thought (depth of responses)	4	3	2	1
5. Shows fluency of ideas (many responses)	4	3	2	1

TOTAL SCORE

_____ ELIGIBLE (_____ or more points)

_____ INELIGIBLE (less than _____ points)

Additional Copies Available From
SLOSSON EDUCATIONAL PUBLICATIONS, INC.
P.O. Box 280, East Aurora, New York 14052

Figure 5.9. Eby Unit and Selection Matrix.
Reprinted with permission of Slosson Educational Publications, Inc.

of the services of the gifted program, but at different levels and in different talent areas (Cox, Daniel, and Boston 1985, p. 159).

To design such a comprehensive gifted program, it is necessary to design identification systems for each level. For example, a district might use the IEP Model of identification and program prescription for the tiny population of highly gifted students whose needs cannot be met in the child's own grade level or school. Case histories would be reviewed by a pupil personnel team to decide on appropriate placement for each student. The same district might use Specific Academic Aptitudes as the basis for selecting a middle group of children. Using aptitude and criterion-referenced testing, students with unusual talents in math would be placed in an accelerated math program; children with unusual verbal talents would be selected for an enriched language arts program; and children with a special aptitude in any other talent area would be selected for extra programming in that subject or field. At the base of the pyramid, the district's gifted program might choose to offer all children enriched experiences designed to enhance their higher-level thinking skills or creative problem-solving abilities. Alternatively, the base of the pyramid might be served by offering the entire school population the opportunity to take part in gifted programming with final selection determined by the "pre-task" identification method.

IDENTIFICATION ISSUES

Identification raises some of the most critical issues facing gifted education today. Decisions about identification can have an unknown but undoubtedly powerful effect upon a child's self-concept and school career. In our view, gifted program administrators have frequently mishandled their power over children's lives through casually constructed and often quite arbitrary identification plans. Children have been labeled either "gifted" or "nongifted" based on misused tests and hastily created identification procedures.

Unless we reexamine our attitudes and procedures about identification, the entire field of gifted education is at risk. A thoughtful, common-sense, and caring attitude is an absolutely necessary attribute of any gifted program teacher or administrator. We must be aware, at all times, of how our decisions affect the children we serve and the ones we choose not to serve.

We must learn how to communicate effectively with the students' parents about crucial placement and selection decisions. Too often, parents' views are neglected or discounted in the identification procedures. We must recognize that parents are naturally going to advocate for their child in any competitive situation. Parents of handicapped children were powerful advocates for special education programs. Parents can also become powerful allies in our efforts to fund and maintain high-quality gifted programs. But, if we make our identification procedures competitive, many parents will struggle to get their child included, using any means that work. This struggle is the greatest source of risk to gifted programs as they exist today.

Parents of children who are excluded may question our rationale for identification decisions. If they are not satisfied with our answers, they may use a variety of political processes to change the program so that it will include their children. They may call or visit the superintendent of schools or members of the board of education. They may also undermine our efforts by sharing their own dissatisfaction with other parents in such a way that the program is generally viewed as negative or ineffective.

There are ways to deal effectively with parents on identification issues. One way is to create a wide base of support for the program by gathering and using community input in articulating the basic program philosophy and definitions. If the identification procedures are congruent with the program philosophy, they will also be understood and supported by the community. As new program initiatives are considered, the community must be informed about the rationale and substance of any and all changes. Two-way communication with the entire school community is essential for program maintenance.

A second way to satisfy most parents on identification issues is to provide a comprehensive program, like the one described above, that has many alternatives open to children with many different gifts and talents. When different levels of programming are provided, so that there is an appropriate program for each child, the fierce competition for selection is eliminated. Parents can then become allies in the decision about which placement is most suitable for their children.

Related to the issue of effective two-way communication is the issue of labeling. Some parents have supported and encouraged the use of labeling because of the reflected glory they experience by discussing their "gifted child" and her "gifted program." Others have literally refused to have their eminently well-qualified children enrolled in a program because they do not wish to have them labeled. This issue may cause divisiveness because of its damaging effects on children's lives. The field of gifted education may have been initiated by Terman's rudimentary IQ test and his arbitrary label that a child with an IQ above 130 was a gifted child, but in the present day both IQ and the gifted label are oversimplifications of a complex set of talents and motivating forces that may be expressed in an infinite variety of ways depending upon the environment.

Less damaging is the use of the word "gifted" to describe specific talents, aptitudes, or commitments, such as gifted musician, artist, or mathematician. As Bloom found in his talent development study and Feldman noted in his studies of child prodigies, there is a turning point when the child begins to think of herself as a talented pianist, an unusually good mathematician, or a budding scientist or artist. When this occurs, the child may become more intrinsically motivated to practice and perfect her potential talent. We can therefore advocate the use of the term "gifted" as an adjective for a specific talent to encourage a child to make a greater commitment to the development of her potential in that field.

We advocate the use of the term "gifted" to describe a set of behaviors that are used by individuals to bring a budding talent to full fruition. "Gifted behavior" does not separate or distinguish children on the basis of who they are as people. It is also useful in that it can be applied to any talent field. More importantly, this term can be operationally defined, which leads directly to the selection of appropriate identification procedures, program goals, and evaluation techniques. Once defined, it can be used with relative precision to assess and discuss the child's growth and development in meaningful ways with other program personnel, with parents, and even with the children themselves.

Operationally, gifted behavior is defined as the "perceptive, active, reflective, independent and persistent commitment to create an original product in a self-selected talent area, to evaluate it, and to communicate the findings to others" (Eby 1986, p. 41). This definition statement includes ten behavioral variables that have been shown to be associated with the creation of high-quality, original products in several talent areas. In a chronological list, the behaviors are:

Perceptiveness	Goal orientation
Active interaction with environment	Originality
Reflectiveness	Productivity
Persistence (commitment)	Self-evaluation
Independence	Effective communication of findings

To fit this operational definition, the following identification processes are used:

1. Evaluation of children's products in the talent area they have selected, looking for unusually high quality and originality
2. Teacher, parent, and self-evaluations of the extent to which these gifted behaviors are used and demonstrated by the child
3. Criterion-referenced tests of aptitude in the specific talent areas considered to be important by the school community.

In subsequent chapters, we will describe the way in which we use these ten behaviors as the basis for educational objectives and program evaluation, for one of the major advantages of this system is that it allows for the consistent development of all aspects of the program from selection to evaluation.

You are encouraged to gather and use community input in the origination or adaptation of your own program philosophy, definitions, goals, and procedures. Create your own operational definition of gifted behavior. In surveys or in meetings, ask members of your community to brainstorm those behaviors that lead to the full use of one's talents and abilities. The list of behaviors your group develops may have similarities to the one presented here, but won't match it completely. Which one should you use? Use the best of both. Use our list as a starting place and add any behaviors that your community prizes but that we have neglected to include. You may choose to add more affective behaviors than we have done, such as tolerance for others with lesser talents, or you may want to be more specific about the creative process by including such behaviors as curiosity or using one's imagination.

Your list of behaviors should be long enough to be comprehensive and include the many priorities of your diverse school community, but short enough so that it can be remembered. The purpose of the definition is to unify your program and make each separate decision meaningful to the whole. A long list of behaviors may suffer from the same fate as Guilford's list of the 120 components of the Structure of the Intellect. How many can you name? A list of 8 to 12 behaviors, arranged in some type of logical order will allow you to establish priorities and make decisions regarding identification instruments, programming goals, and evaluation procedures.

OPPORTUNITIES FOR DISCUSSION AND ACTION

1. As a class, brainstorm the behaviors that you would include in an operational definition of gifted behavior. We suggest that you use the following procedures:
   a. Allow 5–10 minutes of quiet reflective thinking for each individual to write his or her own list of behaviors that lead to the full use of an individual's potential in a self-selected talent area. The lists should include those behaviors that must be used in order to create a high-quality, original product.
   b. In groups of three or four people, discuss your lists, noting similarities and differences. Combine your lists to create one list of the behaviors that all of you consider to be important.

    c. Give each small group five blank 4-by-6-inch cards. Using only one word or a very short phrase (e.g., "active interaction with the environment"), write one behavior on each card.

    d. First, collect the card from each group that is the clearest and most easily understood. Using tape, put these cards up on a blank wall, in a horizontal row. If two cards are similar in meaning or intent, put them into a column.

    e. Next, collect the card from each group that is the most important to that group. Put these up on the wall. If a card is unique in meaning it is put into its own column. If it is similar in meaning to a card already up on the wall, it becomes part of that column. Let the group be actively involved in deciding whether a card is similar or different. If there is a difference of opinion, allow the group who wrote the card to decide where it is placed.

    f. The third card collected should be one that is most different from any other cards already up on the wall. Continue to make rows and columns, but restrict the number of columns to about ten columns. The group must decide which behaviors are similar enough to move into existing rows so that no more than ten rows are used.

    g. The fourth and fifth cards from each group are then placed on the wall as the group determines. Cards may be moved from column to column at any time until there is consensus that the cards are in the correct columns.

    h. Finally, create one new label card for each column. By looking at all the behaviors listed in each column, decide what general term or behavior best describes all of the elements in that column. Start with the easiest column first. Gradually work toward the harder, more diverse columns. You may continue to move cards around until the last moment to reach a group consensus on the labels for each column.

    i. Conclude by reviewing the ten behaviors on the label cards as the starting point of a group definition of gifted behavior, unique for that group, but probably sharing some important similarities with definitions that would be created by other similar groups of educators.

2. Take this same process and use it in your own school setting with a group of stakeholders who have both interest and expertise in the field of gifted education and in the development of a successful gifted program for your district.

REFERENCES

Bloom, B. 1963. Report by the examiner's office of the University of Chicago. In *Scientific creativity,* ed. C. Taylor. New York: John Wiley.

Clark, B. 1983. *Growing up gifted,* 2nd ed. Columbus, Ohio: Merrill.

Cox, J., N. Daniel, and B. Boston. 1985. *Educating able learners.* Austin, Tex.: University of Texas Press.

Eby, J. 1983. Gifted behavior—A non-elitist approach, *Educational Leadership* 40 (no.8): 30–36.

———. 1984. Developing gifted behavior, *Educational Leadership* 41 (no.7): 35–43.

————. 1986. The relationship between gifted behavioral processes observed in students and the quality and originality of the products they create. Ann Arbor, Mich.: University Microfilms.

Fiske, D. 1971. *Measuring the concepts of personality.* Chicago: Aldine.

Gallagher, J. 1979. *Teaching the gifted child,* 2nd ed. Boston: Allyn & Unwin.

Hoy, W., and C. Miskel. 1978. *Educational administration: Theory, Research, and Practice.* New York: Random House.

Illinois State Board of Education. 1985. Illinois Administrative Code, Section 227-10.

Mitchell, J. ed. 1985. *The Ninth Mental Measurements Yearbook.* Lincoln, Neb.: University of Nebraska Press.

Renzulli, J. 1981. *The revolving door identification model.* Mansfield Center, Conn.: Creative Learning Press.

Taylor, C. 1986. Cultivate both knowledge and talents—not one without the other. *Illinois Council for the Gifted Journal.* Palatine, Ill.: Illinois Council for the Gifted.

U. S. Congress. 1981. Education Consolidation and Improvement Act. Public Law 97-35.

CHAPTER 6

Special Needs of Talented Minority Children in Gifted Education

A teacher, a program director, and a community member are rifling through applications for a special one-month program for talented minority students.

TEACHER: Maribel performs well in mathematics and art, but her reading lags behind, and the scores we have here indicate a potential problem.

COMMUNITY MEMBER: These tests can be misleading. Maribel does what many bilingual children do when they have to read material above their level of fluency. They simply provide background information to fill the gaps. I do not believe this score means Maribel is a poor reader.

TEACHER: But Maribel has lived here for a long time, and speaks well.

PROGRAM DIRECTOR: But she also has a family that rarely speaks English. This also needs to be taken into account. Also, gifted children do not necessarily read well anyway. I think we should interview Maribel, and talk to people from the community center as well.

COMMUNITY MEMBER: Well, now what shall we do with this application from Alfred Thompson? He has little to recommend him as far as the school is concerned . . . very average grades, except in history. His social studies teacher claims that his projects were by far the most thorough and innovative. But look at his grades and scores. Is this kid gifted?

TEACHER: Well, in all fairness, I must admit I'm impressed by this recommendation from the church youth group. The director of the youth program says that Alfred's leadership ability, perception of other people, and ability to "make things happen" are remarkable.

PROGRAM DIRECTOR: I'm concerned that my program might be too academic for him, although I also have an arts component in the course selections. Would he feel out of place with all children interested in subject areas? We could investigate his case too.

TEACHER: Wow, look at this child's scores! His name is Khieu . . . from Cambodia. He has only lived here a year and and a half and his scores are higher than the children from the top schools. Why don't the other minority kids perform like him?

PROGRAM DIRECTOR: Many Asian children have parents who want them to excel in the mainstream culture, and so they are encouraged to learn English quickly.

TEACHER: That's true. My new Asian students walk around with dictionaries and notebooks.

PROGRAM DIRECTOR: But many of them lack experience in more creative work. The ones in my program often opt for the science subjects, because that is what they think will please their parents. But then they discover that in my program, math and science are creative subjects, too . . . I think this child would benefit from our approach.

WHAT DO YOU THINK?

1.   How can the mainstream culture identify talent among minority students?

2. In what areas aside from the academic realm might talent be found in nonmainstream students?
3. Should children from cultures that discourage assimilation be excluded from a gifted program simply because they do not have the mastery of English or writing that the majority culture sees as a sign of intelligence? Should children from populations that encourage assimilation be preferred over those who do not?
4. Should we continue to motivate Asian students to excel in math and science? Is there a danger that doing so might contribute to the stereotyping that prevents them from the proper nurturance of their creative being?
5. How much weight should mainstream definitions of intelligence have in the selection of students from minority groups?

INTRODUCTION

Until recently, the talents of minority children have largely remained an unmined resource. In the early 1900s, these children were an invisible population to all but a few. One of those few, W. E. B. Du Bois saw in bright children the future possibility for the newly freed black race. He wrote: "The problem of education, then, among Negroes must first of all deal with the Talented Tenth; it is the problem of developing the Best of this race that they may guide the Mass away from the contamination and death of the Worst, in their own and other races" (1903, p. 33). But his proposal went against the grain of an emerging class of influential researchers, who were busy gathering data on how intelligence is distributed among races, as we saw in Chapter 2. Their findings alluded to a genetic inferiority in the IQ level of minorities, particularly in black, Spanish, Indian, and Eastern European groups (Kamin 1974). This testing movement was a drastic setback for gifted minorities. The damage would take many years to repair.

A few voices began to speak out against the cultural bias of testing as early as the 1930s (Samuda 1975), but they never gained a hearing until the tide began to turn in the 1960s and 1970s. Pioneer efforts like those of Klineberg (quoted in Samuda 1975, p. 2), for example, clearly documented the impact that cultural differences of Dakota Indians and blacks had on their performance on mainstream, white tests. But such research was minimal. Not until the 1960s and 1970s did accumulating proofs of test bias force educators to seek alternatives. Mounting criticism of the mythological "objective" test produced abundant studies challenging the hereditarian concept of intelligence.

The world of education was torn between old familiar assumptions about testing and intelligence and new ones. In the process of creating new tests for special populations, culture-sensitive educators began to scrutinize a number of sacred cows:

The assumption that only the mainstream definition of intelligence is valid
The assumption that tests could actually measure the whole of individual mental ability, as a fixed entity
The assumption that talented minority students should be educated to imitate

the mainstream culture and bury their cultural differences as hindrances to mainstream achievement

The culture-sensitive researchers of the 1960s, 1970s, and 1980s have challenged the conviction that tests should dictate who is talented and who is not. The devastating impact that scientific blunders have had on children has created an attitude of healthy skepticism and a new realization of how hidden bias affects the way data is analyzed and interpreted.

REVIEW OF THE PROBLEM

A brief review of educational reports on culturally different groups over the past 200 years will quickly reveal a dearth of information on giftedness within minority groups. In fact, as mentioned in Chapter 2, early testing proved to be disastrous for minority and disadvantaged groups. The studies of Lewis Terman, one of the chief importers of the Binet test, concluded that the lower IQ "is very, very common among Spanish-Indian and Mexican families of the Southwest and also among Negroes. Their dullness seems to be racial. . . . The whole question of racial differences in mental traits will have to be taken up anew. . . . The writer predicts that when this is done there will be discovered enormously significant racial differences in general intelligence" (quoted in Kamin 1974, p. 6).

An accumulation of proof in support of such sentiments poured out of the laboratories of zealous eugenicists, who quickly added other cultural groups immigrating from Eastern Europe to their list of mentally deficient populations. Widely publicized documents such as Professor Brigham's rating of the Nordic race as superior to Alpine, Slavic, and Jewish groups, for instance, helped to establish the Johnson-Lodge Immigration Act of 1924 (Kamin 1974, p. 21). Immigrants fleeing Europe were forced to return and thousands fell victim to the Nazi biological theorists. No one questioned the eugenical experimenters or their evidence. It was evidence that government officials wanted to hear. As Walter Lippmann observed, "If the tester would made good his claim, he would soon occupy a position of power which no intellectual has held since the collapse of theocracy. The vista is intoxicating enough. . . . The unconscious temptation is too strong for the ordinary critical defenses of the scientific methods" (quoted in Gould 1981, p. 180).

Testing began as a biased system. It is now evolving into one that attempts to diagnose minority children more fairly and defend them against the possibility of misjudgment by teachers and/or school officials whose definition of "talent" narrows itself to mainstream academic skill. Any test, however, no matter how culture-sensitive it is, lends itself to biased decision making if it is the only indicator used to measure talent.

NEW DEFINITIONS AND ASSESSMENT PROCEDURES

In 1968, the Association of Black Psychologists reacted against the ethnocentric nature of standardized measurements and declared a moratorium on testing

(Samuda 1975, p. 4). Before the moratorium went into effect, the search for a broader definition of intelligence had already begun. It started with culture-free tests, such as those developed by Davis and Eels (Samuda 1975, p. 133). The makers of these new instruments attempted to strip away cultural influences in order to measure innate intelligence. In so doing, however, they did not depart fundamentally from the hereditarian concept of intelligence. They assumed that culture could be clearly separated from the mind that it influenced and, more importantly, that intelligence was measurable as a fixed entity. This conventional idea began to give way to broader definitions with the introduction of Guilford's Structure of the Intellect Model, as well as the innovative work of Torrance (1977). Torrance, Passow, Bruch, Bernal, and others felt that identifying giftedness within other cultures should not be undertaken without consulting the definitions of talent and ability that prevail in these cultures (Bernal 1981). Proof kept turning up that cultural values determine the kinds of talents expressed by bright people. The conclusion was that those values, rather than mainstream values, should be used to identify giftedness in children from other cultures.

Spanning the last 30 years, the new testing movement has tried to remedy bias due to such factors as language differences, the ethnocentric nature of test items and the mental operations required to answer them, inappropriate norm samplings, and issues of test administration itself (time limits, lack of motivation, test anxiety, etc.). Wechsler was translated into Spanish, the instructions and time limits adjusted, and specific items replaced with more culturally appropriate ones. The Arthur Point Scale of Performance Tests, the Chicago Non-Verbal Examination, the IPAT Culture Fair Intelligence Test, the Leiter International Performance Scale, the Abbreviated Binet for the Disadvantaged, Raven's Progressive Matrices Test, the Alpha Biographical Inventory and Test of General Ability, as well as Williams' culture-specific BITCH test (Black Intelligence Test of Cultural Homogeneity), SOMPA (the System of Multicultural Pluralistic Assessment), PAPI (a Piagetian-based Assessment Pupil Instruction system), SOI-LA (Structure of the Intellect—Learning Abilities), and Torrance's Tests of Creative Thinking all responded to the need to craft tests sensitive to the special environmental and cultural differences of nonmainstream groups. Torrance's research on the "creative positives" of the culturally different forced the education field to confront its own ethnocentric concept of the human intellect.

The freedom educators felt to conduct research within new parameters gradually shifted the focus of psychometrics from testing for prediction to testing for description (Samuda 1975); from identifying what other cultures lacked to identifying what they had; from perceiving a deficit in minority children to perceiving a difference. Samuda felt that the whole question of innate potential was far less crucial than the more pressing issue: "how can we stem the waste of human potential and bring hope and motivation where frustration and despair exist?" (1975, p. 151). Reports such as a recent one from the U.S. Department of Education noting that the percentage of minorities in gifted programs (with the exception of Asians) falls far below the percentage in total school enrollment (Barstow 1987) indicate that this waste continues and that conventional methods of identifying giftedness have failed.

A NEW SELECTION PROCESS

Pioneers in gifted education saw that the only way to reverse the trend of neglect was to make the identification process more flexible and less test-bound. Through the years, a number of programs have instituted policies that minimize narrow, one-sided assessments. The "Encendiendo Una Llama," a national bilingual program based in Hartford, Connecticut, uses many indicators of ability without arbitrarily assigning values to any. Barstow (1987) recommends trial participation as a reliable way of experiencing a child's work first hand. Dorothy Sisk (1981), in her work among the poor, identified gifted children by employing theater techniques, cultural positives, and the ABDA (Abbreviated Binet) to gain a more comprehensive picture of each child's ability.

To test or not to test is no longer the question. Today, many programs are asking how they can develop selection practices that help stop large numbers of minority children from slipping through the cracks of a blind system. The test, which still has a mystique for many school practitioners, has become but one of many criteria in the more open-ended programs. The realization that children's talents come to life in very different settings and circumstances has reduced the importance assigned to any one setting or circumstance. Encendiendo Una Llama used the three characteristics of talent designated by Renzulli: above-average ability, creativity, and task commitment. The program conducted an "open recruitment," where children who demonstrated their abilities through one of many channels available would be eligible to participate in one or more of the special services. The program used as many indicators of ability as possible: trial performance in the resource room; culture-sensitive tests, such as the Torrance Tests of Creative Thinking; teacher/parent/peer recommendations; work samples; and cumulative record. The more sources available about each child, the more reliable the information.

Program directors need to be sensitive to environmental and cultural factors affecting minority student performance in order to escape misleading assumptions that accompany low grades and test scores (Baldwin 1985). Many talented children from culturally different backgrounds may live with parents who speak no English, who cannot or do not provide resources (toys, books, etc.) that stimulate cognitive growth, and who do not approve of social behaviors that interfere with the minority cultural values. In addition, children from other cultures may have experienced prejudice, life hardships of many kinds (e.g., the Vietnamese refugee children; gifted illegal aliens; talented youth from gang neighborhoods; etc.), and may also have an oral history that discourages extensive involvement with reading materials. The talents of these vital children can flourish in special programs developed to meet their needs without sacrificing their cultural uniqueness and commitment to their own community values and traditions. But it takes sensitivity to make this happen.

Project '86, '87, and '88 in Winnetka, Illinois, a yearly three-week summer institute with follow-up sessions through each year for talented minority and white sixth through tenth graders, consulted with Asian, black, and Hispanic community leaders, social workers, parents, teachers, and community art and drop-in centers to investigate candidates fairly and thoroughly. Smutny and her staff also used work samples, checklists (developed specifically for culturally different populations), and parent and student interviews. They briefed school officials, psychologists, class-room teachers, and parents on how talents of nonmainstream populations often go unseen under conventional definitions. Drawing on Gay's (1978) six-step plan for identifying black talent, Kitano's (1986) study on high-achieving Asian students, Baldwin's (1985) review of selection and curriculum issues for minority talented children, and her own experience with nonmainstream talent, Smutny held work-shops for parents, community leaders, and bilingual teachers that helped diffuse popular myths about children with special abilities. While these methods of selection and communication are not particularly new, her program abides by some general principles that avoid identification pitfalls. Here are some crucial ones:

> Identification is an individual matter and should never depend on a test score. If anything, it should depend more on the conclusions of teachers or special-ists who are either trained to work with talented minority children, or sensi-tive to the less obvious "signs" of talent.
>
> All staff involved in the identification process should know how to work with talented children from very diverse backgrounds. So ingrained is the conven-tional concept of "gifted" that efforts to broaden that concept and sensitize staff to the unusual ways that giftedness may show itself should be ongoing. For that reason, Project '86, '87, and '88 held regular meetings with commu-nity liaisons and teachers to review the performance of identified students and to problem-solve ways to encourage students who needed extra support.
>
> Program directors should know the cultures they are inviting to participate and have minority contacts assigned to help identify students and support those who attend. Liaisons know how other cultures express their talents and can orient the director and staff to their values and viewpoints. If possible, sur-veys, questionnaires, and/or interviews should further inform directors about cultural values and strengths.

MINORITY GIFTED PROGRAMS: ASSIMILATIONISTS VS. CULTURAL PLURALISTS

Procedures for the identification and education of talented minority students vary from place to place, depending on the philosophical bias of the program. The ulti-mate educational goal for these students has become a point of dispute. The disput-ers fall roughly into two categories. One side contends that only through assimila-tion will minority talent thrive in the big world. This side claims that cultural strengths that served these children in their home environments hinder them in soci-ety (Smilansky and Nevo 1979). The opposing side insists that learning the ropes of mainstream culture should never require imitation. Cultural strengths, far from disabling, empower minorities to excel in mainstream contexts, as amply demon-strated by Torrance, Bernal, Bruch, Rimm, and Sisk, among others. Presently, bilingual-bicultural education programs have become the center of this debate (Davis and Rimm 1985).

While the dust over the bilingual education issue is far from settled, imitation or assimilation has not come any closer to becoming a proven method of educating the culturally different. Programs that pressure minorities to catch up with their white, middle-class competitors by filling them up with mainstream values, facts, and figures may gain them positions in a fast-paced, industrial society. But cultural pluralists weigh the gains of such an approach against the losses. What has the child sacrificed in the process of imitating the majority culture? The message to the child is: to succeed with us, you must be like us. The message to the child's community is: you are keeping this child back. However sensitive their teachers or program directors may be, the children cannot avoid the sense of lack and deficiency that are built into the program's approach.

The family and community cannot avoid it either. Frequently assimilationist programs confine family or community involvement to supporting their children's progress into white, middle-class America. But progress, in this case, means adopting the dominant culture. Enthusiastic parents may not realize the distinction between helping children escape poverty or lack of opportunity and schooling them in such a way that they give up their culture and community. Although traditional programs may not intend for minority children to reject their own culture, such programs ultimately have this effect. In open-ended programs, on the other hand, families participate in an effort to support cultural strengths and cultural identity in their children, and the translation of their talents into mainstream contexts. The use of cultural strengths and community involvement underlies most open-ended programs for minority talent.

CULTURAL STRENGTHS

Program directors and specialists know that children respond to the way they are defined. Torrance (1985), reviewing the case of John Torres, a 12-year-old sixth grader highly gifted in leadership, psychomotor activities, art, and mechanics, but less so in reading and writing, asked: "Was John Torres gifted? Would it be better to treat John as gifted in the psychomotor and leadership areas or as a retarded non-reader and a behavior disorder case? Which is in John's best interest? Which is in society's best interest?" (p. 2). The school's recognition of John's ability changed his attitude radically. He took his work more seriously, began to see new possibilities for his talents, and quickly improved his reading as well. John Torres was an asset to his school and to other children. A false assessment of John would have squelched his talents and created a loss for those around him.

A young Native American child who demonstrated exceptional ability, yet was seriously deficient in academic skill areas, was described in an article by Scruggs and Cohn (1983). These authors developed an individualized program that capitalized on his talents and employed his interests to involve him in the skill development process. He improved rapidly in skill areas and discovered other latent abilities and interests, because of the open-ended nature of his program. His mentors placed him at advantage, rather than disadvantage.

A journalist in Nairobi, Kenya, noticed a phenomenon among children in the shanties there (Gacheru 1985). Lacking toys or playthings, these "child engineers," as they were called, consumed long hours fashioning trucks and cars out of bits of tin and scraps. Not one had ever sat in a car or even stood close enough to see how they operate. Yet they constructed autos with movable wheels, steering wheels that maneuvered the front wheels, brakes, and other attachments. The local school-master reported that these children surpassed their classmates because of their advanced creative thinking. The schoolmaster saw the advantage the "child engineers" had; assimilationists would see only the disadvantage. Should this talent be disregarded as valueless?

The cultural strengths of minority children influenced the curriculum of Project '88. Bilingual students with special talents had innovative instruction that not only increased their ability to use English in abstract reasoning activities and conceptual discussions, but was sensitive to their background, community values, environmental resources, and learning styles. The curriculum centered around hands-on experience, rather than language-based introduction of abstract concepts. In Economics, for example, students assumed the roles of business leaders, investors, consumers, and workers through a series of simulations that plunged them into the concerns of people in fast-paced fiscal quarters. Over the three weeks, the class grappled with the intriguing relationships between money supply, inflation, the GNP, the national debt, and unemployment. In Futuristics, children imaginatively conceived of a world where cyborgs, androids, automatons, and robots work side by side with human beings. A woman who had formerly taught college mathematics offered a class in Mathematical Curves, which involved students in a progression of explorations from the simplest circles to the trigonometric function curves and exotic cycloid and spiral curves. Finding curves in spider webs, soundwaves, and galaxies, as demonstrated in class activities, stimulated learning in many children who might ordinarily lose interest in abstract mathematical thinking. Having the class explore modern mathematical applications in the Golden Gate Bridge or automobile headlights further expanded and enlivened course content for students with less experience in Algebra.

Bilingual teaching colleagues in Project '88 and other programs for students with limited English proficiency (LEP) assisted instructors by participating directly in class sessions, counseling LEP students and offering help with lesson plans when needed. Their close association with the children proved to be a valuable source of information for many teachers and staff in planning and adjusting each day's activities. Consistently, these colleagues encouraged practical application of course content. Math classes, for example, focused on the development of geometric intuition and the use of math skills already in place as a way to discover new mathematical principles. A class on energy looked at current uses of energy and its application to everyday life and developed a bilingual dictionary of energy and ecology terms. Building a solar cooker, designing an energy system for the future, and performing experiment to study interventions in a minibiosphere gave realism and urgency to their study.

Project '88's range of class offerings, as in the previous year, allowed children talented in different areas to share their strengths and experience a diversity not possible in homogenous programs. Both suburban white and minority students grew from the presence of many cultures. Though initially tentative with one another, both groups began discovering what they had in common and how their differences contributed to the richness of the program. Urban students benefited from the knowledge that they could attend classes side by side with suburban children and not come out on the bottom. Suburban students found the freedom and innovative spirit of urban students refreshing and illuminating. In fact, one suburban seventh grader insisted on riding the bus with the urban children to the other side of town, just to be with them longer.

Teachers noticed that even though some urban students did not have the academic background in several subject areas that suburban students did, they quickly assimilated what was needed to do the project before them and tried some approaches that the more knowledgeable might not have considered. The process of working together eliminated the strain of having one's academic background (or lack thereof) exposed. Researching the ecosystems of rivers, lakes, and ponds in an Aquatic Biology class in 1987 left little room for worrying about academic level. Students were simply too busy working together, testing water samples, and engaging in joint inquiry. Minority students, who in formal settings might cringe before pen and paper, wrote furiously for three weeks in a creative writing class where a visiting journalist from Kenya talked about writing in Africa. They assembled a 200-page, illustrated magazine in three weeks.

The urban students in Project '88 discovered new channels for their strengths. If these children had attended formal academic classes emphasizing a purely abstract, linear approach, they might not have shown any talent at all. Culturally different children need opportunities to use their bold improvisational powers, their quick verbal wits, their inventive spirit, and their creative thinking. Suburban children likewise need to see the disadvantage of relying on mere factual knowledge, and the advantage of allowing themselves the freedoms that their restrictive schooling has at times stifled out of learning.

COMMUNITY OUTREACH

All cultures need role models and leaders. The talent in a community is its potential leadership. Although many assimilationist programs for talented minority students maintain strong ties with parents and communities, they limit the degree to which the parents and communities can participate in the actual education of their children. This diminishes the likelihood of these children growing up to assume a strong leadership role in the community. What child will want to lead a community with which he or she no longer identifies? What community member will follow someone who has been physically or mentally removed, only to return as a white, mainstream makeover? Education for assimilation tells children that they must begin all over. In the process of beginning all over, however, they leave their culture behind.

Alternative programs insist on strong, consistent family and community outreach. Parents and neighborhoods can make the difference for the minority participants in a program. Rather than approaching parents with the request that they support the program, the program should consult with parents about the needs of their children and should use community people as counselors and teaching colleagues. When the Encendiendo project discovered through community contacts that bright Hispanic children often express their talent by helping other classmates, the program quickly capitalized on this quality in class projects and activities.

When Project '86, '87, and '88 surveyed communities to construct an accurate picture of the needs and strengths of this highly diverse student body, Smutny soon discovered that—in order to reach the wide spectrum of talents, interests, and backgrounds—course content would have to cover a range of subjects from performing arts to advanced mathematics. Families and community organizers offered advice about the needs of the children, their learning styles, and their prior exposure to subject matter. Liaisons and teaching colleagues were crucial communicators for parents and students through the three weeks and reported progress and/or problems to Smutny and her staff.

Parents attended the open house and observed their children in action—on the dance floor, on stage, in the laboratory, in print. Teachers made a point to give parents specific suggestions about resources for their children during the year. The follow-up sessions through the year served to keep many parents and community people current about career facts, schools, and universities. Minority adults and contacts in various professions helped to dislodge some deep-seated preconceptions about what sorts of careers are "appropriate" or "realistic" for nonmainstream groups.

Other open-ended programs such as Project LEAP in Connecticut, HEP-UP in Pennsylvania, Project SEED and SEPE in California, and the New Orleans Center for Creative Arts have successfully developed contacts with communities in similar ways (Sisk 1981). Without this component, children will often withdraw due to family resistance to something they do not understand. A program should not wait for parents to come to it. The program should go to the parents and make them a vital part of the development of their children. If parents and communities have an investment in the program and own it, others will follow. The program will then become something they can be proud of, rather than something that makes them feel inferior.

A FINAL NOTE

Talented culturally different children have stirred up old ways of thinking in gifted education. Their differences question societal definitions and values and the status quo that predominates in a fast-paced, technologically intensive environment.

Talented minorities have a twofold challenge. On the one hand, they need to achieve within the dominant culture in order to grow and contribute. On the other hand, they want to maintain the cultural distinction that differentiates them from white, middle-class values. For a long time, society simply excluded them from the wealth of resources available to middle-class white children. Then it conceded that minorities could join the ranks of professions formerly considered "white," but only by imitation and assimilation.

Now, more and more, society is including nonmainstream groups on their own terms. On some level, these groups remind "progressive" culture of what it lacks, and what other cultures can contribute if given the chance to do so. Given the mounting challenges that can only be answered by inspired, creative thinkers, gifted educators cannot afford to overlook the tragic loss of hidden potential lying waste in many minority communities.

OPPORTUNITIES FOR DISCUSSION AND ACTION

1. What kinds of talents are valued by mainstream society? How do these values determine how the mainstream educational system identifies ability in both white middle-class and culturally different children?

2. Do you notice any pitfalls in identifying talent in culturally different children through the use of criteria established by mainstream culture? Cite examples. Think of test instruments, class assignments, or activities that might make culturally different students appear deficient rather than able. What methods might you use to discover abilities of the nonmainstream? How would you nurture these talents?

3. Talk to representatives from different cultural groups to determine which talents these groups value in their children, and how they identify these unique abilities.

4. Talk to and invite to your class outstanding members of nonmainstream cultures and ask them to share their experiences as they pursued the career of their choice. What prejudices did they have to confront? How did they overcome obstacles thrown in their path by those who did not feel they could excel in the area they had chosen?

5. Imagine yourself in a new country where you do not know the language or culture of a people (e.g., China, the African continent, the Philippines, Mexico). Imagine that you have been asked to participate in an event, the significance of which you do not understand. How would you look to that culture? Do you think you would appear skilled and talented, or deficient and awkward? Write down your imaginary account of your experiences and share with each other.

REFERENCES

Baldwin, A. Y. 1985. Programs for the gifted and talented: Issues concerning minority populations. In *The gifted and the talented: Developmental perspectives,* ed. F. D. Horowitz and M. O'Brien. Washington D.C.: American Psychological Association.

Barstow, D. 1987. Serve disadvantaged and serve all gifted. *Gifted Child Monthly* 8, no. 10: pp. 1–3.

Bernal, E. M. 1981. Special problems and procedures for identifying minority gifted students. Paper presented at the Council for Exceptional Children Conference on the Exceptional Bilingual Child, New Orleans, La.

Bruch, C. B. 1975. Assessment of creativity in culturally different children, *Gifted Child Quarterly* 19: 164–74.

Cooke, G. J., and A. Y. Baldwin. 1979. Unique needs of a special population. In *The gifted and the talented: Their education and development,* ed. A. H. Passow. Chicago: University of Chicago Press.

Davis, G. A., and S. B. Rimm. 1985. *Education of the gifted and talented.* Englewood Cliffs, N.J.: Prentice-Hall.

Du Bois, W. E. B. 1903. The Talented Tenth. In *The negro problem: A series of articles by representative American negroes of to-day,* ed. B. T. Washington. New York: James Pott and Co.

Feldhusen, J. F., and D. J. Treffinger. 1980. Special needs of minority and disadvantaged gifted students. In *Creative thinking and problem solving in gifted education.* Dubuque, Iowa: Kendal/Hunt Publishing Co.

Gacheru, M. 1985. Children of Nairobi. *Illinois Council for Gifted Journal* 4: 5–7.

Gay, J. E. 1978. A proposed plan for identifying black gifted children, *Gifted Child Quarterly* 22: 353–60.

Gould, S. J. 1981. *The mismeasure of man.* New York: W. W. Norton.

Kamin, L. J. 1974. *The science and politics of IQ.* Potomac, Md.: Lawrence Erlbaum Assoc., Inc.

Kitano, M. K., and P. C. Chinn. 1986. *Exceptional Asian children and youth.* Reston, VA.: Council for Exceptional Children.

Rimm, S. B. 1985. Identifying underachievement: The characteristics approach, *G/C/T* November–December, pp. 2–5.

———. 1987. Creative underachievers: Marching to the beat of a different drummer, *Gifted Child Today,* November–December, pp. 2–6.

Samuda, R. J. 1975. *Psychological testing of American minorities: Issues and consequences.* New York: Dood, Mead.

Scruggs, T. E., and S. J. Cohn. 1983. A university-based summer program for a highly able but poorly achieving Indian child, *Gifted Child Quarterly* 27: 90–93.

Sisk, D. 1981. The challenge of educating the gifted among the poor. In *Gifted children: Challenging their potential—New perspectives and alternatives,* ed. A. H. Kramer et al. New York: Trillium Press.

Smilansky, M., and D. Nevo. 1979. *The gifted disadvantaged: A ten year longitudinal study of compensatory education in Israel.* New York: Gordon and Breach, Science Publishers, Inc.

Sternberg, R. J. 1982. Lies we live by: Misapplication of tests in identifying gifted, *Gifted Child Quarterly* 26: 157–61.

Thomson, B. M., and E. Cisternas. 1981. Strategies for identification and academic development of the gifted/talented bilingual student. Paper presented at the Council for Exceptional Children Conference on the Exceptional Bilingual Child, New Orleans, La.

Torrance, E. P. 1977. *Discovery and nurturance of giftedness in the culturally different.* Reston, Va.: Council for Exceptional Children.

———. 1985. Who is gifted? *Illinois Council for the Gifted Journal* 4: 2–3.

CHAPTER 7

Special Needs of Girls in Gifted Education

A group of parents, each of whom has a daughter participating in a district program for gifted students, are discussing their gifted adolescents.

> PARENT A: About the time she began eighth grade, my daughter's academic performance declined markedly. Her grades are still OK, but the social side of school is her current priority.
>
> PARENT B: My daughter Sarah has a full load of honors courses; however, she refuses to take calculus. She just doesn't enjoy it. Like mother like daughter, I guess.
>
> PARENT C: I wouldn't take dropping out of math so casually. By forgoing calculus your daughter is eliminating a whole range of possibilities. I skipped math my senior year and then I regretted it in college.
>
> PARENT D: Our high school daughter is a gifted and committed student, determined to succeed at everything. In fact, I worry about the pressure she puts on herself. She leaves early every morning to attend her two advanced placement classes and stays late for drama club, volleyball practice, and student council meetings. Our older daughter was that way, too, but she dropped out of a master's program when her husband got a good job offer on the other side of the country. She does a little freelancing now, but basically she is a full-time mother.
>
> PARENT A: That's fine. You can creatively use your gifts as a wife and mother, too. I think I have. Education is never wasted.
>
> PARENT D: Can a gifted woman be truly satisfied at home like that? I have a lot of regrets about my life. I don't want Lupe to make the same mistakes.
>
> PARENT C: I think some women are happy at home, but I worry that girls and young women are being forced to make compromises they don't want to make.
>
> PARENT A: Being gifted doesn't mean you can have it all. We all make choices.

WHAT DO YOU THINK?

1. Do talented girls and talented boys have different intellectual abilities?
2. What are some possible reasons for the underachievement of talented girls?
3. Are male and female students served equally well by the same sort of gifted programming? Are they served equally well by the same sort of mainstream classroom?

INTRODUCTION

Children with unusual strengths hold the promise of vision, perception, and endless wonder. They are often the inquisitive ones who seek new paths, break down barriers, and fearlessly improvise when no solution seems possible. They see through appearances to insights others overlook. If they are loved and granted room to grow, they become our best leaders, humanitarians, artists, physicists, writers, inventors, and teachers. They open doors that others have closed. Often they delight and anger simultaneously those who work with them, play with them, and parent them.

The very characteristics that make these children exceptional, however, also give them challenges in a society that values conformity over creativity. Girls face a double dilemma where their gifts not only do mischief to many adult expectations, but also render them "unfemale" in the conventional sense. Many face the prospect of becoming ostracized if they assert themselves too much or dare to enter fields that seem to be reserved for boys. Their lives can quickly become a process of treading water or forging upstream alone. Many of them eventually succumb to the current. They may forsake their own talents to support their husband's or surrender family and motherhood to be career women. The message society unconsciously conveys to them is: you either be a real girl and keep quiet, or be active in the ways boys are, but don't expect to be treated with respect. Another version of this might be: women can have women's talents such as intuition, sympathy, and creativity in the arts, but they should not express too much competence in mathematics or science, which are men's fields.

In this chapter we attempt to expose fallacies such as these. We review the problems and describe current efforts to reverse the trends of the past. Most importantly, we see how gifted education is expanding itself to help girls formerly neglected. Program directors are becoming sensitive to the unusual challenges facing them and are seeking ways to circumvent bias and stereotyping. The great loss of talent due to narrow assessment and sex bias has jolted current practitioners to salvage the talent in these children before they give up. The results of more open-ended gifted programs have shown what can happen when these talented girls have the freedom, opportunity, and unbiased mentoring to grow and contribute.

TALENTED GIRLS

Most members of contemporary society would not dare publicly echo the sentiments of Euripides (484–406 B.C.), who wrote: "A woman should be good for everything at home, but good for nothing abroad." We are confident enough in our own enlightenment that we can laugh at J. R. R. Tolkien's condemnation of the female intellect: "How quickly an intelligent woman can be taught, grasp the teacher's ideas, see his point—and how (with some exceptions) they can go no further when they leave his hand, or when they cease to take a personal interest in him. It is their gift to be receptive, stimulated, fertilized (in many other matters than the physical) by the male" (quoted in Carpenter 1978, p. 185).

Americans can point with pride at the various achievements of women, giving special attention to the firsts: the first woman Supreme Court Justice, the first woman astronaut, the first woman mayor. The percentage of college degrees earned by women has consistently increased since the turn of the century, so that they now receive bachelor's and master's degrees with greater frequency than do men, and 38 percent of doctorate degrees, from 6 percent in 1900 (U.S. Department of Education

1988). Between 1970 and 1980, the number of women lawyers and judges in the experienced civilian labor force increased 500 percent, while the number of men in the same professions did not even double (U.S. Department of Commerce 1984).

But these statistics are not the harbingers of equity, nor do the eminent accomplishments of deservedly famous women signal smooth sailing for talented girls. We have added a new twist to Euripides' dictum: women are still supposed to "be good for everything at home," but now they are expected to be productive and capable "abroad" in the world of work as well.

At the same time, today's schools may be subtly spreading Tolkien's message that intelligent women cannot produce in the world without the direction of men. Women remain underrepresented in high-status occupations. A review of outstanding creative and intellectual contributions, as demonstrated by both product and recognition (awards, published books, Ph.D.'s, *Who's Who* listings, etc.), quickly reveals that whether the field is science, art, literature, or affairs of state, men continue to achieve more than women. Underachievement among talented women is particularly tragic, because when women of such unusual intellectual and creative talent are denied opportunity, the loss is felt both by the individual and all of American society.

In this chapter we will review the evidence of underachievement among girls with special abilities and consider factors contributing to it. We will examine the status of women in the work force, the world into which most talented girls are headed. We will explore ways in which school environment is a factor in underachievement and discuss systematic and curricular changes, special programs, and counseling services benefiting girls who display giftedness in various areas.

UNDERACHIEVEMENT IN FEMALE STUDENTS

Viewed as a discrepancy between a child's performance at school and her intellectual ability, underachievement may appear to be an easy phenomenon to identify. Of course, it isn't. Accurately assessing school performance is difficult. Grades are a limited shorthand description of accomplishment, although augmenting grades with teacher and parent observations and evaluations of student products (projects, writing samples, etc.) provides a clearer picture of student performance. As we discovered in Chapter 4, we still have only primitive tools for indexing human ability. While these can help in assessment, formal tools should not be the only evidence considered in identifying underachieving children. A simple hunch by a parent or teacher that a child is underachieving in school should be given credence. In the experience of Sylvia Rimm (1984), a psychologist specializing in the needs of underachieving children, such hunches are almost always on the mark. Grades, on the other hand, tell only part of the story. An academically gifted girl earning A's is not necessarily working at, or near, her potential, and grading schemes may not be able adequately to measure the achievements of her creative classmate who brings home report cards peppered with B's and C's.

An achievement and ability discrepancy that is reflected by grades and scores is what educators and the public are most often referring to when they talk about underachievement, but that is a narrow way of defining the syndrome. The research of Stockard and Wood (1984) and Achenbach (1970) indicates that, within school settings, boys are more often underachievers. However, professional achievement is lower among women. A comprehensive working definition of underachievement, therefore, needs to encompass men and women who underachieve in adult life as well as children and young people who fall short of their academic potentials.

Lacking the old standby assessment tools of grades and standardized tests, evaluations of underachievement in adulthood rely on career status and professional accomplishments, work-related productivity (e.g., the number of journal articles published), directory listings, and awards. We must be wary of such an exclusively masculine definition of achievement (Friedan 1981). As Sally Reis (1987) notes, "The realization of giftedness in women may need to be redefined to include the nurturance of one's children and family, the success of being an outstanding teacher or the joy of accomplishment from the pursuit of a career that still allows time for a satisfying personal life" (p. 84). However, she goes on to warn that we must be certain that gifted young women are fully cognizant of their options and we must support them in whatever endeavors they choose.

UNDERACHIEVING GIFTED WOMEN: A PATTERN WITH A PRECEDENT

Women are underrepresented in high-status occupations and executive positions; traditionally, female work is grossly underpaid. But labor force statistics exclude two important populations. A significant, but undetermined, number of workers (by some accounts, 10 million) are self-employed, working out of their own homes, and for tax or zoning reasons keeping quiet about the arrangement (Bolles 1986). Among this number must be many achieving women who are not included in labor force statistics but who may be involved in highly creative or entrepreneurial pursuits. In a second, more familiar group, many homemakers care for their families, staff the school library, and spend two days a week at the Humane Society trying to place unwanted cats. They are not compensated financially for their work and their contributions are rarely recognized statistically.

Even considering these "closet" workers, it is clear that women—especially talented women—are underachieving. The landmark longitudinal study of Lewis Terman and his associates contains a wealth of information about the work histories of highly intelligent adults. As college students, the men and women in Terman's sample chose different majors. Forty-two percent of undergraduate men majored in a biological or physical science or in engineering. Twelve percent of women chose science or engineering majors. In graduate school the ratio shifted only slightly. Thirty-eight percent of male subjects and 14 percent of female subjects pursued postgraduate degrees in science or engineering (Oden 1968). In 1960, when the subjects were between 46 and 54 years old, 15 percent of the men were employed as scientists, engineers, or architects while only 1 percent of the women (only 2 women) were working in one of those fields.

Twenty-four percent of Terman's women earned graduate degrees, compared to 40 percent of the men who completed a postgraduate education (Eccles 1985). In 1960, 97 percent of the men were employed but only 42 percent of the women were wage earners (Oden 1968).

Though many more women today receive doctoral degrees, a recent report by the Congressional Office of Technology Assessment stated that "it takes 2,000 ninth-grade girls to produce one woman with a doctorate in science or engineering" (Winter 1988). The percentage of women completing doctorates in math and science has tripled since the early 1970s, according to this report, but their actual number does not total more than 200 per 1000. A recent survey at Stanford University and MIT showed that women do not receive the professional support that their male counterparts do (Winter 1988). To find out about financial support for scientific research, opportunities to publish, or potentially valuable academic resources, women must forage on their own.

CAUSES OF UNDERACHIEVEMENT

Why this prevailing pattern of underachievement? Educators have identified a variety of internal and external factors in the underachievement of talented girls and women.

Sex-role stereotyping predominates in our media-oriented society. The average kindergartener has already watched 5000 hours of television (Trelease 1985). While some textbook series have made remarkable strides, others still give the impression that physicists should be men and preschool teachers should be women. Melvin Maddocks (1988) recently pointed out in the *Christian Science Monitor* the ironies of women detectives in characters like Agatha Christie's Miss Marple, Dorothy Sayers' Harriet Vane, and Margaret Colin in the now-defunct series "Leg Work." Underneath their intelligence and spunk, the old message still prevails: women should not tamper with men's work. The process of justice is better suited for men with their superior reasoning and analytical ability. "With reasoning like this," comments Maddocks, "male detectives need all the help they can get."

School does little to erase this myth of male superiority. Carol Shakeshaft (1986) contends that the structure of schools, instructional methods, teacher-student interaction, curriculum, and the very goals of education respond to male needs. In her view, the curricular schedule of schools is based on a model of male development. Math concepts are introduced when boys are most likely to be ready for them. Social studies scopes and sequences are determined with boys' needs and interests in mind. According to Shakeshaft, "the result is that girls are often ahead of the game in some areas and never in the game in others. Some grow bored, others give up, but most learn to hold back, be quiet, and smile" (p. 500).

Carol Gilligan's (1982) research on the moral psychology of women has broad implications for present-day curriculum. According to her studies, the majority of girls tend to act according to an ethic of caring for others, rather than one based on absolutes of right and wrong. Because much of the curriculum is developed along the lines of a predominantly male moral psychology, females may find themselves adrift in class discussions.

The research of Myra and David Sadker (1986) indicates that classrooms, be they in kindergarten or college, are inequitable environments in which male students receive more teacher attention and are more often allowed to speak than female students. Teachers spend more time interacting with male students, and more of that time is effective interaction. High-achieving females are the least likely of all student subgroups to receive constructive interaction.

Competition is a prevailing instructional method in most schools. Yet Carol Gilligan (1982) and Janet Lever (1976), among others, indicate that competition is not an effective instructional technique for most girls. Girls respond better to cooperative approaches to learning. The Horner effect explains the tendency of women to avoid success in mixed sex competitions (Horner 1972). This presents a special problem for women with special talents, who feel torn between the pressure to compete and the pressure not to. Society sends them mixed messages. Because of their abilities, they are expected to assert themselves like men, work hard, and find a high-powered position. But the call to be nurturing and passive in a traditional marriage and home life drives them equally hard to set aside their own ambitions for the sake of their husbands and children. Even the most creative child would be unable to completely reconcile those two sets of expectations.

EMINENT WOMEN: HIGH ACHIEVERS

In an effort to discover why some talented girls not only avoided the underachievement trap but translated their gifts into outstanding achievement, Barbara Kerr (1985) examined the biographies of 31 eminent women, including Maya Angelou, Eleanor Roosevelt, Margaret Fuller, Florence Nightingale, Virginia Woolf, Margaret Mead, Mary Cassatt, Simone de Beauvoir, Anne Morrow Lindbergh, Golda Meir, Indira Gandhi, Jane Addams, and Edith Sitwell. Kerr discovered some distinctive and basic commonalities in the lives of the women she studied:

As girls, they spent time alone. Kerr speculates this time allowed them to read and think and enabled them to learn how to set independent goals, assess their own success, and reward themselves.

As children and as adults, they read voraciously. Kerr contends that authors became their guides and counselors.

They felt different or special. Some felt physically anomalous, others felt they had unusual families, several recognized that their talents made them unique.

As girls, they received a lot of individualized instruction. For some it was in a field for which they eventually gained reknown. Others received general home schooling. Kerr speculates that individualized instruction reduced boredom, increased knowledge, and provided mentors and models.

With one exception, each of these women had a difficult adolescence resulting in a sense of alienation or separateness that brought them to an understanding of the cost and rewards of following a "different drummer." It also gave them more of that valuable "alone" time.

They had a sense of their own identity, independent of anyone else's. They took responsibility for themselves.

The intellectual and romantic lives of these women were bound together; they often discovered love through their work.

They were able to fall in love with an idea. Kerr regards passion for a subject as vital to the achievements of these celebrated women.

They ignored the societal confines of womanhood. They did not allow themselves to be limited by traditions and expectations.

Some of the women in Kerr's sample were brusque, sarcastic, and intolerant. Kerr calls this "growing thorns" and considers it a reflection of their passion and intensity. Other women needed to "grow shells" to compensate for shyness and uncertainty.

The women Kerr studied chose lives replete with companions, friends, and children. They managed to integrate these responsibilities with professional achievement and did not view it as a regrettable hardship. "None of these women were complaining 'superwomen,' either self-pitying or martyrs; instead, they were strong women who decided calmly, if boldly, to use life to its fullest" (Kerr 1985, p. 72).

TALENTED GIRLS AND THE CLASSROOM: WHAT CAN BE DONE?

Minimizing Competition

The first principle in nurturing talent in girls is to minimize competition by structuring classes around group work, hands-on experiments and projects, and the process of finding new solutions rather than on any one final answer. The Center for Gifted at National College of Education, Evanston, Illinois, abides by this principle in all programs. Joan Smutny, director of the Center, encourages teachers to integrate group work and creative problem solving in all laboratory experiments and projects. To break down the stereotype that boys excel in mathematics more than do girls, teachers need to break down the stereotypical math class. The problem of competition needs to be addressed organically. Girls who lack experience in applied mathematics or science need hands-on activities that develop a more advanced understanding of, for example, spatial skills. Without the equalizing effect of more innovative and experimental class sessions, efforts to encourage girls in mathematics or science will merely be cosmetic.

Creative programming alters the dynamics in a classroom. In Worlds of Wisdom and Wonder, a yearly program in Illinois for four- and five-year-olds and first through sixth graders, Smutny offers math and science classes that have drawn as many girls as boys. Courses entitled "Geometric Patterns and Constructions," "In Touch with Science: Projects and Experiments," "Microbiology," "Chemistry: Air, Water and Fire," "Intuitive Math: Logic and Problem Solving," and "Archeology: Fossils, Dinosaurs and Digs" gave mathematically curious girls plenty of intriguing choices. Working together on projects and experiments proved to be an equalizer. The children unraveled the mysteries of math and discovered abstract formulas through an inductive process. The class format eliminated the structured, competitive arrangement where verbal boys silence mathematically timid girls. Children clustered informally around activities that focused on finding many solutions rather than producing right answers.

Providing Role Models and Mentors in Science and Math

The second principle in nurturing talent in girls is to provide opportunities for them to see women in math and science fields, and to find female teachers and mentors. The value for female students of seeing women of all races, nationalities, and ethnic backgrounds performing successfully in the math and science professions cannot be overstated. Teachers in the sciences often perceive the vital link between course work and the professions, but students, particularly female ones, often do not. "Beyond Theory: Math and Science Related to Industry and Community," another summer program offered by the Center for Gifted, combined business and educational resources to service 120 students entering seventh, eighth, and ninth grade. Girls represented almost half of the program and participated in actual problems and applications as they occurred in industry and business. They met women in fields dominated more or less by men, and saw what it took for them to gain their positions.

In spite of the fact that gifted programs often emphasize acceleration in math and science, professionals from the Water Department; the Commodities Exchange; Skidmore, Owings & Merrill; and the *Chicago Sun Times* stressed the need for innovative thinkers, advanced analysts, and pioneering executives. The field is glutted with gifted technicians who have little innovative thinking ability, they commented. Daily contact with the professional applications of math and science in Beyond Theory clearly demonstrated what was missing for girls in traditional gifted programs. Talented girls who might ordinarily lose interest in a purely academic, technological approach were intrigued by current ecological problems in the Water Department, by the complexity of financial mathematics in the Commodities Exchange, and by the latest innovations in the *Chicago Tribune's* computer system. The exposure to real problems, and to the women tackling them, whetted their appetites for math and science study.

Without a strong creative component, training in math and science misleads and eventually discourages girls. The cutting edge of the math and science fields requires boldness in creative thinking and the ability to pierce through technological training to the perception of new strategies for solving persistent problems. This cannot happen if girls do not have the opportunity to take bold, risky steps in an open classroom setting. In Smutny's Project '88, a summer institute for talented sixth through tenth graders, physics, mathematics, and computer courses were taught by women who had their fingers on the developments of business and industry. Consequently, class activities and projects used real-life situations that grappled with abstract math and science concepts on a tangible level. They ousted the one-answer syndrome that dominates the conventional classroom and asked: where do we go from here?

Developing Strong Contacts with Parents

Parents need to be conscious of the potential underachievement pitfalls their daughters face. Project '88 discovered that counseling parents was not sufficient. They needed to see what their daughters could do in science and math, as well as in creative writing, art, and performance. For this reason, parents spent time observing classes (on specified days), and attended an open house where their children exhibited and explained their projects, inventions, and discoveries.

The uninhibited, energetic style of girls, as well as of boys, became evident during the program. In spite of the fact that Project '88 students were at the age where the issue of sex roles becomes exaggerated, parents consistently noticed the freedom, spontaneity, and daring of their usually intimidated or subdued daughters. Girls forgot themselves while performing, inventing, or creating, and conformed less to the stereotypical schoolgirl image. Teachers and mentors counseled parents on resources that would support the talents of their children during the school year, specifically those talents that might not receive attention by conventional educators. The opportunity for parents to meet female teachers and mentors active in fields usually associated with men had a powerful impact on how they envisioned their daughters' futures. Parents who preferred certain talents over others began to realize how stereotyping dictated this preference and influenced their daughters' aspirations. This happened to a mother who had never taken her daughter's science interest seriously. Seeing the capabilities of her daughter's gift in science at the open house, the mother talked with her teacher about ways to support that interest during the year.

Because parents and students benefit from ongoing guidance and support, Project '88 offered follow-up sessions during the school year to reinforce parents' efforts to keep their children's eyes on future possibilities. These sessions allowed participants to see men and women in diverse roles (such as male dancers, female judges and lawyers, male makeup artists), to broaden the range of choice for both girls and boys. Contact with professionals and college counselors gave students and their families a close look at their options and helped to focus their interests.

Incorporating women's studies into the curriculum, inviting women speakers and professionals to lecture or work with children, creating lesson plans that are consistently open-ended and not written with boys in mind, and maintaining contact with parents will not make a significant impact on how girls regard math and science or affect their participation in it, unless programs disassemble the old classroom structure. Math and science have to become something completely different in order to eliminate the old relationship that boys and girls have involuntarily maintained toward these subjects. Most importantly, teachers need to live what they teach so that both girls and boys begin to see the fallacy behind sex stereotyping. Girls need to know that math and science are not a forbidding or tedious list of facts and figures, but a fascinating set of discoveries emerging from a highly creative, analytical thinking process. Women have much to offer these and other "male" fields and should not be turned away, as they usually are, by misinterpretation and stereotyping. Teachers and parents can work together to halt the loss of talent in women, and help them assume leadership where they have earned it.

OPPORTUNITIES FOR DISCUSSION AND ACTION

1. Think of talented women you know, and how they have forged their own path in society. What, in your estimate, were some of the major challenges they had to face? Did they, for example, have to manage family and career simultaneously? Did they have to cope with sexual discrimination? Did these women have to sacrifice anything important to them in order to pursue their interests?

2. Can you see any subtle or not so subtle ways in which schools encourage girls to veer away from certain subjects (e.g., math or science) and adopt more "feminine" tastes? Have you ever noticed parents influencing their daughters to stay away from interests that they believed should be reserved for boys?

3. Can the learning styles of girls be distinguished from those of boys? In your estimation, does the curriculum you use respond more to boys' or to girls' needs and interests?

4. What stereotypes have you encountered in your career choice as a teacher? In Africa, teaching is a predominantly male profession. In America, particularly in the elementary grades, more women teach than men. How do you account for this? Consider other professions (such as media executives, corporate managers, etc.) where you tend to think automatically of men rather than women. What stereotypes about men and women have contributed to this?

5. Read biographies of talented women who work in predominantly male fields. What challenges, in your assessment, have they had to confront? What would you say are the disadvantages of working in such fields? What are the advantages to the field and to talented girls?

6. How would you identify and foster math and science talent in girls? Consult with women in these fields to determine how you could help girls with special talents pursue their math or science interests. Find out what these women needed when they were schoolchildren (i.e., what would have made a difference to them in school?). This might include inviting them to your class and organizing field experiences or mentorships.

REFERENCES

Achenbach, T. M. 1970. Standardization of a research instrument for identifying associate responding in children. *Development Psychology* 2: 283–91.

Barstow, D. 1987. Serve disadvantaged and serve all gifted. *Gifted Child Monthly* 8: 1–3.

Benbow, C. P., and J. C. Stanley, 1982. Intellectually talented boys and girls: Educational profiles, *Gifted Child Quarterly* 26: 82–88.

Bolles, R. N. 1986. Epilogue: The progress of women, so far, in the workplace. In *What color is your parachute?* Berkeley, Calif.: Ten Speed Press.

Campbell, P. B. 1986. What's a nice girl like you doing in a math class? *Phi Delta Kappan* 67, no. 7: 516–20.

Carpenter, H. 1978. *The inklings: C. S. Lewis, J. R. R. Tolkien, Charles Williams and their friends.* London: George Allen and Unwin.

Eccles, J. S. 1985. Why doesn't Jane run? Sex differences in educational and occupational patterns. In *The gifted and talented: Developmental perspectives,* ed. F. D. Horowitz and M. O'Brien, Washington D.C.: American Psychological Association.

Friedan, B. 1981. *The second stage.* New York: Summit Books.

Gardner, J. W. 1984. *Excellence.* New York: W. W. Norton.

Gilligan, C. 1982. *In a different voice.* Cambridge, Mass.: Harvard University Press.

Goldberg, K. 1988. Among girls, ethic of caring may stifle classroom competitiveness, study shows, *Educational Week* 7: 31.

Harvey, G. 1986. Finding reality among the myths: Why what you thought about sex equity in education isn't so, *Phi Delta Kappan* 67, no. 7: 509–12.

Hollinger, C. L., and E. S. Fleming. 1983. Internal barriers to the realization of potential: Correlates and interrelationships among gifted and talented female adolescents, *Gifted Child Quarterly* 27: 157–61.

Horner, M. 1972. Toward an understanding of achievement related conflicts in women. *Journal of Social Issues* 28: 157–75.

Kerr, B. 1985. *Smart girls, gifted women.* Columbus, Ohio: Ohio Psychology Publishing Co.

Lever, J. 1976. Sex differences in games children play, *Social Problems* 23: 478–487.

Maddocks, M. 1988. The new direction. *Christian Science Monitor,* Jan. 22, p. 19.

Mitchell, B. M., and W. G. Williams. 1987. Education of gifted and talented in the world community, *Phi Delta Kappan* 68: 531–34.

Oden, M. H. 1968. The fulfillment of promise: 40-year follow-up of the Terman gifted group, Genetic Psychology Mono.

Reis, S. M. 1987. We can't change what we don't recognize: Understanding the special needs of gifted females, *Gifted Child Quarterly* 31: 83–89.

Rimm, S. B. 1984. Underachievement, *Gifted Child Today,* January–February, pp. 26–29.

Sadker, M., and D. Sadker. 1986. Sexism in the classroom: From grade school to graduate school, *Phi Delta Kappan* 67, no. 7: 512–16.

Schwartz, L. L. 1980. Advocacy for the neglected gifted: Females, *Gifted Child Quarterly* 24: 113–17.

Shakeshaft, C. 1986. A gender at risk, *Phi Delta Kappan* 67, no. 7: 499–508.

Stockard, J., and J. W. Wood. 1984. The myth of female underachievement: A reexamination of sex differences in academic underachievement, *American Education Research Journal* 21, (no. 8): 825–38.

Trelease, J. 1985. *The read-aloud handbook.* New York: Penguin Books.

U.S. Department of Commerce. 1984. *1980 Census of Population,* Vol. 1. Washington, D.C.: U.S. Government Printing Office, Table 276.

U.S. Department of Education. 1988. *Digest of Educational Statistics.* Washington, D.C.: U.S. Government Printing Office, p. 189.

Winter, M. 1988. Closing the PhD gender gap, *Christian Science Monitor,* March 18, pp. 19–20.

CHAPTER 8

Alternative Structures for Program Design: Focus on Primary and Preprimary

TEACHER: These children get pulled from my room twice a week. Tell me, what do they get from the gifted program that they don't get in my class?

PARENT: Now that my son is in the gifted program, he has more homework than he can handle. His gifted teacher gives him special assignments, and he has to make up all the work he misses in his regular classroom. We are concerned that his grades have dropped and he is upset about it, too. He likes his gifted classes, but are they worth the sacrifices he has to make?

SCHOOL BOARD MEMBER: The school board is thinking about spending a lot of money on this gifted program. I want to know what of substance we are buying. I can't justify a boondoggle to the community.

SECOND GRADER: When the teacher pays attention to our cluster or we go to the learning center to work with the gifted coordinator, I like school and I learn a lot. If we go to school to learn, why can't the people in charge make it so that it is mostly challenging too? I think it is mostly boring.

Persons working in gifted education, especially at the preprimary and primary levels, are repeatedly confronted by classroom teachers, parents, administrators, and students who want to know if the gifted program in their school is worth the sacrifices (in classroom time, student free-time, or district funds) it requires. Staff members in part-time gifted programs are often asked by talented children and their parents why appropriate instruction is only available a few hours each week. Though pointed, such questions should not be unwelcome. It is important that teachers critically examine their school's gifted program and the role they play in it.

WHAT DO YOU THINK?

1. Does the gifted programming in your school offer something qualitatively different from standard preprimary and primary classroom instruction?

2. Is your gifted program effectively addressing the needs of your gifted students, or is it inadequate but surviving because of inertia and a general conviction that it is better than nothing?

3. Do you choose instructional strategies appropriate for your gifted preprimary or primary students?

4. Do you effectively foster a classroom climate that encourages independence and acceptance?

5. Does the curriculum include provisions for the mastery of skills, the acquisition of basic knowledge, and the application of thinking skills to subject matter, or is it a hodgepodge of unrelated units and thinking games?

6. Do I ask my talented young students to assume unreasonable burdens

or make unfair choices? Do students sometimes regard participation in the gifted program as punishment?

INTRODUCTION

In this chapter we will examine a variety of models in primary gifted programming (grades 1 through 3), considering their relative merits and limitations and offering in each instance ideas for teachers working in similar programs. Very young talented children, long neglected by educators, are the focus of increasing research and debate. The unique characteristics and requirements of bright young children will be discussed in a special section on early childhood gifted education at the conclusion of the chapter.

THE TEACHER'S ROLE

Among the various components that influence student learning the teacher is the principal determinant of success. This fact is both reassuring and daunting. The significance of programming choices should not be understated, but it is important for teachers to recognize that the choices they make within their own spheres of authority are of more consequence to students than those made in district offices and board of education meetings. Even when teachers must work within a programming model they believe to be among the least effectual alternatives, their intelligence, creativity, and resourcefulness in dealing with the constraints the model imposes are the critical factors in student learning.

PROGRAM DESIGN

No two programs for the gifted are alike, and that is exactly as it should be. Just as a good teacher celebrates the uniqueness of each student, an effective gifted program is designed in specific response to the needs and requirements of the community it will serve. Districts and schools should not succumb to the temptation to go ''shopping'' for a gifted program, selecting what appears to be the most appropriate approach and then returning home to try simply to duplicate the model. The knowledge of experts and the experience of other schools and districts are important resources, but they should be treated as schematic designs rather than blueprints.

A well-reasoned educational philosophy and clear objectives are essential for an effective program. The particulars of budgets, staffing, scheduling, and facilities are different in every school and district. If a program for talented students is to thrive, its design must not only reflect educational philosophy and objectives but also creatively address the district's limitations.

Effective gifted programs are not rigid, nor are they static. A vital program is constantly evolving, responding to changing needs and circumstances and continual evaluation. Flexibility is imperative.

Renzulli (1975) identified seven components he deemed fundamental to a successful gifted program:

1. Teacher selection and training
2. Carefully designed curriculum that is both inclusive and methodical and encourages academic and artistic growth
3. Appropriate and varied identification procedures
4. Clearly stated philosophy and objectives
5. Knowledgeable faculty prepared to work together
6. Evaluation plan inherent in the program design
7. Lucid delineation of administrative responsibility

ADMINISTRATIVE MODELS

While Renzulli analyzed programs in their entirety, a study by the New York State Education Department sought to determine what organizational factors were most critical to the development of an effective and viable program for the gifted (Orenstein 1984). Those programs recognized to be "worthy of replication" were more frequently under the direction of a coordinator or teacher, while the less effective programs tended to be more directly administered by a superintendent or assistant superintendent who had also played a greater role in the design of the program.

Secondly, the New York research indicated that effective programs had a high level of involvement from organized parent groups and used independent consultants in program development as well as in-service training. Effective gifted programs were supported by district committees that met frequently and had a diverse membership including persons who were not district employees, school board members, or otherwise involved in the formal organization of the district. The programs cited for excellence offered a variety of options to students, and included programming for kindergarteners.

In 1981 the Sid W. Richardson Foundation began a four-year national study of existing programming for able learners. Not since Commissioner of Education Sidney Marland prepared his 1972 Report to Congress had there been any comprehensive examination of the particulars of programming for able learners. The directors of the Richardson Survey chose to use the term "able learners" for two reasons: (1) because of the range of meanings educators assign to the labels "gifted" and "talented"; and (2) because the directors intended to focus on a substantially larger group than the 3 to 5 percent to whom the terms "gifted" and "talented" commonly refer. It was the intent of the foundation to investigate three central questions (Cox, Daniel, and Boston 1985):

1. What programs for able learners exist and where are they located?
2. Of the existing models, which are most effective and offer the best chance for adaptation in many school environments?
3. Can new ground be broken in the field and can we provide recommendations to assist all types of schools in serving able learners?

The findings of the Richardson research are important and will be discussed throughout the chapter. The methodology is also significant. A base survey was sent to each of the 16,000 public and parochial school districts in the nation. The Richardson Foundation received 4000 responses. A lengthy questionnaire, based on the original survey, was then sent to each of 4000 respondents. The analysis was based on the 1572 replies to the second questionnaire. While making no claim to statistical reliability (the respondents were self-selecting and not necessarily a representative sample of the nation's schools), the Richardson Study does seem to offer the most accurate picture to date of available programming for able learners.

The Pull-Out Model

Seventy percent of the districts responding to the Richardson Survey indicated that the pull-out model was in use in their district (Cox, Daniel, and Boston 1985). As the name implies, a pull-out program is one in which talented students spend most of their time in a heterogeneous classroom but are "pulled out" to attend special classes with other talented students. These special classes may be held in the student's home school or children may travel to another school in the district. The amount of instructional time spent in gifted classes ranges from as little as one hour to as much as one full day each week.

The predominance of pull-out programs should not be regarded as evidence of their superiority. There are serious deficiencies in the pull-out model. Nevertheless, it is not without advantages (Belcastro 1987):

1. Talented students have the benefit of time with their intellectual peers as well as contact with their regular classmates.
2. During the periods in which talented children are out of the regular classroom the teacher has the opportunity to work within a more narrow ability and skill range and has more time for individual instruction. In addition, other students who may feel their abilities are eclipsed by particularly gifted classmates have a chance to shine.
3. The fact that the gifted teacher is not responsible for basic skill instruction allows him or her to focus on independent projects and student interests. Teachers have more freedom in formulating curriculum.

Pull-out programs have a number of disadvantages:

1. The periodic departure from the classroom of students participating in a pull-out program may trigger resentment in their classmates. Talented students may perceive a stigma associated with participation in the program.
2. Frequent absences from their home classroom can result in students missing important instructional time (e.g., the introduction of new concepts or material) and, in addition to special projects for their gifted classes, students are often required to make up work they missed in their regular class. Many are asked to complete what is an inappropriate amount of homework for primary students. The result of this extra burden is often lower grades.
3. Students may regard the gifted classes as more exciting than their regular

class, a demoralizing attitude for the regular teacher who is struggling with the burden of a more structured and content-oriented curriculum and the challenges of a heterogeneous classroom.

4. Because basic skills and content areas are considered the purview of the regular teacher's domain. One result is that thinking skills are not taught substantive and emphasize thinking skills but that don't intrude upon the regular teachers' domain. One result is that thinking skills are not taught contextually: students learn to apply them to the logic games in the gifted class but not to the social studies unit in their regular classroom. This is especially unfortunate for primary students who miss out on excellent opportunities for integrated and interdisciplinary learning.

5. Because most pull-out classes do not meet daily and many occur only once a week, students and teacher must struggle with a lack of continuity (especially frustrating for primary students), the disruption of intervening days, and a very inflexible time schedule. Even if students are having a particularly successful discussion, when it is time to return to the regular classroom they must leave. Gifted teachers work without the option of postponing the current events period or delaying the mathematics lesson. And for first and second graders, the length of time between meetings is particularly challenging.

6. Just as the pull-out model may be unfair to the regular classroom teacher, it often places unrealistic expectations on the gifted teacher. He or she is often responsible for pull-out programs at every grade level in the school or may even be itinerant, splitting the workday between several schools in the district.

7. The dominant deficiency in the pull-out approach is that it is a part-time response to a full-time condition. Even if many of the disadvantages listed above are overcome, students are likely to be spending the majority of their day in an environment not geared to meeting their specific needs.

The Popularity of the Pull-Out Model.   Given its difficulties, why has the pull-out model continued to dominate primary gifted education? One reason is that it is thought to be relatively easy to implement and less costly than alternative models. However, most pull-out programs require hiring additional staff; even in a small program at least one new teacher is required to serve as gifted coordinator or instructor. A stronger, less costly program may be achieved by reassigning gifted students of one or two grade levels to a full-time gifted classroom staffed by a single teacher.

Much of the pull-out model's popularity may be simply the perception that it does something—but not an excessive amount—for talented children. Administrators and board members often feel unable to justify a more substantive program for a group the community regards as already advantaged. This is especially true of programming at the primary level where gifted education is often regarded as less critical. The pull-out program is, in these instances, regarded as a diplomatic solution. Finally, the pull-out model is old and familiar and some of its continuing use should be attributed to inertia.

Making the Most of a Pull-Out Program.   There are four steps that primary gifted teachers working in pull-out programs can take to make the pull-out model a much better option for their students.

First, the gifted teacher should make an effort to coordinate curricular offerings with the regular teacher. If, for example, the third grade students are studying the culture of the Inuit (Eskimos of North America or Greenland) as part of a unit on Alaska in their regular class, the gifted teacher could consider a unit exploring the culture of the Aleuts (Eskimos native to the Aleutian Islands) emphasizing cross-cultural comparisons. This will allow thinking skills to be taught contextually.

Opportunities for curricular coordination exist within every subject area. A regular classroom unit on electricity could be complemented by an in-depth study of hydroelectric power. An emphasis on geography would serve as a good basis for an exploration of cartography. In addition to promoting the primary goals of curricular continuity and the integration of thinking skills, coordinating with the regular teacher may lead to a strengthened relationship that will only benefit the students.

Second, the gifted teacher should consider the workload of his or her students and be willing to serve as their advocate if it becomes unfairly heavy. Participation in the pull-out program should not be punitive. Once again, coordination with the regular teacher (projects accepted for credit in both classrooms, excusing students from further work on mastered math facts to focus on a number theory project, etc.) is critical.

Third, the gifted teacher should explore ways of providing Saturday learning experiences, which are invaluable opportunities for student growth on intellectual and emotional levels. Six or eight hours of uninterrupted time offer a wealth of options not available within the constraints of Monday through Friday scheduling. More time together with their intellectual peers and an opportunity for teachers and students to develop stronger relationships will be important to individual primary students as well as strengthening the pull-out program.

A good alternative is to encourage students to participate in appropriate college-sponsored supplemental programs, museum workshops, and similar enrichment activities. When teachers go beyond distributing brochures, by contacting parents or suggesting car pooling, the degree of student involvement in supplemental programs rises substantially.

Fourth, if the gifted teacher senses that students have concerns about the pull-out program, he or she should provide opportunities to discuss these concerns, as a class and privately. The teacher may not share her students' perceptions of an unfair work load, a stigma associated with participating in the program, or discrimination from a classroom teacher, but she must be ready to accept as valid her students' feelings.

The Cluster Model

In a cluster program, a small group of talented students are "clustered" together in a heterogeneous classroom. Most often the classroom teacher is responsible for planning and implementing programming (generally enrichment) for the talented students in the classroom, although there are some cluster programs in which a gifted coordinator or consultant does much of the planning and the classroom teacher is in charge of implementation.

Much of the success of cluster programs depends on how the classroom is organized and the abilities of the teacher. A classroom in which group instruction is the norm is simply not a good place for gifted students and a cluster is likely to do little to change that. If the classroom is essentially individualized, the cluster model will be more successful.

Clustering offers these advantages:

1. Students benefit from extended contact with gifted peers.
2. Cluster programs are easy to implement, require little change in the structure of schools or districts, and may be less expensive than some models, for example, pull-out programs and special schools.
3. Students can move in and out of the gifted cluster, and identification may be less rigid, resulting in a more inclusive program. There are those who argue that identification of young students is particularly unreliable (Siegelbaum and Rotner 1983). Flexible clustering addresses those concerns.
4. Clustering enables less able students to benefit from the thoughts and interests of their more able peers.

Beyond the basic inadequacies of all part-time programs, the cluster model creates some distinctive problems:

1. Clustering increases the instructional burden for teachers who may already be overtaxed.
2. Gifted instruction is often relegated to snatched moments. It may be the last scheduled and the first cancelled, and—because it applies to only a handful of students in the classroom—planning and preparing for the cluster may fall near the bottom of the teacher's priority list.
3. Although in the cluster model a single teacher is responsible for both basic curriculum and gifted instruction, cluster curriculum, like that of the pull-out program, tends to consist of isolated enrichment units that emphasize thinking skills but are not well integrated into basic subject matter.

Cluster and pull-out programs often operate in tandem. Able children are clustered in one classroom and then pulled out as a unit. It is a natural pairing that offers some advantages. Participants in a cluster/pull-out program have more time with their peers. The gifted teacher or coordinator has fewer classroom teachers to work with, and can therefore work more effectively with each teacher.

The Special Class Model

When a district has made the philosophical and financial commitment to gifted education required to establish a combination cluster/pull-out program, the next logical step is to establish special classes for gifted students. The special class model, although found far less frequently than pull-out and cluster programs (under 40 percent of districts responding to the Richardson Survey had full-time special classes), offers many advantages for talented primary students (Belcastro 1987):

1. Special classes are an attempt to meet the full-time needs of talented primary students.
2. Full-time special classes enable important bonding among students and between students and teacher. This is especially critical for primary children.
3. The curriculum can be integrated and interdisciplinary. Thinking skills can be taught through and applied to the complete range of subjects and disciplines.

Special full-time classes for able students do not guarantee effective programming. The structure and curriculum must be thoughtfully prepared and appropriate for primary students, and teachers must be well equipped for the assignment. If not, the resulting learning environment, though populated exclusively by able students, may be unsuitable for them.

The Special School Model

Fewer than 5 percent of districts responding to the Richardson Survey featured specialized schools as part of their gifted programming. Cox, Daniel, and Boston (1985) cited specialized schools as a particularly attractive option for learners of high ability. There are a number of advantages to this approach (Cox, Daniel, and Boston, 1985; Clark 1983; Belcastro 1987). Specialized schools vary widely. For older gifted students there are science academies, performing arts centers, and a variety of other special schools that focus on outstanding abilities in certain disciplines. But for primary students the differences are more often found in their philosophies, structures, and methods.

Many special schools are sponsored by districts or even regions. Others are independent, some affiliated with colleges or universities. Sometimes special schools take the form of schools within schools, fairly autonomous learning environments operating within a larger school. This model is more common at the junior high and high school levels than at elementary level.

Many of the advantages of the special class model are also features of the special school approach. However, the special school does offer several unique benefits:

1. The program of the entire school can be designed to meet the needs of gifted students. This may include flexible scheduling, integrated curriculum, learning contracts, and opportunities for cooperative planning. A flexible pacing or nongraded approach (highly recommended in the Richardson Foundation report) is an exciting option available to special schools.
2. Bringing together the gifted education resources of an entire district results in new organizational and curricular possibilities: a sophisticated science lab and skilled science teacher, a full-time writing lab, a strong fine arts program.
3. Talented students are stimulated by one another. The special school model

allows for sustained interaction among a number of talented students. Depending on admissions policies and integration plans, a special school may bring together a more ethnically and economically diverse group of students than might meet in a special class program.

Special schools bring with them particular challenges:

1. Special schools elicit a variety of reactions from the communities they serve. Districts must be prepared to address charges of elitism and brain drain. Parents of children not in the gifted program may feel that their children are being unfairly denied access to district services. Administration, parents, and staff may share a concern that the best and the brightest of district faculty will be lured away from local elementary schools and take appointments at the special school.
2. Because of the large outlay of funds required, special schools may be an easy target for budget balancers. Gifted education, especially for younger children, may be seen as desirable, but dispensable. If the bond issue fails, the special school may be the first thing to go.
3. Students often dislike the complete segregation of special schools. In addition, able students enrolled in special schools miss the opportunity to learn to appreciate the abilities of their less talented peers.

While special classes and special schools seem to be generally better options for talented primary students than pull-out and cluster programs, there are steps teachers can take to make each model more effective.

SUMMER PROGRAMS AND OTHER SUPPLEMENTAL LEARNING OPPORTUNITIES

Supplemental programs, while not supplanting school-day offerings, are often sources of stimulation and satisfaction for able primary students. Weekend classes, summer workshops, and museum programs can be pivotal experiences for such students. An example of a highly successful weekend program is described below.

Worlds of Wisdom and Wonder Program

On eight consecutive Sunday afternoons in the late fall and early winter, teachers arrive at a suburban junior high school carrying cardboard boxes containing science experiments, art supplies, and room environments. An hour and a half later, 300 able students in grades 1 through 6 have gathered at the school. Each child has selected from 12 options a schedule of four classes that he or she will attend every Sunday. Classes are 40 minutes long and during passing periods the halls are filled with the enthusiastic conversation of children who are doing exciting things.

Worlds of Wisdom and Wonder, sponsored by the Center for Gifted at National College of Education in Evanston, Illinois, is a supplemental program for elementary students. For the last ten years, eight to ten class sessions have been offered on weekends during the school year and on weekdays in the summer. The program faculty and staff do not regard it as a substitute for school-sponsored gifted programs, but rather intend it to supplement the gifted offerings of public school districts and independent schools. Nevertheless, for many of the students Worlds of Wisdom and Wonder is the only gifted programming in which they participate.

Students are admitted on the basis of standardized test scores, teacher and parent nominations, special talents and abilities, and in some instances staff interviews.

Teachers are chosen carefully and work with the program director to develop their own curriculum. They are allowed a great deal of latitude but must design classes that are intriguing to the children, intellectually and creatively challenging (special emphasis is placed on honing thinking skills within the context of a subject or discipline), and offer plenty of opportunities for hands-on learning. Teachers are encouraged to select subject areas that excite them. In a typical semester students might be offered the following selection:

Creative Writing: Poems and Stories
Math Constructions: Paper, String & Straw
Math Games & Strategies
Geology: Rocks, Minerals, and Crystals
From Teeth to Toes: Science and the Five Senses
Experimenting with Ubleck
Science Spies: Observe, Test & Conclude
Science of Flight
Passport to People: A Multi-Cultural Immersion
Shipwrecked! Stranded on a Desert Island
Build a Future City
Introductory French
Improvisational Theater
Art: Paint, Plaster & Clay

There is no homework, although students leave each class with suggestions for independent projects. There are no tests or grades. Students are given the opportunity to evaluate the program at the conclusion of the semester and teachers compile brief narratives on the children with whom they have worked. These narratives are not evaluations, but rather descriptions of the teachers' perceptions of the child's experience in the class.

For students, the classes are a time when "school" is stimulating and fun. Parents and teachers report that enthusiasm for these Sunday sessions carries over into weekday schooling as well.

In a supportive and flexible setting, teachers find the freedom to experiment with different approaches and develop new curricular units. Ideas are shared freely and strong collegial relationships develop.

During the course of each semester several parent seminars are offered while students are attending classes. Speakers address a variety of issues concerning parenting a bright child, but what parents value most are the discussion groups that accompany each seminar. Even on days when parent seminars are not taking place, the parent lounge is the site of lively and supportive discussion.

Planning a Supplemental Program

Supplemental programs like Worlds of Wisdom and Wonder may be sponsored by a district but can also be organized by an independent coalition of parents and teachers. Often independent supplemental programs serve children from several districts. There are obvious advantages to district-sponsored programs. Districts can provide funding, facilities, equipment, and staff support. An independent approach (parents and teachers, sometimes in conjunction with a local college or university) offers the latitude to respond flexibly and creatively amid fewer bureaucratic constraints.

Effective supplemental programs are no different from school-day programs in requiring well-conceived and clearly stated objectives, an accepting atmosphere that encourages independence, an integrated curriculum, and appropriate learning strategies. Programs can be as simple as a two-Sunday workshop on archeology organized by a handful of parents and teachers for a small group of interested primary students or as elaborate as a summer daycamp involving hundreds of children from several school districts. If you are involved in planning a supplemental program, among the important features you will need to consider are faculty, admissions, location, recruitment, and evaluation.

Faculty. Full-time teachers are not the only persons qualified to teach children. Give serious thought to pairing experienced teachers with carefully selected adults working in other areas.

Teaming teachers in less familiar combinations can result in synergism. For example, a math teacher and English teacher might choose to jointly lead an exploration of the math, science, and poetry of time.

Admissions. If your program is operating independently or involving children from more than one district, be ready to establish a flexible admissions criteria. Not all schools and districts use the same standardized tests. Behavioral checklists; parent, teacher, and student nominations; and interviews with students are tools to consider.

Think about what your policy will be on admitting children who do not meet the eligibility requirements of their school gifted programs. There is potential for a conflict between a commitment to inclusiveness and credibility with schools and districts.

Location. Public and independent schools, community centers, libraries, churches and synagogues, and colleges are good places to consider. If you are offering a multidistrict program, look for a central, easy-to-get-to location. The best spaces to rent are often the most unorthodox. Warehouse or basement space that is clean and reasonably comfortable can allow activities that would be difficult to execute in a rented classroom.

Recruitment.   If the program is offered independently of a school district, recruitment can be critical. Brochures should outline the program's objectives, provide detailed information on its design, include cost and admissions criteria, and even an application blank. Distribute brochures to gifted coordinators, principals, librarians, pediatricians, advocacy groups, college education departments, dance and art studios, and museums.

Evaluation.   Evaluation is as essential for a supplemental program as it is for a school-day program. Be sure to include parents and students in the evaluation process. Consider hiring an independent evaluator; plan to distribute carefully formulated questionnaires to teachers, parents, and students; and make sure the staff schedules classroom observations. Informal evaluation methods are also important. Spot interviews by the director with parents after one or two class meetings can be invaluable, providing valuable information to the program staff and also communicating to parents your interest in their opinions. Be responsive. Sometimes changes do need to be made in midstream.

EVALUATION

No matter what sort of program a district or school implements, provisions for ongoing evaluation should be inherent in the design. Before beginning, baseline data should be gathered. Internal evaluation should occur regularly and involve teachers, parents, and students. External evaluation is essential, although it doesn't need to be as frequent as internal review. An external assessment can be a tremendous asset to any program, providing objective observations and adding credibility to internal evaluation reports.

When provided with ample time and appropriate tools, children are most anxious to share their thoughts about the programs in which they participate. For younger children, consider providing scribes (dictation takers) or tape recorders rather than asking students to undertake the laborious task of writing out their responses. If you make responding easier, you will be rewarded with more and better information. If scribes are persons involved in the program, children will censor their responses. Junior high or high school students are often effective in this role.

EARLY CHILDHOOD GIFTED EDUCATION

Max

Max is an energetic, thoughtful, and attentive 3-year-old. His vocabulary is unusually advanced and his speech is peppered with similes. He is fascinated by systems and processes and will happily explain to any interested adult the route a letter takes from the neighborhood mail box to grandfather's house. Max has an unusually long attention span, loves books, dinosaurs, and building. Max has a zany sense of humor that puzzles many adults but delights his parents. Sometimes Max gets angry and frustrated when his art or building projects don't look like he hoped they would. When given a choice he seeks out older children as playmates.

Max's parents chose a good neighborhood nursery school. School wasn't as exciting as Max expected, but he didn't mind going. Sometimes he was bored. Often he was frustrated because his classmates didn't understand the words he chose and lost interest in projects more quickly than he did. Max's teacher recognized that Max was a particularly bright child and knew that he needed something extra, but she wasn't quite sure what that something extra was or where it could be found.

Neglected Needs

No one would argue that a child becomes gifted on the eve of the first day of second grade or third grade or whenever gifted programming in his or her school district happens to begin. Benjamin Bloom's (1964) assertion (discussed in Chapter 2) that 50 percent of the IQ that an individual will acquire by age 17 is developed before the fourth birthday has become broadly accepted by educators. But despite a general acknowledgment of the importance of early childhood, early childhood teachers remain the most poorly paid of educators, and preprimary programs, parent and child programs, and school-sponsored play groups are among the first places districts look when they are forced to trim the budget. When early childhood education remains a low social priority, it should be no surprise that in most communities it is very difficult to find a program equipped to nurture a child like Max.

Why has there not been more dramatic growth in the provision of services to very young talented children? A dearth of adequately prepared teachers has been part of the problem (Karnes, Shwedel, and Kemp 1985). Teachers with advanced training in gifted education are rarely early childhood education specialists, while those who have pursued a career in early childhood education usually lack equivalent training and experience in gifted education. Infrequent state funding for preprimary gifted education has been another limiting factor.

Securing the funds necessary to institute appropriate gifted programming for preprimary students will require a concerted effort to alert administrators, school board members, and legislators to the needs of these young children. Pilot programs and a larger database, including more longitudinal studies, will be important in this regard. Quite understandably, decision makers want evidence of the efficacy of preprimary gifted programming. Identification, a concern in any gifted program, can be an especially difficult issue in designing, funding and implementing preprimary programs.

Identification

Early identification encourages parents to seek out professional assistance in nurturing their child's talents and enables parents and professionals to make informed and appropriate choices in early school experiences. The identification of talented preschoolers has been the topic of much controversy. The views of educators range from those who advocate a rigorous battery of standardized tests to those who feel that behavioral characteristics are a more discerning and inclusive identification method.

Formal standardized testing most frequently is preceded by a general screening using group intelligence tests or nominations by parents and teachers. Individual tests typically used with preprimary students include the Stanford Binet Intelligence Test, the Goodenough-Harris Draw-A-Person Test, Torrance's Thinking Creatively in Action and Movement Test, Raven's Progressive Matrices, and the Woodcock-Johnson Psycho-Educational Battery.

There are many unanswered questions concerning the validity of existing testing instruments used with preprimary children. Do they effectively identify children with gifts that are not strictly intellectual, such as the creatively gifted and gifted leaders? Do the tests tend to exclude children of low socioeconomic or ethnic minority backgrounds? Are there bright young children whose emotional development stands in the way of a satisfactory performance in standardized testing situations?

For many districts and independent preschools the accuracy of standardized preprimary testing is not an issue because the school or district simply does not have the funds and adequately trained personnel to consider testing. Several educators have developed behavioral characteristic checklists that may be used by parents or teachers to identify giftedness in young children. Kitano (1982) offers a synthesis of their work:

Behaviors and Traits of the Young Gifted Child

Intellectual and Academic
Is attentive, alert
Possesses advanced vocabulary for age
Shows early interest in books and reading
Learns rapidly
Has high level of curiosity
Enjoys being with older children
Pursues interests; collects things
Has long attention span
Possesses high standards
Shows mature sense of humor for age
Prefers new and challenging experiences
Retains information
Displays high level of planning, problem solving, and abstract thinking compared to peers

Creative
Asks many questions
Does things in own way (independent)
May prefer to work alone
Experiments with whatever is at hand
Is highly imaginative
Thinks up many ways to accomplish a goal
May respond with unexpected, smart-alec answers
Produces original ideas

Leadership
Is frequently sought out by peers
Interacts easily with other children and adults
Adapts easily to new situations
Can influence others to work toward goals—desirable or undesirable
Is looked to by others for ideas and decisions
Is chosen first by peers

Music
Makes up original tunes
Shows degree of tonal memory
Enjoys musical activities
Responds sensitively to music
Easily repeats rhythm patterns
Easily discriminates tones, melodies, rhythm patterns

Art
Fills extra time by drawing, painting, etc.
Draws a variety of things—not just people, horses, flowers
Remembers things in detail
Takes art activities seriously and derives satisfaction from them
Has long attention span for art activities
Shows planning in composing the artwork

Parents often have more knowledge and understanding of their young child than any other adult. This fact has been hard for educators to accept, although a growing body of research bears it out. Jacobs (1971) found that parents identified 61 percent of the gifted children in a group of kindergarteners, while teachers identified only 4 percent of the same group. Karnes (1985) reports that 41 percent of the children assessed, at the request of parents, for admission into a gifted preprimary program met eligibility criteria. Ciha et al. (1974) found that even teachers who had knowledge of the characteristics of giftedness identified gifted children with only one third the frequency of untrained parents. It is evident that parents must be included in the identification process and their knowledge and understanding of their children must not only be respected when offered but actively sought

Enriched Heterogeneous Preprimary Programs

Almost every childhood class includes children with special talents. There are those who argue that rather than focusing on identifying talented preprimary students and setting up special programs to serve them, educators should focus on making all early childhood classrooms a nurturing environment for these children (Kitano 1982).

There is a great deal early childhood educators can do to make classrooms stimulating and challenging to talented young children. It is important to note that preschoolers, when they are permitted to select independently, do not choose activities that are too difficult for them. By allowing children to choose from a range of activities appropriate to varying stages of development, teachers stimulate particularly able students without frustrating other members of the group.

Kitano (1982) has assembled some specific techniques that teachers can employ to make their classrooms better suited to serve talented students. These are listed below along with examples of specific ways these techniques could be employed.

1. Develop creativity through activities that encourage a broad range of responses rather than those that solicit a single correct answer. Activities should address various aspects of creative thinking, including fluency, flexibility, originality, and elaboration.

   Example: Enhance fluency by asking students to list all the methods of transportation the class could use to get to the park. Affirm every response, and don't be frustrated if the first few attempts bring rather pedantic suggestions (take a bus, walk, my mom could drive). Repeated efforts to encourage freer thought will result in children slithering like snakes, taking spaceships, riding magic carpets, or swimming through the drainage pipes.

   Example: Nurture originality by avoiding follow-the-model art activities (a good rule for all preprimary and primary teachers) and celebrating the uniqueness of each child's creation.

   Example: Encourage elaboration by working together with the children to embellish a story or imagine detail for something visually quite simple. Spend a few minutes on a breezy spring day cloud gazing with children. "That one looks like a dragon." "What is the dragon doing?" "Going to get pizza, that's why he is smiling." Once again, affirm each response and let the children see your delight in their efforts.

   Example: Foster flexibility by encouraging children to see things from a new perspective. "Pretend you are a cornflake living in a cereal box. What are you thinking about?" Give children the opportunity to be (move, speak, etc.) like the cornflake or bubble or banana.

2. Develop higher cognitive processes through activities that enhance knowledge, comprehension, application, analysis, synthesis, and finally evaluation. (See discussion of Bloom's Taxonomy in Chapter 9.)

   Example: Almost any classroom activity can be an occasion to use higher cognitive processes. When making corn muffins with the class, ask, pointing to the corn meal, what is this? (Knowledge) How is corn meal made? (Comprehension) What are some uses for corn meal? Yes, we could fill the water table with it. Yes, we could make tortillas. Yes, we could make muffins. We have the ingredients for muffins, let's make some together. (Application) How does the corn meal feel? Is it an important ingredient in this recipe? What would the batter be like if we didn't add corn meal? (Analysis) Corn is ground to make corn meal. Are there other vegetables and fruit we mash or grind? Are mashed potatoes still potatoes? Do you think apple sauce is still apples? (Synthesis) How do they taste? What makes our muffins taste like that? How could we make them better? How could we make them different? (Evaluation)

3. Provide activities that encourage forecasting, planning, and decision making.

    Example: Ask "What would happen if . . . ?" questions, both fanciful (what would happen if you could make your tricycle fly) and more actual (if it snows tonight, how will your day be different tomorrow). Use forecasting as a catalyst for art and group writing projects.

4. Encourage inquiry and problem solving.

    Example: Work with the scientific method (observe, hypothesize, experiment, and evaluate). The water table is a natural focus center for a float-and-sink investigation. Work with students to record observations and hypotheses as well as results. Familiar school problems offer exciting opportunities to foster inquiry and problem-solving skills. Why are we having so many collisions in the play yard? Observe, hypothesize, and experiment. You must, however, be willing to try the children's traffic flow suggestions and discuss seriously rule changes they propose.

5. Provide activities that nurture affective growth.

    Example: Hypothetical situations and children's literature are two particularly effective ways to nurture affective development.

The enriched classroom model has several advantages:

1. Every child in the group benefits from the enrichment techniques the teacher employs.
2. The model avoids the necessity of rigid selection guidelines and offers developmental opportunities to children that established identification procedures might miss.
3. The model can be applied in small towns and rural communities where small populations of young children would make implementing a special school or classroom model difficult.

Cluster and Pull-Out Programs

While rarely employed for 3- and 4-year-old preschoolers, cluster and pull-out models have been used in kindergartens. The advantages and disadvantages for kindergarteners are much the same as they are for primary students. Clustering in a preprimary classroom need not be formalized. If children are clustered in a decentralized classroom where the teacher has designed a program that is suitably stimulating for able young children, clustering can have the added benefit of providing these children with a small community of their peers.

It is essential that kindergarten pull-out classes not imitate first grade programs emphasizing reading, addition, and subtraction. Enriching activities like those suggested in the previous section are far more appropriate than traditional first grade curriculum for bright kindergarteners.

Special Classes for Talented Preprimary Students

Some independent and college-affiliated preschools as well as school districts offer special classes for talented students. In some instances these are self-contained early childhood classrooms and in other schools there is movement between rooms and teachers. Although the special class model is most prevalent in public kindergartens, the State of Louisiana has embarked on a pioneering effort to provide special education services for all preprimary students with special abilities. Special classes for 3-, 4-, and 5-year-olds are included in the state's comprehensive plan. Special classes can be an excellent option for young children, but simply bringing together 12 talented preprimary students is no guarantee of an effective program. Teachers with strong backgrounds in both early childhood and gifted education are a special asset.

When talented preprimary students participate in a special class it is especially important to make sure they are moving into a kindergarten or first grade program equipped to challenge and stimulate them. All too often, students move from an appropriate, and therefore stimulating, environment into one unable to meet their needs.

Gifted Early Childhood Education and the Superbaby Syndrome

At every level, much of what is best about gifted education has been borrowed from early childhood educators. Many of the basic features of a nourishing preprimary learning environment are also elemental for effective primary and secondary gifted programming. Preprimary gifted education must remain firmly grounded in early childhood philosophy and methods. Bright young children are young children first and bright children second.

"Superbaby" programs that replace cardboard boxes, blocks, and dress-up corners with flashcards and reading charts are misguided and pernicious. Although every young child has an individual developmental timetable, "superbaby" programs impose adult agendas on their young participants and forget that children learn best through experience. A collection of boxes can be a castle, a fort, a pontoon plane, or mom's office building. Making corn muffins is a treat for the senses, an opportunity to measure, and a wonderful science experiment. On the other hand, you can't build much of anything with flashcards and they aren't good to eat! It is important that gifted early childhood education carefully distinguish itself from programs taking the "superbaby" approach.

Parent Education

Teaching parenting (which includes teaching parents to teach) is an important educational arena of the future. The future has been slow in coming, but the New Parents as Teachers project in Missouri and other similar programs are significant developments.

New Parents as Teachers Project.   A collaborative effort that included the Missouri director of Early Childhood Education, the commissioner of education, the Danforth Foundation, and the governor, the New Parents as Teachers program was designed by Michael Meyerhoff and Burton White (1985a, 1985b) of the Center for Parent Education in Newton, Massachusetts. Founded on the notion that parents are children's first and most important teachers, the project aimed to provide parents with information and support to help them to do that job well.

Four school districts (rural, small town, suburban, and urban) hosted the three-year pilot project. A resource center, staffed by two full-time parent educators, was established in each district. All first-time parents were invited to participate. Small group meetings (10 to 12 parents) at the resource center and home visits began in the third trimester of pregnancy and continued until the child was 3 years old. After six months, home visits increased and parent educators visited most families for at least an hour once a month. Home visits and group sessions provided basic information on child development. The resource center featured books, magazines, and toys related to very early childhood.

To measure the results of the project, 75 randomly selected participating children were compared with a matched sample of children from districts not involved in the project. The participating children appeared to be ahead of their peers in social development, although Meyerhoff and White lacked a method of measuring this scientifically. The Kauffman Assessment Battery for Children and the Zimmermann Preschool Language Scales were administered to the children. Project participants scored significantly higher on both tests. Parents were pleased with the project as evidenced by their overwhelming affirmative evaluations and a project retention rate of almost 90 percent.

Implications for Education.   Programs like New Parents as Teachers are important because they lead to the nurturing and healthy development of all children. For talented children, parent education programs may be especially critical, particularly if they lead to early identification of their special abilities and needs. Imagine a program similar to the Missouri model, in which well-trained staff members were able to say to the parents of especially bright 3-year-olds completing the program, "We think you should investigate the school district program for gifted 3-year-olds and their parents." It is the sort of continuum of appropriate services that persons concerned with able children must seek to establish.

A Program for Gifted Preschoolers and Their Parents

In 1975 the Rockford Public School District in Illinois instituted a program for preschool (3-, 4-, and 5-year-olds) potentially gifted children and their parents (Harris and Bauer 1983). The parent component of the program shares many of the goals of the Missouri project, such as teaching parenting skills and providing parents with a support group. It also teaches parents about giftedness, gives them specific strategies for home learning experiences, and introduces them to the options in gifted programming within the school district. Parents meet for one-half day each week and concurrent programming is offered for children.

As the central figures in the lives of their children parents are, of course, their primary teachers. It is natural that parent education should become a focus of gifted early childhood education. Programs like those in Rockford, Illinois, and Missouri are logical responses to all we know about child development and gifted education.

OPPORTUNITIES FOR DISCUSSION AND ACTION

1. Why do you think society is so reluctant to identify talents and abilities among preprimary and primary children?

2. Do you detect any evidence of prejudice or limited points of view from nursery schools, kindergartens, or day-care centers? Why do you think this is so?

3. We have stated that the parent is the person who can most accurately identify the gifts and talents of the preprimary and primary child. Do you agree with this? Why or why not?

4. From an educational point of view, what do you notice most about very young children? Is there a way to encourage their high motivation, curiosity, and enthusiasm without pressuring them or succumbing to the super-baby syndrome?

5. Observe preprimary and primary children in an educational setting. Based on what you see, how would you identify ability in this young age group? Do the children appear interested and engaged? Do they get bored quickly? Do you notice any particularly curious, inventive, imaginative, and enthusiastic children? Are there times when any of the children seem captivated for a longer period of time with the work before them (so that they do not want to stop)? Notice your own criteria in this process. Do you find it difficult to judge children this young? Do you think that this is due to the fact that the children are too young, or that the criteria we are accustomed to using depend on narrow academic standards?

6. Talk to a young child who you have decided is talented in some way. What behaviors stand out to you? Do you assess the child's ability based on reading and verbal talent, or are you open to other kinds of talent? Early reading and expressive speech are automatically associated with talent. Notice if that criterion is operating in your judgments. What other sorts of ability might preschool children have that may have little to do with reading or verbal expression?

REFERENCES

Bailey, D. B., and J. Leonard. 1977. A model for adapting Bloom's taxonomy to a preschool curriculum for the gifted, *Gifted Child Quarterly,* 21 (no. 1): 97–103.

Belcastro, F. 1987. Elementary pull-out program for the intellectually gifted—Boon or bane? *Roeper Review* 9 (no. 4): 208–12.

Bloom, B. 1964. *Stability and change in human characteristics.* New York: John Wiley.

Bryant, M. 1987. Meeting the needs of gifted first grade children in a heterogeneous classroom, *Roeper Review* 9 (no. 4): 214–16.

Christian Science Monitor. 1986. Schooling: When should it begin? March 28, pp. B1–B12.

Ciha, T. E., R. Harns, C. Hoffman, and H. W. Poher. 1974. Parents as identifiers of giftedness, ignored but accurate, *Gifted Child Quarterly* 18 (no. 3): 191–95.

Clark, B. 1983 and 1988. *Growing up gifted.* Columbus, Ohio: Chas. E. Merrill.

Cox, J., N. Daniel, and B. Boston. 1985. *Educating able learners.* Austin, Tex.: University of Texas Press.

Davis, G., and S. Rimm. 1985. *Education of the gifted and talented.* Englewood Cliffs, N.J.: Prentice-Hall.

Delahanty, R. 1984. Challenge, opportunity, and frustration: Developing a gifted program for kindergarteners, *Roeper Review* 6 (no. 4): 206–8.

Elkind, D. 1976. *Child development and education: A Piagetian perspective.* New York: Oxford University Press.

———. 1986. Formal education and early childhood education: An essential difference, *Phi Delta Kappan* 67 (no. 9): 631–36.

Feldhusen, J., and M. Kroll. 1985. Parent perceptions of gifted children's educational needs, *Roeper Review* 7 (no. 4): 249–52.

Feldhusen, J., and M. Kolloff. 1981. Me: A self-concept scale for gifted students, *Perceptual and Motor Skills* 53: 319–23.

Gillman, J., and H. Hansen. 1987. Gifted education in Minnesota kindergartens, *Roeper Review* 9 (no. 4): 212–14.

Green, M. 1985. Bringing out the best in gifted children, *Contemporary Pediatrics,* October, pp. 66–74.

Harris, R., and H. Bauer. 1983. A program for parents of gifted preschoolers, *Roeper Review* 5 (no. 4): 18–19.

Hollinger, C., and S. Kosek. 1985. Early identification of the gifted and talented, *Gifted Child Quarterly* 29 (no. 4): 168–71.

Jacobs, J. 1971. Effectiveness of teacher and parent identification of gifted children as a function of school level, *Psychology in the Schools* 8: 140–42.

Johnson, L. 1983. Giftedness in preschool: A better time for development than identification, *Roeper Review* 5 (no. 4): 13–15.

Kamii, C. 1985. Leading primary education toward excellence, *Young Children,* September, pp. 3–9.

Karnes, M. 1985. Preschool: Programming for the young gifted child: Maximizing the potential of the young gifted child, *Roeper Review* 7 (no. 4): 204.

———, A. Shwedel, and P. Kemp. 1985. Maximizing the potential of the young gifted child, *Roeper Review* 7 (no. 4): 204–9.

Karnes, M., A. Shwedel, and S. Linnemeyer. 1982. The young gifted/talented child: Programs at the University of Illinois, *Elementary School Journal* 82 (no. 3): 195–213.

Kitano, M. 1982. Young gifted children: Strategies for preschool teachers, *Young Children,* May, pp. 14–22.

———. 1985a. Issues and problems in establishing preschool programs for the gifted, *Roeper Review* 7 (no. 4): 212–13.

———. 1985b. Ethnography of a preschool for the gifted: What gifted young children actually do, *Gifted Child Quarterly* 29 (no. 2): 67–71.

Leyden, S. 1985. *Helping the child of exceptional ability.* London: Croom Helm.

Lorton, J., and B. Walley. 1979. *Introduction to early childhood education.* New York: D. Van Nostrand.

McHardy, R. 1983. Providing for preschool gifted children on a statewide basis, *G/C/T,* no. 29, September–October, pp. 24–27.

Malone, C., and W. Moonan. 1975. Behavioral identification of gifted children, *Gifted Child Quarterly* 19 (no. 4): 301–6.

Marks, W., and R. Nystrand. 1981. *Strategies for educational change: Recognizing the gifts and talents of all children.* New York: Macmillan.

Meyerhoff, M., and B. White. 1986a. Making the grade as parents, *Psychology Today,* September, pp. 38–45.

———. 1986b. New parents as teachers, *Educational Leadership,* November, pp. 42–46.

Orenstein, A. 1984. What organizational characteristics are important in planning, implementing, and maintaining programs for the gifted, *Gifted Child Quarterly* 28 (no. 3): 99–101.

Piechowski, M., and N. Colangelo. 1984. Developmental potential of the gifted, *Gifted Child Quarterly* 28 (no. 2): 80–88.

Renzulli, J. 1975. Identifying key features in programs for the gifted. In *Psychology and education of the gifted,* ed. W. Barbe and J. Renzulli. New York: Irvington Publishing.

———. 1977. *The Enrichment Triad Model: A guide for developing defensible programs for the gifted and talented,* Mansfield Center Conn.: Creative Learning Press, 1977.

Richert, E. 1985. Identification of gifted students: An update, *Roeper Review* 8 (no. 2): 68–72.

Shorr, D., N. Jackson, and A. Robinson. 1980. Achievement test performance of intellectually advanced preschool children, *Exceptional Children* 46 (no. 8): 646–48.

Siegelbaum, L., and S. Rotner. 1983. Ideas and activities for parents of preschool gifted children, *G/C/T,* January–February, pp. 40–44.

Sloan, C., and U. Stedtnitz. The Enrichment Triad Model for the very young gifted. *Roeper Review* 6 (no. 4): 204–6.

Torrance, E. 1977. *Discovery and nurturance of giftedness in the culturally different.* Reston, Va.: Council for Exceptional Children.

Turner, P., and M. Harris. 1984. Parental attitudes and preschool children's social competence, *Journal of Genetic Psychology* 144: 105–13.

CHAPTER 9

Program Models and Curriculum Development: Focus on Elementary and Secondary

Several teachers from neighboring school districts are having lunch together on the first day of their state's Gifted Conference. As they eat, they discuss the profusion of curriculum materials available at the conference.

> **TEACHER A:**   What sessions did you go to this morning? Did anyone get to the materials display yet?
>
> **TEACHER B:**   I took a quick look, but it would take a full day to go through all the materials on display.
>
> **TEACHER C:**   I went to an interesting session on the Future Problem Solving Bowl. That would be a nice addition to my program because I don't have anything on science for my students.
>
> **TEACHER D:**   I'm looking for math materials. Has anyone spotted any materials appropriate for an accelerated math curriculum at the elementary level?
>
> **TEACHER A:**   We don't add any new materials to our math curriculum. We simply let children work in the textbooks a grade or two ahead of their own grade level.
>
> **TEACHER B:**   We tried that, but those kids can move so fast through the textbooks that we'd have them in calculus by sixth grade. So we are supplementing with computer software math programs.
>
> **TEACHER C:**   Of course the new emphasis is on problem solving in math. We get our kids involved in surveys and graphs of real issues and problems confronting our school and community.
>
> **TEACHER D:**   All of those ideas sound so good. How will I ever decide which materials and which types of programs to buy for my program?
>
> **TEACHER A:**   I know what you mean. The choices can seem overwhelming at times.

WHAT DO YOU THINK?

1. How do you distinguish among dozens of program options to determine which fit the needs of your school district?
2. What are the advantages and disadvantages of incorporating nationally organized programs into your gifted curriculum?
3. Are you comfortable with the way you select educational materials?
4. How can you establish valid criteria for the selection of materials?
5. Can you name some educational fads that have occurred in gifted education recently? How can you distinguish between a fleeting fad and a substantial and meaningful program?

INTRODUCTION

Although the choices can seem overwhelming, there are systematic ways to plan and organize learning experiences and choose appropriate educational materials. In this chapter, we will review the current state of curriculum planning in elementary and secondary programs around the country and then examine some methods for making a viable and defensible curriculum plan for your own program.

First, it is essential that you understand that the basic questions curriculum planners ask determine the types of choices they finally make. In the past two decades, the debate about curriculum development for gifted programs has been in response to the general focus question: what type of differentiated curriculum is appropriate for gifted students? As might be expected, this question evokes a variety of responses, reflecting widely disparate philosophies and definitions of the term "gifted students."

Three Curriculum Categories

One general response has been that students identified as "gifted" need *accelerated* curricula that allow them to move at rapid pace through a subject or field of study. It is believed that they will be more appropriately served by providing them with challenging learning experiences beyond their own grade level. This strategy is thought to be especially important in school subjects or talent fields that are sequential in nature, such as mathematics. Students with special aptitudes in these subjects easily master the grade level material and become bored and restless when held back to wait for their classmates. Implicit in this response to the focus question is the definition of the "gifted student" as a student who learns more rapidly than his or her peers.

Another general response to the focus question has been that students identified as "gifted" need *enriched* curricula made up of learning experiences with greater depth and/or breadth than their classmates want or need. Literature, science, and social studies are subjects that lend themselves to the development of enriched curricula. Students with special aptitudes in these areas respond with enthusiasm to programs that allow them to deal with complex and abstract ideas. The implicit definition of "gifted student" in this context is the student who understands abstract ideas, enjoys complexity, and has either deeper or a wider range of interests than the average student.

A third general response to the question is that students identified as "gifted" require *individualized* curricula that emphasize independent study on self-selected topics or interest areas. Implicit in this view is the definition of "gifted students" as those who have one or more extraordinary talents or special interests that should be supported in the school setting even if they don't fit into the regular curriculum. Curricula developed to meet the needs of this type of student are quite open-ended. Students are encouraged to pursue their own interests with support and guidance from gifted program personnel. The independent study curriculum is more process-oriented than the acceleration or enrichment models, and its goal is to provide the student with skills that allow him or her to function as an independent researcher or creator in any self-selected talent area.

These three responses represent three different basic categories of curriculum models for gifted education. All three have had enormous influence on gifted program development and have generated a number of interesting and unique curriculum models for both elementary and secondary schools. However, they have also caused divisive rifts among researchers and specialists in the field and resulted in confusion on the part of gifted program personnel at the local district level. When resources are limited (as they almost always are), choices must be made. Some school districts choose to develop programs that fall into one of the three categories described above. Others attempt to field three separate programs for three different types of giftedness. Still others attempt to combine the philosophies into a single curriculum or program. Variations are endless.

Donald Neuman (1981), professor of Curriculum and Instruction for the University of Wisconsin at Milwaukee, visited every school district in his large metropolitan area in order to determine how and why their gifted programs had been established, and who and what influenced the decisions regarding programming. To his dismay, he found that his interviews with teachers, administrators, students, and parents, and his own observations of classroom activities resulted in:

> . . . more questions needing answers than answers to my initial questions. Instead of common practices flowing from general principles and definitions, there was substantial diversity in the programs. Instead of basic agreement on issues of theory, organization, and practice, I found, for the most part, disagreement. (p. 114)

The Sid Richardson Foundation supported a nationwide survey in the early 1980s to describe the variation of gifted programs throughout the United States. Wide variation was discovered both in program structures and in curriculum goals and objectives. The report of this survey has been published in a paperback book entitled *Educating Able Learners* (Cox, Daniel, and Boston 1985), which also contains recommendations of the most "promising practices" observed by the researchers conducting the survey.

In order to provide a comprehensive overview of options in gifted program curriculum development, this chapter will describe the most frequently used and best researched curriculum models offered in all three of the broad curriculum categories described above. You will then be able to select and modify various existing models to fit the unique needs of your district.

ACCELERATION CURRICULUM MODELS

Johns Hopkins Studies of Mathematically Precocious Youth

The Math Talent Search, which resulted from the Study of Mathematically Talented Youth (SMPY), is perhaps the most widely recognized and emulated gifted program in the United States today. Developed at Johns Hopkins University by Julian Stanley, the program is designed to provide "mathematically precocious" students with a radically accelerated mathematics curriculum. Stanley's research demonstrated that mathematically precocious students are able to master the content of courses that have been compressed and accelerated (Stanley, Keating, and Fox 1974). A similar Study of Verbally Gifted Youth (SVGY) is designed to identify and serve students with unusual verbal abilities. Since its organization at Johns Hopkins, the program has been duplicated at Northwestern University, Duke University, and

Denver University and serves students in all 50 states through these regional sites.

To identify students for this program, junior high students who score above the 95th percentile on their district's standardized achievement tests are eligible to take the math or verbal batteries of the Scholastic Aptitude (SAT-M or SAT-V). The Test of Standard Written English (TSWE) is also considered for identification of verbally gifted youth. Those whose scores meet the criteria established at the regional center are provided with direct services in the form of accelerated math or language curricula. The services vary from site to site, but are typically opportunities to take advanced courses in math, literature, science, or languages at a nearby participating college or university. In this way, the students are allowed to move at a faster pace and master more challenging content than would normally be possible in their own schools.

Other acceleration methods employed by schools are full-time honors classes that allow the student to take accelerated course work within his or her own school building. Minicourses, seminars, or other temporary special classes are frequently provided to allow students to work at an accelerated pace in one topic for a given length of time. In high school, students are often given the opportunity to take advanced placement courses, which may earn college credit.

Radical Acceleration

Another set of methods that result in the radical acceleration of an individual's curriculum is to move the child into a higher grade level than his or her agemates. Early entrance to kindergarten, double promotions to skip a grade level altogether, and early admission to college are examples of radical acceleration that may be employed to provide a suitably challenging program for a mature and capable student. There are many social implications to be carefully considered in each individual case. While many educators believe that social interactions with peers are too important to warrant such a step, Julian Stanley believes that the child's true peers are his intellectual peers rather than his chronological agemates.

Compacting Curriculum

Joseph Renzulli suggests that the gifted program coordinator act as an intermediary or advocate for the students in the gifted program by approaching classroom teachers and requesting that the regular curriculum be compacted to allow time for more advanced work in a subject area. Using a form such as *The Compactor* (see Figure 9.1) allows the adults to negotiate and agree upon criteria for demonstration of mastery of the regular curriculum, the content to be eliminated, and the content to be added to the child's school program.

Mastery Learning

Mastery learning is a system that allows students to move at their own pace through a body of knowledge and is used primarily in subjects that are sequential in nature. Students with high ability and interest in an area of study are allowed to progress rapidly through the material that is already known to them. They take "pre-tests"

INDIVIDUAL EDUCATIONAL PROGRAMMING GUIDE
The Compactor

Prepared by: Joseph S. Renzulli
Linda H. Smith

NAME _____ AGE _____ TEACHER(S) _____ Individual Conference Dates And Persons Participating In Planning Of IEP

SCHOOL _____ GRADE _____ PARENT(S) _____

CURRICULUM AREAS TO BE CONSIDERED FOR COMPACTING Provide a brief description of basic material to be covered during this marking period and the assessment information or evidence that suggests the need for compacting.	PROCEDURES FOR COMPACTING BASIC MATERIAL Describe activities that will be used to guarantee proficiency in basic curricular areas.	ACCELERATION AND/OR ENRICHMENT ACTIVITIES Describe activities that will be used to provide advanced level learning experiences in each area of the regular curriculum.

☐ Check here if additional information is recorded on the reverse side.

Copyright © 1978 by Creative Learning Press, Inc. P.O. Box 320 Mansfield Center, Ct. 06250. All rights reserved.

Figure 9.1
The compactor (actual size, 11 × 17) by Dr. Joseph Renzulli and Dr. Linda Smith. Copyright © 1978 by Creative Learning Press, Inc., Mansfield Center, Conn. All rights reserved. Reprinted with permission of the publisher and the authors.

for each new concept or skill. If the results of the pre-test demonstrate that they have already mastered the skill, they are allowed to move on to the next skill in the sequence.

Mastery learning is not a new educational concept. Parents use it in the home to teach their children basic skills and ideas. A skill such as tying shoes is introduced to the child. Once the child masters the skill, the parent goes on to teach other things. The child is not retaught the learned skill over and over every year. In schools, highly able children are often asked to sit through repetitive reteaching and practice sessions of skills and concepts they have mastered long ago.

Also known as continuous progress, mastery learning programs are being used in school programs today in such subject areas as math, reading, and computer science. The structure of such programs varies enormously. In some instances, a classroom teacher is responsible for managing the system and teaching the non-graded material to all the students in his or her class. In other variations, teachers from different grade levels cooperate, and the children move from class to class. To accomplish this, the school day must be scheduled so that certain subjects are taught to all children in the building at the same time of day.

For example, the school day may be divided into time blocks corresponding to the basic curriculum areas involved in the continuous progress program. Reading and language arts may be taught in the early morning; math may be taught in the late morning; and computer science or any other selected subject may be taught in the late afternoon. During these periods of time, children move from their "home room" to the appropriate classroom where their own level of math, reading, or computer science is being taught. Children move from level to level by demonstrating mastery of the subject matter and skills taught at that level.

While difficult to schedule (especially around gym and music classes), this continuous progress system is highly recommended to meet the needs of children with unusual talents and aptitudes. Eager to learn new and appropriately challenging material, they thrive in this type of system. Correspondingly, this program has the added benefit of meeting the needs of average and below-average learners as well. All students benefit by being taught at the appropriate level and allowed to progress at their own rates.

At the high school level, mastery learning objectives are typically achieved by offering different tracks or levels of each course to students with different aptitudes for the subject. Honors and advanced placement courses are, in effect, examples of combined acceleration and enrichment programs and, as such, certainly deserve to be included in the description of the district's gifted programming.

ENRICHMENT CURRICULUM MODELS

Pull-Out Programs

Enrichment programs are frequently offered in school gifted programs as part of a pull-out program. Students selected for the program are allowed to leave the regular classroom for an hour or two once or twice a week to meet with the gifted resource teacher. Curriculum designers choose a topic such as architecture or electricity and provide students with a series of activities related to the topic. Frequently these programs involve interesting outside speakers and field trips to sites related to the topic. While these programs are viewed as positive and enjoyable by the students who take part, there is little research to demonstrate their long-term effects. Furthermore, these programs frequently cause criticism by outsiders who observe that any child could benefit from and enjoy such a program.

Prepublished Enrichment Packages

Another frequently offered form of enrichment involves the adoption of prepublished programs, such as the *Great Books Program,* as part of the gifted program curriculum, and limiting access to it to those students who have been identified as "gifted." The curriculum planning in this instance is quite simple, since the teacher may use the guidelines established by the Great Books Program Guides. However, the use of this program with identified children only can also generate negative criticism since it is philosophically developed to enrich the literary experience of all students, not a selected few.

There are a number of other national programs and projects that can be adopted as part of a gifted curriculum. *Odyssey of the Mind* (Micklus 1986) is an excellent example. Featured in science magazines and newspapers and on a Bill Moyers television special on creativity, the curricular goals of this program are to increase the creative problem-solving ability of children by challenging them with complex and unusual problems to solve in original ways.

Working as a team, students brainstorm possible solutions to the problems, select their best solution, and create the machinery or process needed to put their solution into action. Their ideas are then compared and tested in competitions with teams from other schools. The curriculum of this program is modeled after the hands-on problem-solving curricula of the physics departments of some of the best engineering schools in the country. The competitive structure of the program is modeled after sports programs and the Olympics.

A similarly structured national program is the Future Problem Solving Bowl developed by E. Paul Torrance. In this competitive program, students are trained in creative problem-solving skills. After training, teams of students are given tough and complex real-life problems facing humankind in the near future. Within a time limit, the students research the problem, generate solutions, test and select their best solution, and write it up to enter in a regional competition. The curriculum goals of this project emphasize research and communication skills as well as teaching creative problem-solving techniques.

Curriculum Emphasizing the Higher Levels of Bloom's Taxonomy

Long recognized as a powerful curriculum development structure, the Taxonomy of Educational Objectives (Cognitive Domain) developed by Benjamin S. Bloom and his colleagues (Bloom et al. 1956) serves as the basis for many curriculum projects throughout the country. Educational experiences are classified in six categories or levels: Knowledge, comprehension, application, analysis, synthesis, and evaluation.

The intention of the authors of the taxonomy was to provide a classification of all possible educational objectives so that curriculum developers could distinguish between important and unimportant learning experiences. Additionally, the taxonomy serves as a common basis for communication about educational evaluations.

Gifted program personnel have used the taxonomy to great advantage. They determined that the educational objectives of the regular curriculum in most schools are written at the knowledge and comprehension levels in most content and subject areas. Gifted program developers recognized that the higher levels of the taxonomy are underutilized in most school curricula. They also recognized that students with special talents or gifts in academic areas are able to master the knowledge and comprehension levels very quickly and accurately. To enrich the regular curriculum, gifted curriculum developers write educational objectives at the four higher levels on the taxonomy: application, analysis, synthesis, and evaluation. In our view, these are among the strongest and most defensible enrichment programs being offered.

In order to systematically design curricula, most teachers prefer to write behavioral objectives and activities for each level of the taxonomy in the Cognitive Domain. Table 9.1 provides a summary of behaviors associated with each level, so that curriculum writers may select and write appropriate behavioral objectives at each level.

Since the taxonomy was designed to be suitable for planning educational objectives, experiences, and evaluations for any content area, curriculum developers can design learning experiences on any topic or subject. For example, the primary social studies curriculum usually includes content on the topic of "communities." While textbooks in the regular classroom cover the basic knowledge and comprehension levels on this topic by providing students with definitions and main ideas, a gifted curriculum can be developed on the topic by writing educational objectives at the higher levels. At the application level, students can be asked to draw a map of their own community. At the analysis level, students can compare and contrast two or more communities. At the synthesis level, students can create a play about important people in a community. At the evaluation level, students can share their opinions about their own community's services.

Enrichment programs emphasizing the higher levels of Bloom's Taxonomy are appropriate for both elementary and secondary schools. Many published curriculum materials and packages are available to educators through publishers of supplementary educational materials such as those listed at the end of this chapter.

At the present time, curricula based upon Bloom's Taxonomy are more frequently offered in elementary schools, but high school teachers are encouraged to incorporate this valuable planning device in their curriculum planning as well. Students do not grow out of the need to apply what they learn to new situations, to analyze and synthesize new solutions to old problems, and to thoughtfully evaluate ideas. On the contrary, these educational experiences are sorely needed by students at the secondary and college levels as much as they are at the elementary level.

High school and college teachers often report that they find a renewed interest in their own specialized field when it is viewed through the taxonomy's lens, and that the needs of students who hunger for a more stimulating and challenging curriculum are better met.

TABLE 9.1. The Cognitive Domain of Bloom's Taxonomy

Definition of Level	Behavioral Terms
1.0 Knowledge Behaviors that emphasize remembering, either by recognition or recall of ideas, material or phenomena	Define, identify, list, label, match, name, outline, recall, reproduce, select, state
2.0 Comprehension Behaviors that represent an understanding of the literal message or main idea contained in a communication	Explain, extrapolate, give example, infer, interpret, paraphrase, rewrite, summarize, translate
3.0 Application Behaviors that require the student to apply or use what (s)he knows and comprehends	Change, compute, demonstrate, manipulate, modify, operate, predict, prepare, produce, show, solve, use
4.0 Analysis Behaviors that emphasize the breakdown of material into its constituent parts and the ways in which it is organized	Categorize, diagram, distinguish, infer unstated assumptions, recognize point of view and bias, relate cause and effect, subdivide
5.0 Synthesis Behaviors that combine elements and parts from many sources into a new and original whole	Combine, compile, compose, create, design, generate, modify, organize, plan, reorganize, revise, write
6.0 Evaluation Behaviors that are used in making judgments about the value of ideas, works, solutions, methods, and materials	Appraise, compare, conclude, criticize, discriminate, judge in terms of criteria, justify, support

Adapted from *Taxonomy of Educational Objectives—Book 1 Cognitive Domain* by Benjamin S. Bloom. Copyright © 1956 by Longman Inc. Reprinted with permission.

Programs to Develop Critical Thinking

The higher levels of Bloom's Taxonomy describe both critical (analysis, evaluation) and creative (application, synthesis) thinking processes. There are many new initiatives designed for those who wish to be more precise in their definitions and program objectives regarding critical thinking.

Richard Paul directs the Center for Critical Thinking and Moral Critique at Sonoma State University in Rohnert Park, California. The annual International Conference on Critical Thinking and Educational Reform held there each summer attracts philosophers and educators from around the world who are interested in defining critical thinking and describing educational programs to develop it.

Paul describes 31 principles of critical thinking (pamphlet available from the Center upon request), which apply to both affective and cognitive thinking processes, and provides accompanying applications in the form of strategies that can be used in an educational setting to encourage their development. The 31 strategies include independent thinking, insight, fair-mindedness, suspending judgment, transference of ideas to new contexts, developing criteria for evaluation, examining assumptions, making inferences, and exploring implications and consequences.

It is Paul's belief that the human population consists of a portion of *uncritical thinkers* whose thought processes are egocentric, careless, and conditioned by unexamined prejudices and irrational impressions. According to Paul, the uncritical thinker is characterized by thinking that is unclear, vague, illogical, unreflective, superficial, inconsistent, inaccurate, or trivial.

In contrast, *fair-minded critical thinkers* exhibit clarity, precision, specificity, accuracy, relevance, consistency, logicalness, depth, completeness, significance, and fairness in their thinking processes. This definition of a fair-minded critical thinker has much in common with many definitions of giftedness.

Paul does not recommend that educators add new critical thinking programs to the already crowded school curriculum, but rather that they "remodel" existing programs in ways that will encourage students to use and apply the 31 thinking strategies he has described. Two handbooks for remodeling existing curricula are available to educators from the Center. One is specifically designed for remodeling K-3 curricula; the other is designed for grades 4-6. Similar principles apply to the junior and senior high curricula and handbooks are being planned for those grades as well.

Robert Swartz (1986) concurs that critical thinking can be readily taught in the context of traditional content. Swartz is the director of the Critical and Creative Thinking Program at the University of Massachusetts, Boston. Neither Paul nor Swartz recommend the purchase of prepackaged programs that purport to teach critical thinking. They are concerned that these programs have very little transference of learning to real-life situations. Swartz believes that teachers who have worked to infuse critical thinking into their own lives are then able to "infuse" their school programs with learning experiences that utilize critical thinking traits and abilities.

John Chaffee (1987), another specialist in critical thinking, has recently published a textbook entitled *Thinking Critically,* which describes his view that real-life problem-solving experiences are the best method of teaching students to begin to think critically. In his own teaching, he began by using puzzles and games, but found that the transference of skills and abilities from these activities to real-life situations was minimal. He then began to use simulated "real" problems such as issues regarding politics or ecology. While the transference improved, it was not as strong as he had hoped. He now begins critical thinking courses by having his students apply problem-solving and critical thinking strategies to problems they are facing in their own lives. After this initial exposure, students appear readily able to adapt the skills and strategies to other issues.

Kate Sandberg, a teacher at the University of Alaska, believes that collaborative learning experiences are essential to the development of critical thinking. She presented her teaching strategies at the Sixth Annual Conference on Critical Thinking and Educational Reform at Sonoma State University in August, 1988. She has developed a technique in which groups of four students work on a problem together. She structures each group to promote positive interdependence: no one person has enough information to solve the problem alone; they must all collaborate and share their information and ideas in order to be successful. In Sandberg's view, there is a strong affective component involved in becoming a critical thinker. Supportive group interaction and discussion of emotional effects as well as cognitive ideas encourages the growth of fair-minded critical thinking.

Lauren Resnick (1987) concurs that the social context of learning is an essential component which allows individuals to build new schema and to reconstruct existing procedures for thinking through complex problems and issues.

Developing Gifted Behaviors—Higher Level Doing Skills

Throughout the United States, it is well accepted by educators that the development of high level, critical and creative thinking skills are an essential and high priority component of gifted program curricula. We concur, but believe that thinking about an issue is only the first step, not the final one in the lives of creative productive individuals, and therefore should be only the first step in gifted program curricula.

The Gifted Behavior curriculum model is proposed as a means of developing patterns of behavior and action in students that lead to the creation of original products in a wide variety of talent fields. It grew out of the author's study of the behaviors used by highly creative productive adults as they create original products. While there are likely to be other behaviors which affect creative productivity, the ten identified here were cited repeatedly in a review of 32 studies of highly creative, intelligent, talented and productive individuals (Eby 1986).

These ten behaviors were operationally defined in a set of seven instruments entitled the Eby Gifted Behavior Index (see an example in Figure 9.2). The definitions of each variable are stated in terms of observable actions, processes, and behaviors which can be readily observed in classroom situations. The concept of multiple intelligences conceptualized by Howard Gardner (1983) influenced the development of the Gifted Behavior instruments. As Gardner's work suggests, an individual may have a different level of ability or talent in a variety of talent areas. Therefore, a separate form is provided for each of six talent areas: Verbal, Math/Science/Problem-solving, Social/Leadership, Visual/Spatial, Music and Mechanical/Inventiveness. As a guide to curriculum development, and evaluation of student progress, the Eby Gifted Behavior Index provides gifted program personnel with a means of charting the development of ten important gifted behaviors in six different talent fields.

Curriculum development which is written to emphasize Bloom's higher level thinking skills can also emphasize "gifted behavioral outcomes" as well. Whatever the topic or subject matter, higher level thinking skills can and should be used to consider, analyze and evaluate the issues related to that issue. The next step is to require that students put their thinking into action, thereby ensuring that students will use and develop gifted behaviors as well.

As with Bloom's Taxonomy, any subject or topic can be used to create a curriculum unit that will nurture and develop the ten gifted behaviors that are rated on the Eby Index. A single teacher or a team of teachers (and their students) may select a topic of interest. Curriculum activities are designed (in four phases) to lead students toward the goal of producing an original, high-quality product related to that

EBY GIFTED BEHAVIOR INDEX
General Checklist

Name_____ Age_____Date_____

School_____Teacher_____Grade or Year_____

Rated by_____Total Score _____

DIRECTIONS: Please rate this student in terms of the following behavioral descriptors. Circle the number which indicates the level or degree of each behavior you have observed .

5=Evidence of this behavior is shown consistently in most activities
4=Evidence of this behavior is shown often in many activities
3=Evidence of this behavior is shown occasionally in some activities
2=Evidence of this behavior is shown infrequently in activities
1=Evidence of this behavior is shown rarely or never

Perceptiveness

1.	Distinguishes between important and unimportant elements, issues and problems	5	4	3	2	1
2.	Perceives and uses subtle and mature patterns, connections and relationships	5	4	3	2	1

Active Interaction with the Environment

3.	Is active rather than passive; Volunteers or chooses to work on self-selected tasks	5	4	3	2	1
4.	Energetically searches for information, ideas and solutions to problems	5	4	3	2	1

Reflectiveness

5.	Shows mature, in-depth understanding of complex ideas in self-selected topics or talent areas	5	4	3	2	1
6.	Works for accuracy; Thinks out the best possible solutions or conclusions	5	4	3	2	1

Persistence

7.	Displays focus, concentration, and absorption on self-selected tasks	5	4	3	2	1
8.	Overcomes problems and difficulties to solve problems and finish products	5	4	3	2	1

Please turn to other side

Figure 9.2
Reprinted with permission of D.O.K. Publishers, East Aurora, N.Y.

EBY GIFTED BEHAVIOR INDEX

General Checklist

Independence

9. Is a self-starter; Works with little or no assistance
    or support   5   4   3   2   1

10. Expresses strong preferences and ideas;
    Redefines goals to fit own interests   5   4   3   2   1

Goal Orientation

11. Has high intrinsic standards; Revises and improves 5   4   3   2   1
    products to meet them

12. Can state and discuss goals and plans to achieve them   5   4   3   2   1

Originality

13. Is a risk-taker; Is willing to experiment with novel ideas
    and forms of expression   5   4   3   2   1

14. Synthesizes elements from many sources into fresh,
    new ideas and products   5   4   3   2   1

Productivity

15. Shows fluency of ideas and/or products; Makes many
    responses to a problem or challenges   5   4   3   2   1

16. Works efficiently; Finishes high quality products on or
    before deadline   5   4   3   2   1

Self-Evaluation

17. Knows own strengths and weaknesses; Uses strengths;
    Selects appropriately challenging tasks   5   4   3   2   1

18. Monitors own progress; Knows when to revise and when
    a product is finished   5   4   3   2   1

Effective Communication of Ideas

19. Ideas and purposes are stated with clarity   5   4   3   2   1

20. Uses appropriate methods and styles of communication
    to match purpose (e.g. illustrations, models , graphs)   5   4   3   2   1

Figure 9.2—Continued

topic or subject area. In the following example, let us imagine that we are creating a gifted behavior unit on the topic of the human brain.

Phase 1 consists of teacher-centered learning experiences that provide students with the necessary knowledge base in that topic. The teacher assigns readings on the brain, schedules films or videotapes on the subject, and perhaps plans a field trip to a science museum or anatomy laboratory. All of these activities are designed to arouse the students' interest in the topic and, at the same time, provide them with current knowledge about the human brain. These activities are designed to fulfill knowledge and comprehension level objectives on Bloom's Taxonomy. They are also nurturing the student's perceptiveness on the Gifted Behavior Index.

During phase 2, the emphasis is shifted from teacher-centered to student-centered activities. Each student is asked to select a specialized subtopic such as memory, dreams, left and right hemispheres or diseases of the brain. Under the teacher's guidance, each student embarks upon an individual search for information, suggests alternative hypotheses or problems to study, and begins to speculate on his or her own unique perspective of the important issues involved in that particular subtopic. These activities fit the application and analysis levels of Bloom's Taxonomy. In addition, during this phase, the gifted behaviors of active interaction with the environment, reflectiveness, and persistence are being encouraged.

Phase 3 is the culmination of the unit. Each student creates an original product related to the subtopic he or she has selected to study. The term "product" is broadly defined to include tangible inventions, models, prototypes, or other physical objects as well as intangible creations such as speeches, stories, dramas, and poems. The product may be a production, such as a videotape, a set of experiments or demonstrations, a school assembly, an election, or other school event planned and implemented by the students.

Renzulli (1977) recommends that students' products be displayed before a real and appropriate audience (p. 50). The audience may consist of peers, parents, and other members of the school community. Knowing that their products will be viewed by others increases the real-life motivation to revise and refine the quality of their original products. In our example of a unit on the brain, we involved the students in planning a "museum of the mind": a day-long exhibit of all their specialized products and projects held in the school's learning center. Classes were scheduled to visit the museum during the school day and parents were invited to attend in the evening.

Phase 3 is a learning opportunity that emphasizes synthesis on Bloom's Taxonomy. It requires that the students use and demonstrate the gifted behaviors of independence, goal orientation, originality, productivity, and effective communication of ideas.

The final phase of the unit consists of a systematic evaluation of the student's products and processes. In individual conferences with their teacher, students are asked to reflect upon the methods used and the results achieved. When the Eby Index is being used to assist in evaluation, students and their teachers each assess the extent to which the student used and demonstrated the ten gifted behaviors on the index. In the example cited here, the study of the brain, the appropriate form of the index to use in evaluating the student's growth is the Math/Science/Problem-

Solving form. If the unit of study had involved literature and writing, the Verbal form would be used. If the unit had involved music, visual/spatial art, mechanical inventiveness or leadership ability, the appropriate form of the Gifted Behavior Index exists to chart the gifted behaviors as they develop.

Curriculum planning emphasizing gifted behavioral outcomes is highly appropriate for students with high aptitudes and talents for a subject. They are already eager to challenge themselves and create original products related to their interest areas. But this curriculum model has the added advantage of being highly motivating to students whose real potential is unknown. Since behaviors are alterable variables, they can be developed through educational experiences in any child we teach. This is true for every age level as well. In our own programs, we have designed curricula with gifted behavioral outcomes for kindergarten, elementary, and high school students. They have also been successfully employed in the design of college and graduate-level courses. The principles are the same for any age group or subject area:

1. Within your subject area, choose a complex theme or topic that appeals to both you and your students. Every academic discipline has a number of such significant themes.
2. Access to the program should be open to all students. In keeping with the philosophy that gifted behaviors can be developed in children with a wide range of ability and interests, all students should be encouraged to engage in such experiences by school personnel.
3. The learning experiences should be designed to develop each of the gifted behaviors selected by program personnel. This may mean that some units are designed to develop a large number of gifted behaviors while other units focus upon a selected behavior.
4. Units of study that have the following elements or phases will readily use and develop all of the ten behaviors in the Eby Gifted Behavior Index:

   Phase 1: Choice of a complex and challenging topic and emphasis on teacher instruction to build a knowledge base.

   Phase 2: Independent student research and investigations.

   Phase 3: Creation of an original product or performance viewed by a real audience of peers, parents, and other invited guests.

   Phase 4: Systematic evaluation of final products and performances in conference with the teacher by the students themselves.

INDEPENDENT STUDY CURRICULUM MODELS

Renzulli's Enrichment Triad

Joseph Renzulli (1977) created the Enrichment Triad Curriculum Model as a significantly differentiated and therefore defensible gifted program model. While Renzulli's model could be seen as an enrichment curriculum model, its primary goal is the development of an individual's ability to research, investigate, and solve real problems. The mechanism for achieving this goal is a curriculum model with three distinct steps or parts.

Type 1 enrichment consists of activities that awaken interests, provoke inquisitiveness, and stimulate children to pursue a new talent or interest area. Field trips, interest centers, visiting resource persons, games, films, and other introductory learning experiences are employed to help students identify interest areas for further study.

Type 2 enrichment consists of training in systems, processes, and skills that enable the student to find information, conduct investigations, and solve problems in any interest area of their choice. Brainstorming, scientific method, and values clarification are examples of the types of processes that may be taught in a systematic way to students engaged in an Enrichment Triad program.

Type 3 enrichment is the ultimate goal of the program. At this stage, the teacher assists the student in selecting a specific interest area and identifying a gap in knowledge or a problem to solve. The student then carries out an independent investigation into the self-selected topic. Student products serve as the means of communication of the student's findings and are evaluated by the program personnel with the goal of helping the student to revise and improve his or her product until it is of high quality.

Renzulli's Triad Enrichment Program is held in high esteem by gifted program personnel, but is often modified in one way or another because of the time, energy, and resources it requires to do well. Each of the three types of enrichment requires the use of significantly different teaching strategies and styles. Renzulli himself encourages teachers to modify and adapt this model to suit the particular needs and resources available to them. He refers to such modifications as type 3 experiences created by the teacher as a result of his or her own independent investigation.

Self-Directed Learning

Donald Treffinger (quoted in Maker 1982) has developed a curriculum model called Self-Directed Learning. In this model, the goal is to increase the independent learning skills of each child. Treffinger recognizes that even children with unusual capacities for learning information and content may not be able to work independently unless they are provided with experiences and training in independent management. He describes three levels of self-direction, and proposes a curriculum model that allows children to progress from level 1 to level 3 through guided experiences.

Using learning contracts, children are given opportunities to work on independent projects at each successive level of self-directedness. For example, at level 1, a child will select a topic to research from a small number of choices created by the teacher. A very specific and concrete contract with timelines is established by the teacher and student so that the student knows exactly what to do in order to succeed with his first project. At level 2, the child and teacher can brainstorm topics together and the child will work cooperatively with the teacher to establish a timeline and contract for the project. At level 3, the child is able to determine the topic he wishes to study and the steps he must take to complete the project. The products of all three levels are evaluated by the student and the teacher, but the child assumes greater responsibility for self-evaluation as he reaches level 3.

Individualized Educational Plans (IEPs)

Many school districts have adapted the special education model of Individualized Educational Plans (IEPs) to their gifted programs. In this structure, the curriculum is decided upon by gifted specialists, psychologists, and other personnel to fit the specific strengths and deficiencies of each identified student. A child's curriculum plan will specify activities, experiences, and expectations tailored specifically to allow her opportunities to use and develop her own unique talents and will specify other learning experiences designed to remediate her weaknesses. For example, a student with special abilities in math and weaknesses in writing will be given highly challenging math opportunities and remediation in writing skills as part of her IEP.

Computer-Aided Gifted Programming

The computer has opened the door to many new worlds for teachers planning gifted curricula. Excellent computer programs are both stimulating and instructive, providing students with individualized experiences that teachers may not otherwise be able to generate. Since the computer was first introduced to elementary schools, there have been significant improvements in the quality of programs available and in the rationale and purposes for its use in educational programs.

In the early 1970s, when minicomputers were made available to schools, the primary curriculum focus was on computer programming itself. Many gifted programs initiated computer classes for their students with the goal of teaching the students how to program a computer in BASIC. This was one of the few options available at the time because software was scarce and limited in scope. While learning how to program a computer does have validity for some students with particular interests in computer science, it is not appropriate for all students.

Currently, because of the widespread availability of excellent educational software, curriculum developers use the computer as a tool or an opportunity to broaden horizons in many subjects and interest areas. While computer-aided instruction could be viewed as an example of either enrichment or acceleration, it is also very much a vehicle for planning independent learning experiences.

Many challenging programs with an emphasis on computation, geometry, algebra, and graph making are available to be used to provide suitable challenges for students with special interests and aptitudes in math. Social studies simulations are available to allow students to participate in problem solving experiences involving economics, geography, map making, communities, and other important social studies concepts. Language arts curricula have been greatly enriched by the addition of computer programs that allow students to use word processing to compose their stories, reports, and letters. Programs are available that allow children to create posters, banners, and invitations. Other programs allow children to create their own newspapers and design their own graphics.

One of the most effective examples of computer-aided instruction that we know about is also one of the simplest. North Junior High School in Crystal Lake, Illinois, uses an integrated computer program that contains a word-processing program combined with a data base and a spreadsheet program. Each student is required to use all three in a creative, individual way. Students use the word processer to write stories, poems, or words for a song. They use the data base to create a file on any subject or topic of interest, such as movies and movie stars, car models, or record albums. They use the spreadsheet to compute budgets or recipes. Once this introductory activity has been completed, the students have the skills needed to use this valuable program in any other investigation they make.

We encourage educators to explore the full range of computer software programs. Look for materials labeled "educational software" in catalogues and software stores, but also look at the wide variety of programs categorized as "entertainment." In our view, some of the entertainment software has great value in gifted programming. Many games are simulations in which the child is allowed to experiment and make choices with immediate consequences. We believe that this type of experience is one way in which gifted behaviors can be developed, and we encourage teachers to incorporate computer games into gifted curricula. The way we use them is to choose a game with a topic or theme related to the unit we are planning. We allow students time to work on the computer activity just as we would any other activity planned for the unit.

Another service that computers provide for teachers is record keeping of individual achievements. Many software programs contain their own record-keeping systems, allowing students to save their own responses to programs and keeping scores and results, which makes individual record keeping easier for teachers.

INTEGRATING CURRICULUM MODELS INTO A PROGRAM THAT MEETS THE NEEDS OF YOUR OWN DISTRICT

For almost two decades, educators have experimented with gifted program models and structures. Most of us have found that no one model meets the needs of the widely diverse student populations we serve. The most comprehensive plan for integrating various methods, approaches, and models into a districtwide program has been proposed by June Cox in *Educating Able Learners*. The final chapters of this book outline "a comprehensive approach to programming that will bring together all the resources of a community to meet as wide a range of abilities as the resources will allow" (Cox, Daniel, and Boston 1985, p. 171) The approach is illustrated by imagining an ideal district with the commitment and resources devoted to discovering and nurturing talent by "casting a wide net" to include all children who might benefit from gifted programming.

Called the Pyramid Project (see Figure 9.3), Cox's approach offers both acceleration and enrichment, and allows for and encourages individual differences. One of the cornerstones of the Pyramid Project is a district commitment to appropriate pacing or continuous progress in academic subjects such as reading and math. As individual students demonstrate mastery in these subjects, they are allowed to progress.

> Whether the districts accelerate the educational process by moving bright students
> to higher grade levels in their areas of accomplishment or by bringing advanced

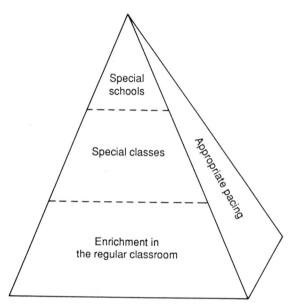

Figure 9.3. Pyramid Concept Model.
Reprinted with permission from *Educating Able Learners: Programs and Promising Practices* by June Cox, Neil Daniel, and Bruce O. Boston (Austin: University of Texas Press, 1985).

materials down to the students, this provision is expected to meet the needs of many able learners in the regular classroom. (Cox, Daniel, and Boston 1985, p. 158)

The broad base of the pyramid represents the enrichment needed by a large number of able learners. Various enrichment activities can be provided to all students in the regular classroom. For example, the type 1 enrichment activities described by Renzulli are appropriate for all learners. Creative problem solving activities are also beneficial. Computer-based learning activities are ideal for enrichment of the regular curriculum.

Additional enrichment opportunities can be made available to those students with particular interests, talents, and willingness to take an active part. Gifted behavior units can be designed to challenge students with special interests. Interscholastic competitions such as science fairs, Future Problem Solving Bowl, and Odyssey of the Mind can be made available to those who are willing to work for them.

The middle tier of the pyramid is designed to provide unusually challenging learning opportunities for the students who require them. Cox suggests the use of honors classes and dual enrollment to provide for students with needs for radical acceleration in certain subjects. Occasionally referred to as the "profoundly gifted," a few elementary students may need placement in middle or high schools to meet their needs in math. A few very extraordinary high school students may need to be enrolled in college-level courses.

The top tier of the pyramid is reserved for students whose needs cannot be adequately met in their existing school or district. These students may need placement in academies and special schools devoted to gifted education of one type or another. States such as North Carolina and Illinois have established special residential high schools for students with extremely high aptitudes in math and science.

In many cities, there are magnet high schools devoted to talent areas such as the performing arts, math and science, or the International Baccalaureate (IB). The IB is a special high school curriculum that was developed in Geneva, Switzerland, in 1970. The IB curriculum requires mastery of two languages and includes special courses in history and the social sciences with a multicultural perspective. High schools that qualify for participation may obtain the course syllabuses and examinations for these courses from the International Baccalaureate North America (IBNA) in New York.

Currently several school districts in and around the Forth Worth, Texas, area are piloting Pyramid Projects. But school districts around the country are urged to synthesize their own responses to such a concept. Many districts may be doing much more than they now recognize in the areas of gifted curricula described in this chapter. The first step in creating your own comprehensive program is to assess what is already being done in your own classrooms that fits these guidelines. Many ad hoc and grassroots efforts to provide children with enriched experiences already exist. You may also find that informal systems are in place that allow children to make continuous progress in subjects such as math and reading.

After surveying programs provided by your own teaching staff, the next step is to conduct needs assessments to determine what needs are not being met. Involve the faculty in a group brainstorming and problem-solving session to determine what new systems can be designed to allow for greater numbers of children to experience continuous progress or enrichment opportunities. Consider alternatives to provide students with unusual talents and abilities the special courses or placements that they need. Design your own pyramid of enriched and accelerated learning experiences.

Many of the weaker programs identified by the Richardson Survey have failed or been inadequate because they spend so much of their resources and time on testing and identification that there is little left for careful and thoughtful design of program options, curriculum planning, and instructional strategies. You may have observed a number of such gifted programs that concentrate their efforts on selecting and labeling the ''gifted children'' and on internal and external struggles to eliminate or reassess those children who don't fit their criteria. Curriculum planning is accomplished after identification procedures are completed, and programs such as these start late in the year and end early.

There is a common philosophy expressed by June Cox as she describes her Pyramid Model for able learners, by Renzulli as he describes the Enrichment Triad and Revolving Door Identification models, by Smutny as she describes the successful summer enrichment programs she founded, and by Eby as she describes units to develop gifted behaviors in children. The intent of these programs is to develop children's talents and abilities. The energy and resources in these programs is concentrated in curriculum development and delivery of services to children rather than in sorting children into in- and out-groups.

Programs such as these involve the whole school community in their efforts.

Classroom teachers are active in the delivery of certain elements of the program while specialists support, coordinate, and teach specialized segments of the program. There is no one best way to create or maintain such a program. Each requires an interactive assessment of needs and gaps in the existing school program, a search for meaningful alternatives to fill these gaps, a strong communication of goals and objectives, and a constant vigilance for ways to improve every element of the program. The result, however, is worth the effort. Children are appropriately served and their needs are met. We should not settle for less.

OPPORTUNITIES FOR DISCUSSION AND ACTION

1. Choose one grade level in your school. Interview the teachers to discover what they are already doing that could be considered examples of either enrichment or acceleration. Are there ways that these individual contributions could be strengthened and supported as part of a comprehensive gifted program?
2. Ask the same group of teachers to brainstorm with you the gaps in the present curriculum. Ask: What are we missing? What areas of our curriculum need enriching? Consider alternative suggestions for each of the gaps you identify.
3. Ask the same group of teachers to discuss ways of promoting mastery learning or continuous progress in subjects such as reading or math. How could the teachers work as a team to accommodate students learning at their own pace? What types of scheduling or grouping changes could be made? How could resources and materials be shared more effectively between grade levels?

REFERENCES

Bloom, B., et al. 1956. *Taxonomy of educational objectives handbook I: The cognitive domain.* White Plains, N.Y.: Longman, Inc.

Chaffee, J. 1987. *Thinking critically.* Boston: Houghton-Mifflin.

Clendening, C., and R. Davies. 1983. *Challenging the gifted.* New York: R. R. Bowker Company.

Cox, J., N. Daniel, and B. Boston. 1985. *Educating able learners.* Austin, Tex.: University of Texas Press.

Eby, J. 1983. Gifted behavior—A non-elitist approach, *Educational Leadership,* May, pp. 30–36.

———. 1984. Developing gifted behavior, *Educational Leadership,* April, pp. 35–43.

———. 1988. *Eby Gifted Behavior Index.* East Aurora, N.Y.: D.O.K. Publishers.

Gardner, H. 1983. *Frames of mind.* New York: Basic Books.

Joyce, B., and M. Weil. 1986. *Models of teaching.* Englewood Cliffs, N.J.: Prentice-Hall.

Maker, C. J. 1982. *Teaching models in education of the gifted.* Rockville, Md.: An Aspen Publication, Aspen System Corporation.

Micklus, S. 1985. *Odyssey of the mind, problems to develop creativity.* Glassboro, N.J.: OM Association.

———. 1986. *OM program handbook.* Glassboro, N.J.: OM Association.

Neuman, D. 1981. It's time to get together on gifted programs, *Curriculum Review,* April, pp. 114–117.

Paul, R. 1988. Critical thinking in the classroom, *Teaching K-8,* April, pp. 49–51.

Paul, R., et al. 1986. *Critical thinking handbooks, K-3, 4-6: A guide for remodelling lesson plans in language arts, social studies and science.* Rohnert Park, Calif.: Center for Critical Thinking and Moral Critique, Sonoma State University.

Renzulli, J. 1977. *The enrichment triad model: A guide for developing defensible programs for the gifted.* Wethersfield, Conn.: Creative Learning Press.

———, L. Smith, and S. Reis. 1982. Curriculum compacting: An essential strategy for working with gifted students, *Elementary School Journal* 82 (no. 3): 185-94.

Resnick, L. 1987. *Education and learning to think.* Washington, D.C.: National Academy Press.

Stanley, J. C., and C. P. Benbow, eds. 1983. *Academic precocity: Aspects of its development, consequences, and nurturance.* Baltimore: Johns Hopkins University Press.

Stanley, J. C., D. P. Keating, and L. H. Fox, eds. 1974. *Mathematical talent: Discovery, description and development.* Baltimore: Johns Hopkins University Press.

Swartz, R. 1986. Restructuring curriculum for critical thinking, *Educational Leadership* 43: 8.

CHAPTER 10

Evaluating Your Gifted Program

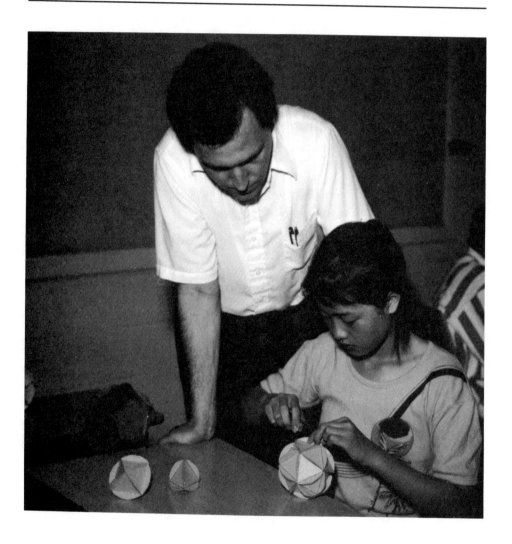

The following scenario presents an extreme example of the low priority that program evaluation may be given. The month is May. The setting is a staff meeting of teachers and administrators who are responsible for the district's gifted program.

GIFTED PROGRAM DIRECTOR: OK, we've got the end-of-the-year field trip all planned and we've discussed the identification screenings for next year. I know it's late, but I need to bring up one more topic today. We need to decide on some type of evaluation of our program before the year is over.

TEACHER A: Listen, I've got to pick up my son at the sitter. Can we talk about this next week?

DIRECTOR: No, we only have four more weeks left in the school year. We've got to deal with it today.

TEACHER B: Well, let's just do what we did last year.

TEACHER C: I'm new this year. What did you do last year?

DIRECTOR: We did two things. We sent home a parent questionnaire and we did a survey of the teachers in the district.

TEACHER C: What kinds of questions were on the parent questionnaire?

DIRECTOR: We used a Lickert scale, asking parents to agree or disagree with about ten items.

TEACHER A: Right, one item was "My child is satisfied with the variety of experiences in the gifted program," and another was "I have enough communication with the staff in the program." You know the kind of thing.

TEACHER C: What did you do with the results?

DIRECTOR: We looked at them last spring to see if there were any real problems, but what we got was the whole range of responses. Some parents are very satisfied with everything and others aren't satisfied with anything about the program.

TEACHER C: Did you make any changes in the program as a result of the questionnaire?

DIRECTOR: That's hard to say. We did make some changes in identification procedures and in the math program itself, but we had already decided to do that before we sent out the questionnaires.

TEACHER C: What did you learn from the survey of the teachers?

DIRECTOR: We got mixed results there too. Some teachers are very critical of the program; some support us and others didn't even care enough to return the survey.

TEACHER B: Well, I understand that. They're busy at the end of the year. There are so many forms to fill out. Ours probably was a low priority for many teachers.

DIRECTOR: That may be. Well, what do you think? We really don't have time to plan anything complicated, but we have to conduct some form of evaluation to get our state aid. How about if we revise the forms we used last year and send them out again?

TEACHER A: That's fine with me. Can I go pick up my son now?

WHAT DO YOU THINK?

1. Have you and your colleagues taken courses or in-service training in program evaluation?
2. Who should organize and administer the evaluation? A school district administrator? The teachers? An outside consultant?
3. Who should be surveyed to evaluate a gifted program? Parents? Students? Teachers? Others in the community?
4. What elements of a program should be evaluated in a given year? Appropriateness of target population? Curriculum? Services? Unintended effects of the program?
5. Which is more valuable: statistics on student achievement or opinion surveys on satisfaction with the program?

INTRODUCTION

Admittedly, the scenario above represents an extreme example of poorly planned program evaluation, and is not characteristic of all or even most gifted programs. But conversations like this do take place in some understaffed or otherwise undersupported programs. Evaluation is the weakest area of most educational programs. As in this scenario, it is sometimes hastily planned at the end of the program, and is seen by the program staff as a necessary evil.

In this chapter, we are going to reassess the whole matter of evaluation. There are many new ideas and theories regarding evaluation that can be applied to gifted programs. You will have an important role in the evaluation process as a gifted program teacher or administrator. The most significant and important contribution you can make to your district's evaluation efforts is to avoid oversimplification. Evaluation is a complex matter. In this chapter, we will provide you with the best-documented new perspectives on the evaluation of educational programs. While we cannot provide you with the answers to your evaluation needs, we can provide you with the appropriate questions. It will be your task to combine these ideas into a usable and productive evaluation system that fits the needs of your district.

APPLYING EVALUATION RESEARCH TO GIFTED EDUCATION

Evaluation of any educational program is difficult under the best of circumstances because of the different values held by each individual or group of individuals who come in contact with the program. The generic term "stakeholder" refers to any person who has a stake in the program being assessed. But stakeholders include both the consumers and the providers of a program, and each one has a very different stake or point of view. School board members, district and program administrators, principals, teachers responsible for delivering the program, teachers whose students are affected by the program, parents of students who are admitted to the program, parents of students who are not admitted to the program, and the admitted and excluded students themselves all have a stake in the success or failure of a district's gifted program.

Each stakeholder defines success and failure quite differently according to long-held beliefs and values about what is important in life, as reflected in a school program and curriculum. As a result, the evaluation of a program often results in mixed reviews, with little or no consensus on what is good and valuable or what needs to be revised and improved.

Two basic (and often unresolved) issues in evaluation are (1) who is the evaluation for? and (2) what type of data should be gathered about the program? After these two issues are resolved, there are still important questions regarding the types of methods used, and the way the results are reported. Whose opinions and views should be taken most seriously? Who should get the results? Who is the actual beneficiary of the evaluation? Who should interpret the results and make decisions regarding program changes? These questions are being studied by educators who specialize in evaluation research.

Evaluation research is a relatively new field of study. As in other newly emerging fields, there is little or no consensus. Researchers who are creating theories of evaluation present dramatically different points of view on the matter. In a highly condensed version, the following are some of the most respected perspectives regarding evaluation.

Client-Centered Evaluation

Michael Scriven (1980) proposes that programs be evaluated from the point of view of the *client*. In the case of a gifted program, the client is the student and his or her parents. An evaluation based upon Scriven's model would be designed to determine whether the client actually receives valuable services or not. To find out, his evaluation plan would attempt to answer these four questions:

1. Who is the target population? How many are served? What are their ability levels? Is there an inequity issue regarding the target population? If so, what is the concern?
2. What does the program do? Is there an adequate quantity of services? How is the quality of services perceived by the client? Are the services appropriate to the stated purpose of the program? Are the costs of the program offset by the gains?
3. How effective is the program? Are gains and growth evident? Are clients satisfied with the program? Is there adequate communication between home and school?
4. What are the unplanned impacts of the program? Are there side effects within the target population? Are there side effects on others not in the program itself? Are there unforeseen problems created by the program?

To answer these questions, a well-designed evaluation would need to be planned before the program is implemented, so that the data can be gathered at appropriate intervals in the school year. Records regarding the target population need to be maintained. Perceptions of the clients need to be ascertained. To gather data regarding the effectiveness of the program would require the use of behavioral objectives written before the program is implemented, with plans for measuring and reporting the results at the end.

For example, if the program has a goal of developing the critical thinking skills of its students, then a behavioral objective might be written to specify that:

> At the end of the school year, 90 percent of the students enrolled in the gifted program for the entire year will achieve a minimum stanine score of 7 on the Watson/Glaser Critical Thinking Appraisal.

At the end of the school term, this objective would be operationalized by testing all the students on this instrument and reporting the results in terms of the established criteria. Who should receive a copy of the report? Scriven believes that this information belongs as much to the clients (the students and their parents) as it does to the program administrators.

Scriven's evaluation plan requires the collection of both "hard" and "soft" data. Scriven would gather hard data regarding the target population of the program, its size and characteristics. He would collect and report statistics regarding the actual accomplishment of program objectives by measuring the gains made by students in the program against a set of criteria of merit and standards for adequacy. Soft data would consist of opinions and reports by clients of the value of the services they received.

Scriven would also gather soft data from the clients by asking the students and their parents to respond to such questions as:

> What do you perceive the program's purpose(s) to be?
> In what ways does it achieve its purpose?
> In what ways does it fail to achieve its purpose?
> Have the purposes of the program been adequately explained to you?
> Have you had adequate opportunities to give input regarding the purposes of this program?

The use of such open-ended questions would allow the program director to gather frank and realistic information about how clients view the program. You should expect that this type of evaluation will yield mixed reviews, depending on the varying biases and philosophies of the clients in your district and the extent to which your program is congruent with their values.

This form of evaluation enhances much needed two-way communication between the clients and program staff. Generalizations regarding the clients' assessments can lead you to make meaningful changes in the program so that over the years the program is more and more tailored to the needs of the clients themselves, for that is the purpose and the philosophy behind Scriven's theory.

Results-Oriented Evaluation

In contrast with Scriven's emphasis on the client's assessment of the effects of the program, Wholey (1983) would design a results-oriented, objectives-based evaluation to meet the needs of the administrators, faculty, and staff of the program. The assumption inherent in this evaluation model is that the program administrators are the "experts" and are therefore better able to judge the results than are the clients. Administrators are accountable for the program and need usable information about the results of the program so that they can make decisions about the program from year to year.

Wholey recognizes, however, that among the program staff there will still be many different points of view and values. To design an evaluation of a program, Wholey begins with an important "preevaluation" by assessing the extent to which the members of the program staff have the same views and understandings about the program. In this vital first step, the entire administrative and teaching staff participate in a lively planning session to discuss and define the program's definitions, assumptions, goals, and methods of achieving them.

In our example of gifted program evaluation, Wholey would suggest that the staff discuss such questions as:

What do you mean by giftedness?
How do you know when someone is gifted?
What are the components of elements of giftedness?
How are they demonstrated?
Which elements are most important?
Can these elements be changed by the environment or are they innate?
How can giftedness be enhanced, supported, or developed?

In Wholey's view, such a discussion results in a greater sense of "ownership" of the program by the staff. As consensus emerges, priorities can be established to determine which objectives are the most highly prized. Then the staff as a whole makes plans to create realistic goals and objectives of the program. The set of objectives that emerges from the preevaluation session may be quite different from the ones originally written by the program developer.

Using his Results-Oriented Management Scale, Wholey suggests the use of the following systematic evaluation scheme, consisting of six steps:

0 Define the program
1 Agree upon the objectives
2 Agree upon a system to assess performance of the objectives
3 Target acceptable levels of performance
4 Agree on a system for using information
5 Gather data on program performance in terms of targets
6 Communicate program performance to administrator or manager

As you can see, many of these important steps take place in the preevaluation process described above. Another key idea in this evaluation theory is that the consensus of a group of experienced administrators and practitioners is stronger and more defensible than the ideas of a single individual. As a group, the planning team agrees upon the objectives, then creates its own assessment system. The important gain made by evaluating a program in this way is that there is greater likelihood that the program will be consistently implemented by the various staff members involved. In programs where such issues are unspoken, where it is assumed that everyone agrees with the written goals and objectives, the actual delivery of the program may be remarkably inconsistent.

The end result of this evaluation would be a report designed by and for program administrators. As such, it would prove very useful to them in understanding the extent to which their own goals were being accomplished. And, while Wholey's model has the attribute of being fairly scientific and precise, it also allows personnel much flexibility in deciding what to do, how to measure results, and how to use the information generated.

The weakness of this model is that program administrators would learn nothing except what they asked for. The perceptions of the client are not given much weight in this scheme. Wholey's evaluation design is most appropriate for ongoing programs that have already demonstrated acceptance by clients and others, since the perceptions of the clients, impacts upon other stakeholders, and other important side effects of the program would not be communicated to the administrator who chooses to use this system alone.

Investigative Evaluation

A third perspective is offered by Guba and Lincoln (1981), who believe that the most effective evaluation is one that is done by outsiders who have no stake in the program at all. In this model, the recipient of the evaluation is the general public rather than the client or the program administrator. Guba believes that taxpayers deserve to know what their tax dollars are buying and that the best way to determine the real, unbiased effects of a program is to conduct an investigation and expose the real facts and effects to the public.

Guba and Lincoln cite as an example of this type of evaluation the work done by investigative newspaper or television reporters, who target a specific public program and go undercover to ferret out the untold facts, figures, and opinions concerning the program. In educational programs, a more typical example is seen when an evaluative team from the state office of education or consultants from universities are hired to conduct an evaluation of a program in a region or district removed from where they themselves live and work. Because they have no stake in the program, these teams represent the public interest.

In the Scriven and Wholey models, program personnel are allowed to generate both the questions to be asked and the data in response. Guba's model assumes that a dimension of conflict exists between the evaluators and the personnel of the program being studied. The goal of this evaluation design is to provide unbiased information to the general public and to the legislative and policy-making bodies who allocate funding to the program.

In the Guba model, the evaluator, rather than evaluating the program on its stated goals and objectives, is encouraged to take on the role of participant-observer to learn about the processes and effects of the program, both intended and unintended. Every program has a "hidden curriculum" that may have effects and consequences as powerful as the planned curriculum. A trained participant-observer would gain information about the program by conducting interviews, making observations, and reviewing all manner of records. The evaluator would be trying to determine:

1. How does this program work?
2. Who gets what services?
3. What are the problems with this program?
4. What is the quality of each element of the program?
5. What are the explanations for what is observed?
6. What changes should be made in this program?

While the goal of this model may be to gain unbiased information, it is not possible to guarantee objectivity. The outside observers may be subject to error if they make judgments prematurely based upon incomplete records, strongly biased interviewees, or other on-site distortions. Any controversial issue would be likely to attract the most attention from the observer. This is especially true if the program is a complex one. The best investigative evaluators return to the site over time to get a more comprehensive view of the program than a single visit would allow.

The strength of this model is that it provides data from original rather than secondary sources. It serves the clients' interests as well as the interests of the rest of the public who is not receiving services from the program. It can also serve the program administrator who is open-minded and willing to learn from outside observers in a nondefensive way.

Practitioner-Centered Evaluation

"Commissioners of evaluations complain that the messages from evaluations are not useful, while evaluators complain that the messages are not used" (Cronbach 1982, p. 29). Cronbach believes that the purpose of evaluation is to improve a social program and, at the same time, add to our generalized knowledge about the phenomenon being evaluated. He believes that improvement depends upon gaining the support of the program deliverers or practitioners.

Cronbach believes that program evaluations conducted by administrators at the federal, state, or district level are less effective than those conducted by practitioners at the local level. In the case of gifted programs, it is the teachers who are best able to evaluate a program since they are the ones who deliver it to the students and are in the best position to understand its positive and negative effects.

An important point made by Cronbach is that even the best evaluation scheme is worthless if the practitioners do not pay attention to the information generated by it. Evaluation reports and studies commissioned by and for administrators may be read and put aside by the local practitioner. Evaluation has little real effect unless it actually changes the behavior and attitudes of the teacher who delivers the program.

Believing that practitioners are the key element in program improvement, Cronbach speaks directly to them. He encourages them to see themselves as responsible for program improvement. The methods he describes include teachers visiting other programs to glean new information and practical knowledge, reading recent accounts of program development in articles, and attending conference presentations that describe and illustrate innovative practices and program models.

Cronbach believes that evaluation is, in fact, occurring whenever teachers read articles, visit other sites, attend conferences, or meet to discuss their program. As they observe or discuss program alternatives, they are actively conducting an inner evaluation of their own programs in comparison to the one they are viewing or reading about. Either through interior dialogues or discussion with other practitioners in small informal groups, teachers discuss the new ideas they've seen and heard. They ask themselves and each other:

1. How does this program really work?
2. Do I like what I see?
3. Would it be good for my students?
4. Would I enjoy teaching a program in this way?
5. Would the parents of my students support this?
6. How much work would it be for me?
7. What's the payoff? Is it worth the extra effort?

If the answers to these queries are fairly positive, the practitioner then proceeds to gain information about the practical matters of incorporating or adapting the improvement to fit into his existing program. He asks:

1. What needs to happen first?
2. What will it cost?
3. What will have to change?
4. What will be the effects?
5. Whose support do I need to get to make this work?

The result is a synthesis of old and new, a unique adaptation of new and existing program elements that will differ from all other programs because of the unique aspects of the site, the students, the materials available, the financial support available, and the interests and values of the teacher.

In this general way, gifted programs change and evolve. To ensure that the changes are positive and valid, Cronbach advises that teachers be trained to be deliberative and discriminating as they observe other programs. He also advises gathering data from a heterogeneous sample of projects, looking for successful and unsuccessful instances of accomplishment, before reaching a conclusion about the value or merit of a program element.

In addition to their role as primary change agents in programs at the local level, Cronbach recommends that successful, innovative teachers can play an important role in the dissemination of information by writing papers or articles, presenting at conferences, and serving as consultants to other districts.

At the beginning, teachers soak up the ideas and information provided to them by more experienced teachers. Gradually, they find themselves contributing examples and ideas to discussions of "what works" and, as they gain sufficient experience and confidence, they become the role models to the next generation. This is just as true in gifted education as it is in the regular classroom. We hope that you will examine where you are in this progression. Are you soaking up ideas to survive your first year in a new position as a teacher in a gifted program? Or are you getting ready to speak out and share what you are doing with your program that is exciting and motivating to your students?

FORMAL AND INFORMAL EVALUATION

Programs are continually evolving. Some changes come about through carefully planned evaluations such as those formal methods described by Scriven and Wholey. Other changes are brought about by the more informal methods described by Guba and Cronbach. It is important to consider how to use both formal and informal evaluation efforts to support and improve your gifted program.

Informal Evaluations

Informal evaluations of a program go on every day. We evaluate options every time we plan a learning event. As we implement our plan, we make alterations due to immediate perceptions of needs; the next time we plan the same event, we make revisions due to the outcome of the first attempt.

In effect, Cronbach's theory of evaluation describes the daily informal evaluations that all teachers use. Programs that acknowledge and support the teacher's ideas and opinions will be stronger than those that tell teachers what to do and how to improve their programs. Teachers should be actively involved in curriculum development. Resources should be budgeted to support teachers in their educational, research, and evaluation efforts.

When the authors read Cronbach's material, we realized that we ourselves had both gone through the processes he describes. Both of us initiated gifted programs by visiting examples and sites of other functioning programs in search of "what works." As we visited each site, we actively questioned and searched for the underlying theoretical meanings, assumptions, planned and unplanned effects that we observed. With no stake in the program that we were observing, we were able, as Guba's theory suggests, to ferret out the many real truths of the program and the values they represented.

We unconsciously compared these observations to our own values, and true to Cronbach, we actively engaged in inner dialogues and discussions with other teachers to evaluate, in detail, the strengths and weaknesses of each program element that we observed or heard about. We attended workshops, classes, and conferences. One highlight of this phase was attending Renzulli's Summer Gifted Confratute in 1978. The Confratute is held at the University of Connecticut every summer in late July and early August. For two weeks, practitioners new to the field of gifted education are offered an enormous variety of program options and models presented by experienced teachers who have participated in actual program development, implementation, and evaluation. It is an exciting environment for teachers at both ends of the spectrum.

Both of us synthesized unique programs to fit our own values, interests, strengths, and weaknesses and the values and needs of the students and the parents in our communities. Over the years, each of us continued to attend conferences and read widely in the gifted literature. So the informal processes described by Guba and Cronbach were important when we initiated our programs and have also been a vital force in the continual evaluation and improvement of our programs.

Staff Meetings

In the administration of an ongoing program, there is a continual need for planned events that allow stakeholders in the program to participate in discussions about the program.

Smutny, who administers several different programs in different sites, involves the staff of each of her programs in an extensive preevaluation assessment at the beginning of each session. She communicates the goals of the program and engages the teachers in active discussions in order to ensure that the program is well defined for each of them. Staff meetings are frequently scheduled and are administered in an open format. She has found that for programs to continue to be fresh and creative over the years, the process of definition and communication must be ongoing as an organic part of the program—one that consistently informs decision makers about adjustments needed on a daily or weekly basis. Continuous assessment has the welfare of the families and teachers at heart.

Parent and Community Meetings

Community support can often make or break a gifted program. For that reason, we recommend monthly or quarterly meetings of parents and other interested members of the community designed to elicit ideas, suggestions, criticisms, and praise in an informal two-way communication process. We have found that these meetings are crucial to the success of an educational program that depends upon community support. When funding is limited, as it almost always is, the board will be more likely to fund a program that has a strong, vocal support group in the community.

The serious mistake that is made all too frequently in conducting parent meetings is the administrator's attempt to control criticism. Administrators and teachers can occasionally become very self-protective and defensive. They have a great sense of ownership in the program they designed and are sometimes unable to share this sense of ownership with the parents. Too often we have seen parent meetings run in a defensive manner. Suggestions by parents are met with staff reactions of "Yes, but . . ." or "We can't do that because . . .," and an attempt to move hastily along to the next raised hand in the audience. We have even observed administrators call on only the parents they want to hear from. If a number of hands are raised on an emotional issue, we have seen administrators say, "We have time for just one more question . . ." When meetings are conducted in this way, the silenced and thwarted audience does not forget easily. A sense of "us against them" begins to develop. If the issues can't be raised publicly, they simply go underground. Parents call each other looking for support. The next day, board members are called. We have all attended meetings run like this and, as members of the audience, you may have felt angry and frustrated. But as you develop expertise in gifted education you will probably find yourself leading such meetings, fielding tough questions, and dealing with complex value-laden issues. We believe that these meetings can be run productively with real benefit to all the stakeholders in the program. To accomplish this, you must recognize an important fact: your stake in this case is the program itself. You helped design it; you administer or teach it; you care very deeply about every element of it. But as important as that is, you must recognize that the parents' stake in the program is even greater—their own children. If you recognize that all parents have the right and the responsibility to speak up for their children, you will feel less defensive when they suggest alternatives you don't agree with.

We like to state this situation out loud at our parent meetings. We openly discuss our own commitment and involvement in the program; we state out loud that each member of the audience has his or her own stake in the program and comes to the meeting with different values and expectations. We state out loud that during discussions of concerns about the program, we *expect differences of opinions on many issues.* We also say that although we can't promise to solve every issue during this one meeting, we can promise to hear them. This openness tends to minimize cutthroat competition and opposition, and turn it into qualified support and cooperation.

The most productive meetings we have run have several different phases. First of all, we assign the task of taking notes to a couple of different people in the audience. On occasion we choose to give this task to the most vocal participant—the one with the strongest opinions. After the meeting we collect these notes and refer to them often. We like to begin with news about the program, and a demonstration or performance by a group of the students. We follow that with the hard part of the meeting, which we frankly and humorously call "onions." After hearing parent's concerns, we raise our own. For example, we may raise the difficult issue of parents helping their students too much, so that the project becomes more the parents' than the child's.

We allow some time for discussion of how these issues might be solved. When issues become heated, we gently listen and say that we understand the speaker's point of view and that our note takers are getting all this down so that we can deal with it effectively in the weeks to come.

We end our meetings on a positive note by asking any member of the audience or staff to pass out some "orchids," by saying something positive that has occurred in the program. We encourage sharing of descriptions of a child's new insight or skill, an enjoyable class, a proud and happy moment. On that note, we adjourn to coffee and cookies. We suggest the following agenda be printed up and distributed at your meetings so that people know from the minute they walk in that their concerns will be heard.

Parent and Community Meeting Agenda

Assign two or three note takers
Announcements
Student performance or demonstration
Onions:
    Update on concerns stated at previous meetings
    Parents' concerns
    Staff concerns
Problem solving to address concerns
Orchids

This type of open forum is an essential part of establishing two-way communication among the stakeholders in a program. Maintaining it is another matter. Follow-up on the issues raised is mandatory. Again, we may not be able to solve every issue, but we can chip away at them, and we must. The telephone plays an important role in maintaining good two-way communication. We encourage you to call the parents who raise issues and listen some more on the phone. We learn new perspectives from them and they learn from us. All of these informal encounters have an impact on the gradual evolution and improvement of the program we run for their children.

Formal Evaluation

The informal evaluation processes described above are energizing and revitalizing to a program and its staff. Constant examination and discussion of the effects of program elements keep programs from becoming stale or rigid. Informal evaluations serve an important function in program improvement, especially in the hands of a dedicated practitioner who is alert for nuances of unmet needs on the part of her clientèle and the district she works for. But they are not sufficient. It is not enough to quietly fine-tune and improve a program. For many reasons documentation of change is required. Written reports are frequently required by the state or the district. Formal evaluation requires careful planning, needs assessments, data gathering, interpretation, and recommendations.

Needs Assessments

Needs assessments are vitally important for both new and continuing gifted programs. Initiating a program requires that the newly appointed staff make hundreds of decisions regarding every important element of the program. They need guidance and information from other stakeholders in order to make decisions that will be supported by the community. They get this guidance and information by conducting an assessment to determine what others need and want from the program.

But what questions should be asked? What are the areas of concern to members of the school community? The first needs assessment must gather information about several important areas of concern:

1. Program philosophy and definition of giftedness
2. Identification of target population
3. Services needed by target population
4. Curriculum to develop giftedness
5. Effects expected from program

The first needs assessment instruments should include queries about the community, perceptions of the definition of "giftedness" and the basic philosophy of the program.

Too often, we have seen program administrators begin with step 2. Many times, program administrators rush through the process of defining the program philosophy and definition of giftedness. They assume that everyone in the district has the same general philosophy that they do; they assume that everyone has a similar definition of giftedness. We have found, as Wholey did in his research, that determining agreement on general terms and definitions is the critical first step in program development and evaluation. When this step is skipped or hastily oversimplified, the whole program is at risk. It is hard to evaluate the effects of a program with no agreement on what the broad goals are to be. When basic definitions are clarified, understood, and accepted by all, the program will be a strong one. When needs are properly assessed, they can be adequately met.

In Chapter 5, you considered your own personal definition of giftedness. In this chapter, we ask you to go a step further. It is necessary to find out the definitions and philosophies of other important people who will be connected with your program. Then, as a group, you must reach a consensus and synthesize these ideas into one coherent statement of philosophy and definition of giftedness.

To gather pertinent and usable information, you will need to plan needs assessment instruments with clear and direct questions. We prefer the use of open-ended questions so that the respondent is allowed to give a full and complete answer to the question. An example of such a needs assessment instrument is in Figure 10.1. It gathers information about each of the five important aspects of program development listed above. To use or adapt it for your program, you would need to add appropriate headings for each group of people (i.e., parents, students, teachers) being assessed and modify the items accordingly.

When the initial needs assessment data has been collected, it must be collated, synthesized, and interpreted. There is no way to do this "objectively." Interpretation of results and the decisions about what to include and what to exclude in a new program are all judgment calls. The needs assessment data do, however, provide you with the information you need to make informed decisions about and for your particular district.

After a program has been successfully launched, the formal evaluation process turns from needs assessments to documentation of the actual population being served, the effectiveness of the services and learning experiences, and the perceptions of other impacts by various stakeholders. State guidelines must be addressed in such summative evaluations, if state funding of the program is granted. If so, the state will provide forms and directions for the collection of data that they require.

I. Program Philosophy and Definition of Giftedness
   A. How do you define giftedness?
   B. List ten adjectives that you believe describe the behaviors gifted people use.

   1.   6.
   2.   7.
   3.   8.
   4.   9.
   5.   10.

   C. Next to each of the following talent areas, tell us which you believe are already
      well served in our district through existing programs (write *Served*) and which are
      underserved (write *Under*)

   _____ Verbal
   _____ Math/Science/Problem/Solving
   _____ Visual Arts
   _____ Social/Leadership
   _____ Music
   _____ Mechanical/Technical Inventiveness

II. Identification of Target Population
    A. Do you agree with the use of quotas in the identification of students for our pro-
       gram? Why or why not?
    B. Do you believe in labeling the selected students "gifted students?" Why or why
       not?
    C. Do you agree with the use of standardized tests as the basis for a long-term identifi-
       cation of students for our program? Why or why not?
    D. Do you agree with the use of students' products as the basis for identification for
       a short term project?
    E. What other identification issues concern you?
III. Services Needed by Target Population
Select the three services that you believe to be the most important for our new program.

   _____ Counseling and guidance
   _____ Individual educational plans
   _____ Individual problem solving and investigative efforts
   _____ Group problem solving and investigative efforts
   _____ Accelerated courses
   _____ Mini courses or seminars on a variety of topics
   _____ Mentor-student relationship
   _____ Regional and statewide competitive events in talent area
   _____ Other _____
   _____ Other _____

IV. Curriculum to Develop Giftedness
Select the three curriculum goals that you consider to be most important for our program.

   _____ Math
   _____ Science
   _____ Reading, literature
   _____ Writing

Figure 10.1. Initial Needs Assessment Instrument

_____ Music
_____ Art
_____ Drama
_____ Leadership, social interaction
_____ Mechanical/Technical
_____ Interdisciplinary curriculum units
_____ Other _____
_____ Other _____

Which do you consider to be most beneficial: acceleration, enrichment, or independent study? Why?

V. Effects Expected from Program
   A. How will we know if our program is a success? What will you expect students to gain in terms of your definition of giftedness?
   B. What negative impacts would you expect to occur when we initiate our program? What can be done to minimize these?

Their requirements may address the same questions that Scriven raises regarding (1) the target population, (2) what the program did or accomplished, (3) how effective the program was.

A FIVE-YEAR EVALUATION PLAN

There are many important issues and elements in a program. To attempt to evaluate everything every year will result only in superficial information. A related concern is that if you choose to evaluate too many elements in a single year, you will be unable to act on them all effectively. Much of the information will sit unused in a file cabinet. For an already established program, you can schedule evaluations of various program elements on a rotating basis. By using a five-year rotation, for example, you could focus on evaluating one of the five major concerns addressed in Table 10.1 each year.

During the first year of the evaluation rotation, assess the community's agreement with the program philosophy and definition and the related questions about which talent areas to serve in the program. Even in a well-established program, these questions may help you discover new information about the talents and unmet needs of the students in your district. Act as soon as possible to refine your philosophy statements and reconsider the talent areas you serve based on the information you receive.

In the second year of the evaluation rotation, conduct needs assessments on identification issues. Act upon those as needed. During the third year, assess the service needs of your clientele. In the fourth year, reconsider curriculum issues. In the fifth year, try to uncover any unplanned effects and impacts of your program that may be undermining your best efforts.

The benefit of this five-year evaluation plan is that each year you can plan and carry out a well-organized and complete analysis of one important aspect of your

TABLE 10.1. A Five-Year Evaluation Plan

Year 1: Philosophy and Definition Issues
   A. Talent areas to be served
   B. Definition of giftedness or talent in each area

Year 2: Identification issues
   A. Target population
      1. Numbers served in each talent area
      2. Numbers served at each grade level
      3. Levels of ability or talent required to be admitted
      4. Criteria for selection established or reviewed
      5. Instruments and other procedures reviewed
   B. Identification of inequity issues among nontarget population

Year 3: Services
   A. Types of services
   B. Quantity of services
   C. Quality of services
   D. Variety of services
   E. Relative costs of services
   F. Satisfaction with services

Year 4: Curriculum Issues
   A. Acceleration, enrichment, or independent study
   B. Curriculum areas
   C. Curriculum goals and objectives
   D. Appropriateness of instructional strategies

Year 5: Effects and Impacts
   A. Planned effects for each talent area served
   B. Unplanned impacts

program. This is a manageable task and the information you receive each year can be acted on to improve that program area.

As our plan suggests, every five years it is important to reconsider and update old decisions. Even the basic questions of philosophy and definitions should be reexamined every five years in light of changes in the community, new personnel, revised board policies, and the most current research.

Identification issues need to be reexamined the following year because they should be directly related to the philosophy and definition statements. In year 2, it is vital to reassess whom your program is serving, and how students are selected. Gather data that show exactly which children are being served by the program. Are there any glaring inequities in the identification procedures? Do children stay in the program or is there a significant dropout rate? Carefully consider whether the real data are congruent with the program's definition of giftedness.

In year 3, consider anew the types of services offered in the program. Conduct a new needs assessment that focuses on the clients' perceptions of these services. Are the types of services offered the same ones the client wants? Are they offered in sufficient quantity to actually bring about a desired effect? Too often gifted programs are offered only a few hours per week. Is this adequate? Is it worth the cost? When you ask these questions, you may find a wide range of responses, but the information can be put to use in order to better serve your clients.

In year 4, reconsider all curriculum issues. Are there other programs in the district that duplicate your curriculum? Are there gaps still unfilled? Should curricula be better connected to the regular program? A complete rewrite of the curriculum goals and objectives will have the effect of revitalizing your program and giving a renewed sense of ownership and interest in the program to the teachers (especially new teachers) who deliver the program to the students.

In year 5, we suggest that you look at longitudinal effects. Collect data from tests, observations, checklists, product evaluations, and other methods of assessing student performance and growth. How do students in the program compare with those who are not in the program? How do students in one part of the program compare with those in another? During this year, also conduct a survey of those outside the program to discover what, if any, unexpected impacts the program has on the school community. Perhaps you will discover that it has a positive impact on the resale of homes in the area. Or perhaps you will find that it causes both identified and unidentified children to seek counseling because of the effects of being labeled "gifted" or "not gifted."

Answers to hard questions like these will lead you to make needed revisions that will make your program stronger and better respected each year. They will also lead you right back to the beginning: you will be well prepared in the following year to reexamine the fundamental issues of philosophy and definition based on your findings regarding actual effects and impacts.

Finally, it is important to consider the need for reliable evaluation reports of gifted programming on the larger field of education. Evaluation is a form of action research. Research on the effects of gifted programs is vitally needed. We encourage you to share the evaluation studies you conduct with others at conferences and in articles. As Cronbach contends, the purpose of evaluation is twofold: to improve our own program and, at the same time, to advance the thinking and knowledge base of the field itself.

OPPORTUNITY FOR DISCUSSION AND ACTION: EVALUATION SIMULATION

Divide the class into groups of eight members each. Given the following roles and conditions, participate in an end-of-the-year evaluation discussion of a gifted program:

Roles:

Gifted program director: Moderates group, asks questions
School principal: Represents others on faculty as well as own ideas
Teacher of the gifted program: Enjoys teaching the program but worries about the reactions of others
Classroom teacher: Is annoyed by having students taken out of her class
Parent A: Is very supportive of these first efforts
Parent B: Is very critical

Student in verbal program: Wants more services
Student in math program: Thinks it's a waste of time

Conditions:

You are all in the same school district, but each of you has a different stake in the district's gifted program. You have been brought together by the gifted program director to help evaluate the first year of the program.

It is a pull-out program for fourth, fifth, and sixth graders. The identification system is a combination of general intellectual ability and achievement. Students are selected using a matrix. No one has ever talked about the philosophy or definition of giftedness very much. The identification system has borrowed from a neighboring district that has had a program for a number of years.

Twenty students with the highest scores in reading and verbal ability are in a Great Books Program that meets once a week for 90 minutes. These children are pulled out of gym, math, science, and reading to take part.

Twenty students are taking a math and problem-solving course that meets once a week for 90 minutes. They are studying graphs, statistics, probability, and logic.

All 40 students meet with the resource teacher together once a week for 50 minutes to work on creative thinking, higher-level thinking skills, and critical thinking activities.

Task:

After 10–15 minutes of role playing, discuss the experiences as a class. Determine what you would do if you were the gifted program director or teacher in that situation.

What would you plan for a more complete evaluation of the program?

REFERENCES

Cronbach, L. 1982. *Designing evaluations of educational and social programs.* San Francisco: Jossey-Bass.

Guba, E., and Y. Lincoln. 1981. *Effective evaluation.* San Francisco: Jossey-Bass.

Patton, M. 1982. *Practical evaluation.* Beverly Hills, Calif.: Sage Publications.

Scriven, M. 1980. *The logic of evaluation.* Inverness, Calif.: Edgepress.

Wholey, J. 1983. *Evaluation and effective public management.* Boston: Little, Brown.

CHAPTER 11

Current Issues in Gifted Education

The following discussion was overheard at a seminar on college selection at a high school.

> **Boy A:** I guess I'll major in business. That's where the money is. If I can get into Harvard's graduate school, I've got it made.
>
> **Girl A:** Business, I never thought you'd be interested in that. All through high school, you've enjoyed the music programs more than anything.
>
> **Boy A:** Well, enjoyment isn't going to pay the bills. I've got to be sensible about my future.
>
> **Girl B:** I know what you mean. I'm planning on law school even though part of me would love to teach kindergarten.
>
> **Girl C:** Yes, teaching school was OK for our mothers, but we almost have an obligation to do something more prestigious because we've been in the gifted program since fourth grade.
>
> **Boy B:** Too bad we didn't ever talk about careers in that program. It was fun, but now what? I got to build that robot in eighth grade and ever since I've wanted to be an inventor, but what type of college program can help me with that goal?
>
> **Girl C:** You're right. The best part of the gifted program for me was writing and producing our own plays, but now how do I make that pay?
>
> **Boy C:** It's confusing, all right. Sometimes I wish we'd never had that program. It was great to be involved in all those extra projects, but someone who wasn't in the program and concentrated on the regular courses got valedictorian, not me.

WHAT DO YOU THINK?

1. How do our cultural values affect the mission and goals of gifted education?
2. How can gifted programs include material on career education?
3. How can gifted programs help children resolve difficult values decisions regarding their life work and the use of their special talents?
4. What types of programs can best serve children whose talents lie in fields such as mechanics, carpentry, and other skills associated with vocational education?
5. Do morals and values educational programs have a place in gifted education?

INTRODUCTION

Educational programs are planned, implemented, and evaluated within a given culture. The mores of the culture are thoroughly embedded in every program decision. Currently, American values define success in terms of money, prestige, power, and material possessions. Because of this, we, as a culture, tend to define "giftedness" in those terms as well.

The child who is seen as the most talented is the one whose goal is to get to the top of a prestigious field in business, athletics, or the entertainment industry. Children with interests in vocational areas or other nonprestigious occupations, including teaching, are usually not viewed as "gifted."

Educators need to be concerned with the difficult choices and circumstances that face young people when they graduate from our schools and gifted programs. Are we adequately preparing them to choose satisfying careers? Are we limiting their choices to a few "prestigious" careers or are we encouraging them to examine their strengths and talents in terms of a wide variety of careers and vocations? Have we given our students sufficient learning experiences to equip them to make wise and thoughtful values decisions? We introduce in this chapter several educational issues that are related to the whole-life education and life satisfaction of the children we teach. We encourage you to consider ways that you can extend your gifted programs to include (1) career education, (2) vocational education, and (3) morals/values education.

CAREER AND VOCATIONAL EDUCATION

Talent is no guarantee of success in life. Many bright children have developed bad habits that dwarf their ability to transfer knowledge and skill to real-life circumstances. This conclusion by researchers investigating the achievement of adults with high IQs throws to the winds the myth that talented people can fend for themselves. "IQ and success in living have little to do with each other," commented Seymour Epstein, a psychologist at the University of Massachusetts (quoted in Goleman 1988). Epstein developed a test measuring "constructive thinking," and found that academically bright children tend to withdraw from challenges that seem dubious. They lack a realism about success (i.e., they exaggerate their ability or lack thereof), and have trouble avoiding self-destructive thought patterns.

Accumulating evidence that promising young children are not always self-sufficient achievers has strong implications for gifted educators and others, who have assumed major roles as caretakers of the nation's talent. Meeting the needs of children with special talents is one of the major justifications for the gifted movement. That many of these children are teetering on the edge of frustration and disillusionment with life rocks the foundation of programs that do not include some form of career education in the curriculum.

More than a quarter of the adult respondents in a study conducted by Post-Kammer and Perrone (1983) said that high school had not prepared them to make any career decisions, and many had no clue as to how their interests or talents related to career possibilities. The children who have the ability to make valuable contributions cannot cope with the realities of their work environments, cannot decide what they want to do or how to research possible avenues for their interests, habitually shy away from challenges that promise no immediate success, and fear the consequences of not deferring to the expectations of others.

The gap between school and the real world, felt intuitively by many children, widens as academia continues to emphasize a linear value of success that ill prepares them for larger life and work issues. From 1970 to the present, approximately 32 career education programs have responded to the demand for better preparation for the world beyond the classroom. This number is minute, however, compared to the abundance of programs that focus on other needs of talented students (Hagen 1982). The importance of career education is still not recognized by the gifted movement, with most of the literature still focusing on identification and instructional methodology. Some find the notion of career education demeaning, especially in relation to talented students, whom they prefer to think of as more self-sufficient than they actually are. For many educators, no consensus has been reached on what "career" means. Definitions range from broad life issues to narrowly specific occupations, and this discrepancy diffuses the impact that career education research could have in the field.

The shift between these two extremes in definition need not be confusing, however. Those who view life as a career must come to grips with the specific kinds of information talented children will need to explore their options. Those who view occupation as career will have to consider the negative impact of self-concept, stereotyping, and societal expectations on career development. "In an effort to maximize the advantages and minimize the difficulties of both extreme definitions, an intermediate position can be taken, such as that in which career is defined in terms of work" (Hoyt and Hebeler 1974, p. 161). Career education should embrace children's needs for more constructive ways of thinking, as well as provide experiences that expose them to specific career possibilities. Arguing over semantics (i.e., the precise definition and purpose of career education) will not help educators to know what to do with a specific group of children in a given program. To avoid this potential confusion, educators can investigate the special needs of talented children as a class for career education, and within that framework also examine the individual needs. Sensitivity to individual needs will keep programs from the triviality or vagueness characteristic of generic responses.

What Are the Special Needs of Talented Children in Career Education?

The need of talented children most often cited in the literature is direction. Because they excel in many areas, these children have trouble deciding where to focus their efforts (Hoyt and Hebeler 1974; Kerr 1981; Post-Kammer and Perrone 1983). Young people agonize over choices for a variety of reasons: they feel torn between two or more equally strong passions; they waiver between doing what others expect of them and acting on their own personal aspirations; they see no alternative to narrowing their focus by excluding all but one option; they accept the stereotypes associated with certain occupations (e.g., male careers, minority careers, vocational careers). These children need guidance and encouragement, but not the kind of guidance that eliminates creative possibilities. One young girl found her own solution to the perplexing problem of choice: "I don't expect to settle down to one occupation and make that the primary interest in life. . . . I may be earning my living doing biochemical research and writing a novel at the same time—or formulating my theory of education while writing a newspaper article on politics. . . . I am not of the opinion that narrowing my fields of endeavor is a good thing—at least not at this time" (quoted in Hoyt and Hebeler 1974, p. 114).

This girl is a rare exception to the general rule. Unlike many able young children, she managed to wrench herself free from the burdensome expectations of others, but without relinquishing her sense of responsibility. Many less fortunate young people have surrendered themselves to adult or peer supremacy before they started, simply because the consequences of a hearty resistance seemed too unbearable. Our society has unusually high expectations of talented children, and an investment in their success which these children feel (Kerr 1981). One young boy reported: "As far as my career is concerned, I know that I have various obligations and duties which must be completed" (quoted in Hoyt and Hebeler 1974, p. 119). The distortion that pressure produces on children's sense of their own worth and future can warp their self-expression permanently (Zorman 1987). To avoid this outcome requires specific and consistent attention. Torrance (1983) believes that one of the world's greatest tragedies can be found in the lives of talented children "who never find the courage to walk away from the games that others want to play, when these games are not really theirs" (p. 74).

Another social pressure molding young people's career choices is the ever-present stereotype. Without much trouble, we can find ample opinion supporting notions such as these: women should not tamper with advanced mathematics; men should not stay home with the children; minorities would do better to stick with vocational education because vocational courses are designed for the less able (a double stereotype); divergent thinkers should consider the arts and convergent thinkers the sciences. Within the gifted population are many who cannot choose how they live their lives unless they receive enough support to overcome these and similar stereotypical notions about the fields that are open to them.

Women in mathematics are a case in point. Many girls withdraw from any math courses that extend beyond the required level (Wilson 1982). Studies reported by Kerr (1981, p. 10) show women still fighting the old bias against female achievement in the work world or, in too many cases, not fighting at all. A similar stereotyping confronts disadvantaged and/or minority students who have a versatile talent for career development but a low self-esteem and lack of family and peer support (Moore 1978). In fact, the communities of many disadvantaged but talented students see the professional interests of their children as alienating (Hagen 1982).

Other less obvious victims of societal pressures and expectations are the conformist and the nonconformist talented child. The conformist fears failure and therefore abruptly dismisses any career possibility that does not promise success. When Nowakowska studied Polish scientists who feared failure he found that they "were likely to advance their careers through attacking simple or trivial problems" (quoted in Kerr 1981, p. 8). Conforming children can easily trivialize their talents by overemphasizing the need for security, and this predisposition will prevent them from feeling satisfied with any achievement or career decision. The nonconforming talented child, on the other hand, often chooses a path so idiosyncratic that it becomes virtually impossible to guide him. This, too, has its problems. Though he asks for no advice or approval, he is in great danger of wandering off the path into a wilderness, unless someone intervenes. The nonconforming or creative child needs structure and discipline to achieve the creative and frequently untraditional goals he cherishes (Hagen 1982).

Perhaps one of the most severely neglected populations is the talented child in vocational education. The reason is simple: vocational education has a "bad name" (Lewis 1988). Children who attend vocational classes do so only because they cannot master an academic course of study, or so claim those prone to intellectual snobbery and elitism. In this way, "vocational" has become synonymous with "less able," even in the face of evidence that high-level work in the occupational clusters demands a mastery unattainable by mediocre thinkers (Milne and Lindekugel 1976). Ample data on career counseling for gifted children show that parents and educators rarely expose them to vocational options, and in many cases practically force them to go to college (Milne 1982). Children whose gifts lie along the lines of vocational study have no recourse from the frustration they experience in a program that does not interest them. Many of this neglected group drop out of school altogether.

How Has Career/Vocational Education Responded to These Needs?

Children love to work on real problems. Nothing thrills a young person more than to be entrusted with a challenge involving real-life circumstances. An article in the *Chicago Sun-Times* (1987) recounts the experience of a 15-year-old who, in addition to maintaining his honors status as a freshman in high school, managed to complete 75 hours of the required classroom training as a tax preparer. During the peak season, he averaged 50 hours a week on returns for actual clients. His high school English teacher said that he studied doubly hard to keep his grades up while doing this intensive course, and that he was "a perfect example of our not giving young people enough credit for what they can actually accomplish." A sixth-grade child who couldn't stay out of trouble, according to an article in the *Christian Science Monitor* (1984), one day decided to respond to an ad for a playwriting contest. That year and the next, the Children's Radio Theatre in Washington, D.C., conferred the coveted prize on his literary efforts, thus changing his status from bored troublemaker into a bona fide playwright.

Samples of real-life occupations give talented children a vision of the future that inspires and heartens them. The students mentioned above gained a sense of direction that children confined to the classroom and isolated from the world do not have. Promising young people often lack a realistic sense of themselves and their talents because achievement has never occurred outside the fabricated walls of school. With no reference point, how can they know what to do outside these walls? They need reality testing, practical experience, and counselors and mentors who will support their individual needs and interests in life.

Most career education programs provide experiences with actual professions in one or more of the following forms: mentorships, internships, courses specifically focused on application (rather than theory), work sessions at occupational sites (e.g., laboratories, newspapers, etc.), and/or extensive contact with artists or scientists in residence. Programs also address the individual counseling needs of students, and many structure concrete activities for constructive self-examination and identification of personal priorities and values. In these ways, students distinguish between their own interests and those adopted in response to expectations of adults and peers. For many children, career education saves them from the fatal mistake of sacrificing their lives for other people's dreams.

Current career education programs vary in length from short, intensive encounters with the work world to longer, year-round efforts, and they also vary in the way they target different populations and occupational interests. These differences reflect the particular needs of specific populations, as well as the philosophy adopted by program staff, and thus provide a valuable choice of alternatives to people who are sensitive to the particular interests and aspirations of different children.

The current efforts are limited, however, by the fact that too few educators are aware of the broader implications of career development in all grade levels and subject areas. These efforts would accomplish more against a widespread background of career awareness and education in the gifted field. But thus far, the profound changes anticipated for the whole educational system as a result of a new career education thrust have not occurred (Hagen 1982). Except for several pockets of informed and committed groups, the gifted education field as a whole is not fully awake to the need for career-oriented teaching and counseling. Those who are awake see the danger of adding yet another movement in gifted education that will ignore the importance of synthesizing program efforts and addressing the individual child. "What is needed is an emphasis on the synthesis of existing programs and on individualizing instruction beyond that which is given in the regular school program. Never before has attention to the individual as a person been so imperative" (Milne and Lindekugel 1976, p. 3).

While the future of career and vocational education programs for talented students remains undefined, the precedent set by efforts we have described has already increased educators' sensitivity to the unique challenges faced by children approaching the world of work. Special awareness of the double challenge faced by talented students from sub-populations, including women, have also resulted in pioneering efforts that can inform future programs. For example, a 1979 project sponsored by Case Western Reserve University, called "Project Choice: Creating Her Options in Career Education" for talented adolescent women, expanded career choices by confronting personal and cultural restrictions over a 14-week period (Kerr 1981). A program designed to reverse the stereotypes about women in science and math careers offered a three-month course to talented girls taught by women (Fox 1976, as reported in Kerr 1981).

Programs for talented disadvantaged and/or minority students have also taken into account the importance of career development. In Project '86, '87, and '88, an ongoing program for talented urban and suburban sixth through tenth graders, Smutny organized sessions throughout the school year for children from all backgrounds to consider the lifestyles and work realities of various occupations. She found the cultural mix an asset to the process. When urban minority students took courses and considered career possibilities in the company of suburban bankers' sons or daughters, they experienced an equality that they would not have felt by themselves. Another program, the Professional Career Exploration Program for Minority and/or Low Income, Gifted and Talented 10th Grade Students (PCEP), which functioned out of two schools in Indiana, involved tenth grade students in active experiences at work sites; close analyses of professional lifestyles, values, and goals; and extensive evaluation of limiting self-concepts, stereotyping, and peer pressures (Moore 1978). Both programs encouraged students to eliminate racial stereotypes in planning the future.

Many career-oriented programs concentrate on specific subject areas such as the arts and sciences. They take various forms, from specialized schools like Interlochen Arts Academy, the High School for Performing Arts in New York, or the Bronx High School of Science, to an assorted variety of intensive workshops such as the career awareness program developed by the Gifted Child Study Group at Johns Hopkins University for the mathematically inclined (Kerr 1981, p. 22), a program at Harvard University involving 60 talented students in advanced instruction by scientists and extensive laboratory work (Hoyt and Hebeler 1974, p. 218), or the project initiated by the Explorer's Club that invites 42 children gifted in the natural sciences to participate in on-site expeditions in archeology, geology, volcanology, and glaciology (p. 222). Programs like these give students who know what interests them firsthand experience in the application of science or mathematics or, in the case of the arts, extensive exposure to the modes of self-expression, production, and performance. The narrow focus of these efforts allows students to examine their subject area in depth.

Innovative responses to a broad spectrum of student needs has given thoughtful program directors useful insights, the most valuable being that they do not have to confine their efforts to any established structure. The difference between programs is primarily a difference of goals. Nash, Borman, and Colson (1980), for example, have refined their own model for senior high school students that attacks the problem of multiple abilities and the dearth of hands-on experiences in many subject areas. The three-phase model provides a guidance laboratory experience, mentorship, and working internships, and is a viable plan for school districts seeking a manageable and affordable solution to the career needs of their most talented students. Perhaps the most expansive program has come out of the Guidance Institute for Talented Students (Kerr 1981, p. 20), which focuses on self-awareness, social planning, and specific plans of action for investigating career options. So far, 3600 talented ninth through twelfth graders have participated. The Artists-in-Schools Program and others like it can make a large dent in the career awareness of children living in isolated rural areas (Yeatts 1980). Novelist-actress Margaret Hill Ritter spent a whole year teaching writing, production, editing, and dramatic presentation and investigating career options for the fledgling writers in her classes. The "Ecternship" Program for gifted high school science students (Anderson 1982) offers an alternative to the scheduling problems inherent in many internship programs. The project expands science curriculum and matches each student with an appropriate "ecternship" sponsor such as a lab technician, geneticist, or veterinarian, but does so within the limits of a more traditional classroom setting. The Executive Intern Program in Hillsborough County, Florida, allows talented high school students to spend a semester with a senior official in government, an educational or cultural institution, a social service organization, or any other organization committed to the public interest (Hoyt and Hebeler 1974, p. 229). Leadership, sensitivity, maturity, and creative thinking ability qualify selected young people for experiences that will expose them to management, executive decision making, budget concerns, and company policies.

A few adventurous projects have taken bold steps to help the talented child in vocational education. Since few people believe that talent can be found in such dubious ground, much of the literature has taken pains to document its existence and society's stolid refusal to recognize the needs of vocationally gifted children. It is simply not prestigious to pursue vocational subjects. According to a startling report in *Education Week* (Welch 1988), Taiwan has seven vocational schools for every academic one, to accommodate the training needs of 70 percent of the school population there. The reverse of this phenomenon seems to be the pattern in the United States, in spite of the fact that 80 percent of all jobs require advanced training in vocational subjects. Advanced technology needs advanced thinkers, but it will not get them unless talented children have the option to pursue another course besides academia. "At the very heart of our problem is a national attitude that says vocational education is designed for somebody else's children. . . . We have promoted the idea that the only good education is an education capped by four years of college" (National Advisory Council on Vocational Education First Annual Report 1969, as quoted in Milne 1982, p. 5).

Forecasting the special demands of this population, Milne (1982) concludes that vocational education for talented students will have to develop clear identification measures beyond the academic ones currently in use, design exploration experiences that expose children to a variety of careers, and train teachers to individualize instruction to challenge the abilities of students. Gustafson (1979) describes Project Sting, a Vermont program that invited 75 gifted eighth graders to a living and learning environment that gave them practical vocational experiences related to six career areas: Automotive Cluster, Building Trades Cluster, Communications/Electronics Cluster, Culinary Arts Cluster, Graphics/Photography Cluster, and Health Careers Cluster. In the building trade section, for example, students constructed a two-room portion of a house, including a bathroom. Giving able children work experiences that capitalize on their problem-solving and divergent thinking abilities will open the door to a whole new world of opportunity for those children (Milne and Lindekugel 1976). Programs for gifted vocational students should include individualized instruction, long time periods for experimenting and testing ideas, and freedom from teaching techniques that stifle or inhibit creativity.

How Can Career Educators Help Talented Students Think Creatively about Work?

A great philosopher named Snoopy once said, "Work is the crabgrass in the lawn of life" (quoted in Hoyt and Hebeler 1974, p. 61). Many people would agree. Because students approaching the work world may shudder at the prospect of a life of boredom, quiet resignation, or frustration, Smutny (1982) developed "Job Creation,'' a program with extensive materials, activities, and teaching strategies that address these concerns. Class activities, imaginative exercises, and personal inventories engage children's creative potential in developing a future career. Job Creation encourages students to consider entrepreneurial options, as well as innovative strategies for creating one's own job within an established profession.

For students who find certain fields too limited for their broader scope, Job Creation unravels a whole other possible scenario in lieu of the narrow, prescriptive ones offered by a linear sense of career options. Smutny's project represents a growing trend to involve the personal and creative interests of students in the process of gaining extensive, practical exposure to a variety of real life work settings. Entrepreneurship, in the earliest stages of our country's development, allowed creative people to respond to economic needs by originating new solutions through invention, experimentation, and production. Back then, individuals followed their creative impulses, acted on their truest ideals and interests, and benefited their communities. Today, education literature treats personal desires separately from the needs of society because they have become separate. Hagen (1982) raises this issue when she comments: ''The idea of career planning raises two questions: Should the planning be guided by what is known about job opportunities? Is the idea of planning ahead for the roles one will take in life appropriate in view of the fact that change seems to be the only modern constant?'' (p. 49). Most of us approach career with the notion of a limited number of slots in each profession, and either an overabundance or a dearth of bodies to fill those preestablished slots. Job Creation asks students to consider the option of creating their own place and filling it.

Smutny divided the project materials into six modules:

1. Identifying personal skills and their relationship to Job Creation
2. Identifying Job Creation opportunities in the community
3. Planning and organizing in Job Creation: selecting goals, determining directions, and organizing and taking a course of action
4. Taking steps of Job Creation: involvement, communicating, risk taking, accomplishing, task performance
5. Evaluation and assessment: assessing one's self and one's readiness for involvement in entrepreneurship, starting and developing new ideas
6. Audio cassette of music: eleven songs; worksheets for teachers and students to complement the first five modules of materials

The emphasis on creativity and originality has helped many high school students to reconsider their visions of the future. The sticky situations described in case histories and minibiographies and confronted in role playing, inventories, assessments, and checklists draw on all areas of career and vocational education, and serve students from all backgrounds. Projecting themselves into the future, students can involve themselves in the unique challenges associated with starting a new business, for example. They consider three basic ways to organize their business and problem-solve the relative merits of each form of organization. This sort of preparation transforms work from desiccated ''crabgrass'' to lush green lawns.

Career education is serious business. Children sense this and assume an appropriate pose. Unfortunately, in adopting the work-oriented values of society, they lose the joy and play of life, and never fall in love with a dream of the future they can recognize as their own (Torrance 1983). This tragic loss in creativity is reflected in the drastic drop in patents issued to U.S. residents, which reached a low ebb in the late 1970s (Michaels, as reported in Torrance 1980). The situation continues to worsen. "What part do play, joy, celebration, and creativity hold in the values of a work-oriented society?" asks Hagen (1982, p. 50).

When Torrance (1980) conducted a 22-year longitudinal study of creative children and traced the paths they followed, he found that many of them felt they had wasted much energy by "playing the games that others have presented, rather than using their own creative strengths" (p. 158). Children need to fall in love with their dreams, but adult society will not let them. The implication of Torrance's study is that our country is pouring its most vital creative resource down the drain. To stop this trend, he concludes, adults can do most by helping these children to "play their own games and to engineer their lives so that they have a chance to do just this— play their own games in their own way, being the very best of whatever they are" (p. 159). He also offers some jewels of wisdom that every counselor, teacher, or parent could use for a troubled or confused child (1983, p. 78):

1. Don't be afraid to fall in love with something and pursue it with intensity and depth.
2. Know, understand, take pride in, practice, develop, use, exploit, and enjoy your greatest strengths.
3. Learn to free yourself from the expectations of others and to walk away from the games that others try to impose upon you. Free yourself to "play your own game" in such a way as to make good use of your gifts. Search out and cultivate great teachers or mentors who will help you accomplish these things.
4. Don't waste a lot of expensive energy trying to do things for which you have little ability or love. Do what you can do well and what you love, giving freely of the infinity of your greatest strengths and most intense loves.

VALUES/MORAL EDUCATION

What Values and Morals Are Prized by Our Culture?

Robert McFarlane, a national security adviser in the Reagan Administration, made a startling confession about his dramatically publicized suicide attempt to the *New York Times*. He admitted to having invested so much of himself in his work that it eventually became the only indicator of his worth as a person (Black 1988). Driven to camouflage his real feelings and intuitions, he early learned, like many talented and sensitive children, the consequences of not obeying adult dictates of super-achievement and success.

Carefully skirting issues of morality and values, our culture has spawned a new breed of talented achievers who follow an ethic of workaholism and moral vacuity.

Children today often seek their fortunes with an almost puritanical austerity, the same value system that kept anyone from noticing that McFarlane's excessive preoccupation with work was abnormal. No one noticed because the problem has become the norm for many people, particularly the high-achieving, talented young. As psychoanalyst Alice Miller (1981) points out, children who scurry around to perpetuate others' admiration for them early discover that it is their qualities that make them lovable, rather than the people they are. These children are continually dogged by a latent suspicion that life ultimately holds no meaning for them. "These dark feelings will come to the fore as soon as the drug of grandiosity fails, as soon as they are not 'on top,' not definitely the 'superstar,' or whenever they suddenly get the feeling they failed to live up to some ideal image and measure they feel they must adhere to" (Miller 1981, p. 6).

How Do We Fill the Moral Vacuum?

Today's critics have much to say about the moral vacuum created by a confluence of several dominant trends: advanced technology with little thought for sticky ethical issues, the legacy of moral relativism and meaninglessness bequeathed to young people by the "values clarification" of the 1960s and 1970s, the disintegration of the home, and the neutral pose officially adopted by the schools on moral and values issues in the curriculum.

There are no easy solutions to today's moral problems. Regret over the rebellion of the 1960s and 1970s has made some observers reminisce over the days when children were good and families stayed together, but nostalgia oversimplifies the complex tangle of moral dilemmas that children have to face today. What are we doing to prepare young scientists, for example, for the unavoidable ethical questions involved in genetic engineering, where a new life form such as the celebrated Harvard mouse can so easily reawake the conflict between intellectual ambition and moral sensibility? How are we helping young actors distinguish between roles that constructively inform, and roles that exploit and demean them? More specifically, as Robert Townsend, the black actor, writer, and producer, implicitly asks in his movie *The Hollywood Shuffle,* how can black performers learn to refuse the roles that stereotype them as pimps, whores, gang members, butlers, or slaves when producing companies tempt them with visions of fame and money? Townsend's movie provides an intimate view of the profound difficulties facing young people, and the kind of courage, self-respect, and values required to resist the easy sellout. In an article called "Restore Ethics as Partner to Intellect" Robert Baker (1987) pinpoints the mistake of emphasizing the mastery of factual information without confronting the questions of meaning and significance.

The problem with nostalgia is that it encourages simplistic notions of both the problem outlined above and its solution. The "back to basics" movement, for example, suggested that all we needed to do to get Johnny reading again was to return to the old routine, forgetting the stultifying methodology that made learning limp and lifeless. The "either/or" approach to moral education offers little room for any but a most superficial treatment of the issues. We suggest that, for talented young people especially, the solution does not lie in resurrecting old forms or in castigating present ones, but in evolving new ways to fill a vacuum created by tossing out the old system. Rather than revert to "back to basic values," talented children need to move "forward" to an ethical sensibility that will help them handle difficult issues at a complex level.

What Is Worth Valuing?

Due to their inherent complexity, human morality issues have always fostered considerable debate. Hence the need, as never before, to confront the issues squarely, rather than avoid them. Values clarification took the moral education of the 1950s to task for its authoritarian and punitive structure, which devalued children's individual insights, intuitions, and feelings. The indoctrination of moralistic sentiments does not lessen the confusion of moral issues that children confront today. "What the world needs is not more closed-minded zealots eager to remake the world in their image but more morally committed rational persons with respect for and insight into the moral judgments and perspectives of others, those least likely to confuse pseudo-with genuine morality" (Paul 1988, p. 11).

By focusing on the process of moral judgment, rather than assigning value to particular judgments and forcing these on children, values clarification tried to restore a sense of worth to individual thought and feeling. Articles on the "hidden curriculum" questioned the role traditionally assumed by schools as perpetrators of "social control" (Vallance 1973). What kinds of people were these institutions creating? From the point of view of the 1980s, values clarification seems at best a naive experiment, but the intentions of Raths, Kirschenbaum, and others was to establish freedom of choice and to encourage that choice through a conscious mental process. Raths (1976) placed children's ideas and interests at the center of the values clarification process, rather than at the periphery.

The consideration of students' cognition of moral issues arose out of the need to address social and political circumstances with something more than blind obedience to absolute principles. Values clarification proponents felt that to surmount the baffling circumstances of the 1960s and 1970s, children had to learn how to think critically. The charge that the values clarification system causes an egocentric, laissez-faire attitude has some validity. But those who formulated it were not interested in producing moral vacuums. Kirschenbaum (1976) specifically addresses the charge of moral relativity, citing the system's central concern for both the personal and social consequences of students' moral positions.

Many critics remain unconvinced on this score. Lockwood (1975) maintains that a system of values education focusing exclusively on the child's preferences and opinions ultimately creates a distorted sense of morality. Despite what Simon or Raths or Kirschenbaum might say, others like Colby (1975) cannot see how to avoid the fuzzy line between a tolerance for different viewpoints, and the assumption that all viewpoints are justifiable, which is the relativist's creed. Critics feel that values clarification does not extend far enough beyond personal opinion or whim to make the distinction between choosing values (which is a difficult and complex process) and choosing objects (which is largely a process of locating preference) (Stewart 1975).

The debate over these issues continues, and, in the midst of it, talented children must decipher the problems and develop their own strategy for finding meaning and value. How can they hope to mold a value system that transcends both the moral relativism and the moral absolutism represented in this arena? To help children grapple with these complexities constructively, C. June Maker (1982) developed a teaching model specifically designed for gifted students. She based her model largely on Kohlberg's research on moral development, conducted in the 1960s, in which he sought to understand the changes in moral reasoning that take place as children mature cognitively. On a philosophical basis, he disagreed both with indoctrination and ethical relativity as viable starting points for values education.

The assumption of certain fundamental, universal ethical principles such as the sanctity of life, for example, underlies Kohlberg's formulation of six distinct stages of moral growth. These stages represent a progressive human development toward a more sophisticated level of thinking and reasoning that enable children to see the value of certain universal principles and make decisions accordingly. Briefly stated, Kohlberg's stages are: (1) orientation to punishment and reward; (2) hedonistic orientation with an instrumental view of human relations; (3) "good boy" orientation where morality is defined by individual ties of relationship; (4) orientation to authority, law, and duty to maintain a fixed order; (5) social contact orientation emphasizing equality and mutual obligation within a democratic order; and (6) morality of individual principles of conscience based on such universals as respecting the rights of others.

To foster the development of moral thinking and reasoning in gifted children, Maker relies on Kohlberg's presentation of moral dilemmas which he designed for class discussion. Although not specifically created with talented students in mind, the format of these dilemmas requires children to engage in problem solving to work through moral questions. His six-step sequence follows: (1) present the dilemma; (2) have students clarify the facts of the situation and identify the issues involved; (3) have students identify a tentative position on the action the central character should take and state one or two reasons for that position; (4) divide the class into small groups (for further discussion of their positions, a particularly useful strategy for shy students); (5) reconvene the class for a full class discussion of the dilemma; and (6) ask students to reevaluate their original positions individually. Teachers who use Kohlberg's model for gifted students can make adjustments in content and process to challenge those who work on a more abstract level of reasoning. Maker recommends, for example, incorporating Taba's process model Resolution of Conflict Strategy into Kohlberg's moral dilemmas to achieve a design for values exploration more suitable for talented students.

Children who fear authority and punishment for most of their lives have little chance of becoming independent thinkers, or of contributing to others in valuable ways. This is the conclusion of Piagetian theory which, if applied to many gifted children today, would probably find more examples of heteronomy (governed by someone else) than autonomy (governed by oneself). Kamil (1984) finds an illustration of the difference between the two in the Watergate case: Elliott Richardson's refusal to obey Nixon and his subsequent resignation exemplified the morality of autonomy, while those who went along with what they knew to be a lie acted on the morality of heteronomy. Children with special talents will face many situations where the moral issue will force them to make crucial decisions. Being gifted does not assume that one will contribute constructively to others. In fact, many of the worst perpetrators of injustice were once gifted children—young people with extraordinary abilities in leadership, creativity, and reasoning who simply used their powers to exploit and abuse others.

Are Developmental Theories of Morality Final?

In spite of all the postbehaviorist research on moral development, many questions remain unanswered. Perhaps the greatest danger lying ahead is in responding formulaically to something we understand so little. So far, we have done just that. The puritanical approach inspired fear more than moral sensibility. Values clarification tried to break the tyranny of a reward-and-punishment morality but introduced its own kind of tyranny. Kohlberg's developmental theories and "moral dilemmas" by themselves also exert a form of authoritarianism, restrict what we can notice in children, and ignore other moral questions. For example, Gilligan (1979) challenged Kohlberg's stage theory on the grounds that all his studies researched the behavior and reasoning of boys, not girls. Girls' values, Gilligan claims, center around the issue of "care" rather than "justice," which explains why female subjects fail to develop according to Kohlberg's system. Gilligan noticed that "the morality of rights differs from the morality of responsibility in its emphasis on separation rather than attachment, in its consideration of the individual rather than the relationship as primary . . ." (p. 222).

One little girl acted in complete defiance of Kohlbergian theory of development. Coles (1986) describes the moral fortitude of a young black girl, one of the first to attend an all-white school. Neither her background, educational or economic, nor her age entitled her to be what she was: a compassionate and understanding child who had the courage to walk into that school every day amidst sneering, spitting crowds and not hate them in return. Coles describes his efforts to "explain" her behavior pedagogically through the eyes of developmental theory and psychological cause and effect, but admits he was unable to do so.

In trying to help talented young people in their struggle with moral issues, we should be willing, at any moment, to change our minds, to admit that perhaps there are things we do not yet know about any given moral question, but are willing to investigate in working with children. Instead of reminiscing over the "good old days," which were not, on second thought, so good, or condemning what we think were the decadent 1960s, we need to respond to the special challenge to help talented students think intelligently and profoundly, rather than superficially, about moral questions. We need to support their efforts to act on their own convictions, rather than surrender to the tyranny of others' opinions. Discussions of "moral dilemmas" in literature, history, or science allow gifted children to reason through difficult issues and develop clear values based on a thorough examination of the problem and consideration of how it affects the people involved. But teaching models are not enough. It is in real-life circumstances that children unravel moral dilemmas. Paul Tillich perhaps said it best:

Morality for ordinary people is not the result of reading books and writing papers, as we're doing. Morality is not a subject; it is a life put to the test in dozens of moments. Morality and social class—that is a subject for us, an important one. For ordinary people it's not a subject; it's life affecting the views of people every day. (Quoted in Coles 1986, p. 16)

Perhaps we can learn from children rather than from books and statistics, paradigms and patterns, as Coles learned from the young black girl in the South. They may surprise us with their searing moral insight, sense of justice, compassion, and intuitive response to others' distresses. Perhaps we have blinded ourselves to the moral capacities of gifted children because of our preoccupation with technical brilliance and material success. By emphasizing achievement, we have forced children to relinquish the best part of themselves to suit our fancy. We have separated their heads from their hearts, and now suddenly we have changed our minds. Children should have hearts after all. Perhaps we need moral education, too.

CONCLUSIONS AND RECOMMENDATIONS

It is well known that educational issues and trends follow a cyclical or pendulum shift pattern. Programs are emphasized and well funded for a time and then tend to fall out of favor with the public and the funding sources. We believe that gifted education is at such a turning point.

In the 1970s and early 1980s, federal and state funds were widely available to support innovative educational programs. Gifted education gained recognition and interest among parents, educators, and governmental funding sources. Gifted programs were added to school districts all over the country. Some of these programs were carefully planned, implemented, and evaluated over the years. They have both consistency and flexibility: a consistent set of underlying principles and definitions and a flexible evaluation system that allows for growth and change. These programs are well supported by the entire school community.

Other programs were hastily planned and implemented. Evaluations have been patchy and inconclusive. These programs have little or no consistency. Their definitions and goals are very general and ambiguous, and their principles cannot be readily articulated. Paradoxically, however, these programs seem rigid rather than flexible. Defensive administrators tend to rigidly defend whatever element of the program is being questioned or criticized by outsiders.

In recent years, federal and state educational funds have been scarce. Programs that serve special needs and subpopulations, such as gifted education does, have had to generate other supplementary means of support. Still, the momentum for gifted education has continued in most states at a level that supports continued services.

But troubling questions about the ultimate value and worth of gifted programs threaten to reduce their status and financial support as we enter the 1990s and the twenty-first century. Are the "right" children being served? Are the services they receive having any real, measurable effects on their lives? Do the troubling side effects of gifted programs outweigh the positive effects?

It will not help our efforts to hide from these issues. Defensive postures can only serve to cause increased threat and a gradual or sudden decline in support. In this book, we have tried to examine our field in an open-minded fashion. We have presented the strengths and the weaknesses of present-day program planning strategies, identification systems, curriculum goals, and evaluation efforts.

We entitled this book *A Thoughtful Overview of Gifted Education* because we intended to provoke our readers into undertaking, along with us, a thoughtful, questioning reexamination of the many issues that are an integral part of gifted education. If we've succeeded, you have reflected upon and discussed the questions we raised with widely different viewpoints expressed among members of your class. If we've succeeded, you've raised new questions that we didn't think of. And if we've succeeded, you see that your role as a teacher or administrator in gifted education is far more complex than it looked before. Perhaps you expected that this book would provide you with a set of specific suggestions for planning and implementing a gifted program. But we haven't provided you with any easy answers or solutions because there aren't any.

Instead, we hope that you'll join us in a search for meaning and purpose in gifted education. We hope that you'll contribute a new way of dealing with one of these challenging issues, so that gifted education can thrive and children will continue to receive educational services that inspire and challenge them to discover and fulfill their infinite potential.

OPPORTUNITIES FOR DISCUSSION AND ACTION

1. Look at your own school. Does your school offer career education that specifically encourages talented children to investigate and pursue their interests?

2. What specific problems do talented children have in making career choices? How early should children start exploring interests that may eventually lead to career development?

3. Do schools, in your opinion, steer talented children away from certain fields, such as industrial arts, architecture, and home arts? How do you account for this?

4. Consider ways that talented children could work on-site on actual problems currently prevalent in various fields. Pretend for the moment that you have unlimited resources with which to plan your academic year. Explore a variety of options in integrating subject matter with field experience for able children. Be imaginative and innovative in your planning!

5. Is there a difference between morals/values education and indoctrination? What is it? In what ways does indoctrination undermine the moral development of children? In what ways can morals/values education help children to escape the "moral relativism" that many today see as an inevitable consequence of the moral vacuum of the 1980s?

6. How does our understanding of children's development of values and morals misinform our actions? Observe children together in various settings.

Do you notice the operation of any moral code or principle? While you do this, also be aware of your assumption of the children's moral state. What are you expecting to see? How do you think Kohlberg's scheme of moral development has affected parent and teacher expectations? How has Gilligan provided an alternative way of assessing the value system of girls?

7. Do you think that some provision should exist for children gifted in the area of moral development, metaphysical insight, intuition, and feeling? Why do you suppose this area has seldom been touched in gifted education? On what basis would a Gandhi be considered talented? Who are individuals representative of this talent area who have contributed greatly to humankind's development?

REFERENCES

Alschuler, A. S. 1982. *Values, concepts and techniques.* Washington, D.C.: National Education Association.

Anderson, T. S. 1982. Real-world science, *Science Teacher,* May, pp. 41–43.

Baker, R. 1987. Restore ethics as partner to intellect, *Christian Science Monitor,* January 30.

Black, B. 1988. Abolish work: Workers of the world, relax, *Utne Reader,* July–August, pp. 48–56.

Christian Science Monitor. 1984. Sixth grader cools the high jinks and settles down to writing plays. May 7, p. 44.

Colby, A. 1975. Two approaches to moral education. In *Moral education . . . It comes with the territory,* ed. D. Purpel and K. Ryan. Berkeley, Calif.: McCutchan Publishing Corp.

Coles, R. 1986. *The moral life of children.* Boston: Atlantic Monthly Press.

Colson, S. 1980. The evaluation of community-based career education program for gifted and talented students as an administrative model for an alternative program, *Gifted Child Quarterly* 24 (no. 3): 101–8.

Edwards, C. P., and P. G. Ramsey. 1986. *Promoting social and moral development in young children.* New York: Teachers College Press.

Gilligan, C. 1979. Woman's place in man's life cycle. In *The hidden curriculum and moral education,* ed. H. Giroux and D. Purpel. Berkeley, Calif.: McCutchan Publishing Corp.

Goleman, D. 1988. High IQ may not make you a genius at life. *Chicago Tribune,* May 6.

Gustafson, R. A. 1979. *Vocational exploration and career development for the gifted and talented in Vermont.* Montpelier, Vt.: Vermont Department of Education.

Hagen, J. C. 1982. Career education for the gifted and talented: An analysis of issues and programs, *Career Education,* November, pp. 48–57.

Hollinger, C. L. 1983. Self-perception and the career aspirations of mathematically talented female adolescents, *Journal of Vocational Behavior* 22: 49–62.

Hoyt, K. B., and J. R. Hebeler. 1974. *Career education for gifted and talented students.* Salt Lake City: Olympus Publishing Co.

Kamil, C. 1984. Autonomy: The aim of education envisioned by Piaget, *Phi Delta Kappan,* February, pp. 410–15.

Kerr, B. A. 1981. *Career education for the gifted and talented.* Columbus, Ohio: Clearinghouse on Adult, Career, and Vocational Education.

Kirschenbaum, H. 1976. Clarifying values clarification: Some theoretical issues. In *Moral education. . . It comes with the territory,* ed. D. Purpel and K. Ryan. Berkeley, Calif.: McCutchan Publishing Corp.

Kohlberg, L. 1975. *Collected papers on moral development and moral education.* Cambridge, Mass.: Moral Education and Research Foundation.

Kristol, I. 1974. Moral and ethical development in a democratic society. In *Moral education . . . It comes with the territory,* ed. D. Purpel and K. Ryan. Berkeley, Calif.: McCutchan Publishing Corp.

Lewis, A. C. 1988. Change is coming to vocational education, *Phi Delta Kappan* 69: 628–29.

Lippmann, W. 1929. *A preface to morals.* New York: Macmillan.

Lockwood, A. L. 1975. A critical view of values clarification. In *Moral education . . . It comes with the territory,* ed. D. Purpel and K. Ryan. Berkeley, Calif.: McCutchan Publishing Corp.

Mahaffey, N. L. 1987. 15-year-old makes grade in taxing field. *Chicago Sun Times,* April 8, p. 44.

Maker, C. J. 1982. *Teaching models in education of the gifted.* Rockville, Md.: Aspen Systems Corp.

Marquand, R. 1987. *Moral education: Has "values neutrality" left students adrift? Christian Science Monitor,* Educational Pullout Section, January 30.

Miller, Alice. 1981. *The drama of the gifted child.* (Translated by Ruth Ward) New York: Basic Books.

Milne, B. G. 1982. *Vocational education for gifted and talented students.* Columbus, Oh.: National Center for Research in Vocational Education, Ohio State University.

——, and K. J. Lindekugel. 1976. *Vocational education: An opportunity for the gifted and the talented students.* Vermillion, S. Dak.: Educational Research and Service Center, The University of South Dakota.

Moore, B. A. 1978. Career education for disadvantaged, gifted high school students, *Gifted Child Quarterly* 22 (no. 3): 332–37.

Nash, W. R., C. Borman, and S. Colson. 1980. Career education for gifted and talented students: A senior high school model, *Exceptional Children* 46 (no. 5): 404–5.

Paul, R. W. 1988. Ethics without indoctrination, *Educational Leadership,* May, pp. 10–19.

Post-Kammer, P., and P. Perrone. 1983. Career perceptions of talented individuals: A follow-up study, *Vocational Guidance Quarterly* March, 203–11.

Purpel, D., and K. Ryan, eds. 1976. *Moral education . . . It comes with the territory.* Berkeley, Calif.: McCutchan Publishing Corp.

Raths, L. E. 1976. Freedom, intelligence, and valuing. In *Values, concepts and techniques,* ed. A. Alschuler. Washington, D. C.: National Education Association.

Smutny, J. 1982. *Job creation: Adult, vocational and technical education.* Illinois State Board of Education.

Stewart, J. S. 1975. Problems and contradictions of values clarification. In *Moral education . . . It comes with the territory,* ed. D. Purpel and K. Ryan. Berkeley, Calif.: McCutchan Publishing Corp.

Tan-Willman, C., and D. Gutteridge. 1981. Creative thinking and moral reasoning of academically gifted secondary school adolescents, *Gifted Child Quarterly* 25 (no. 4): 149–52.

Torrance, E. P. 1980. Growing up creatively gifted: A 22-year longitudinal study, *Creative Child and Adult Quarterly* 5 (no. 3): 148–59.

———. 1983. The importance of falling in love with something, *Creative Child and Adult Quarterly* 8 (no. 2): 72–78.

Vallance, E. 1973. Hiding the hidden curriculum: An interpretation of the language of justification in nineteenth century educational reform. In *The hidden curriculum and moral education,* ed. H. Giroux and D. Purpel. Berkeley, Calif.: McCutchan Publishing Corp.

Watson, J. 1988. Literature and moral growth in children, *Education Week* (no. 28): 36.

Welch, F. G. 1988. The continuing need for vocational education, *Education Week* 7 (no. 27): 32.

Wilson, S. 1982. A new decade: The gifted and career choice, *Vocational Guidance Quarterly,* September, pp. 53–59.

Yeatts, E. H. 1980. The professional artist: A teacher for the gifted, *Gifted Child Quarterly* 24 (no. 3): 133–37.

Zorman, R. 1987. The residential high school for excellence in the arts and in the sciences— A unique experimental model, *Roeper Review* 10 (no. 1): 5–9.

Index

ABDA [Abbreviated Binet for the Disadvantaged], 119, 120

Ability: and achievement, 131–132; and assessment instruments, 63; and creativity, 46; and definition of giftedness, 12, 104, 106; and the development/endowment controversy, 20; general intellectual, 4–5, 63, 72, 94–95, 101; and group intelligence tests, 64, 68–72; and identification, 63, 101, 104, 106, 107; and minority students, 120. *See also name specific assessment instrument*

"Able learners", 35, 143–144

Academic achievement/aptitude, 4–5, 63, 72–78, 94, 154. *See also name of specific assessment instrument*

Accelerated curriculum, 165–169, 181–183

Achenbach, T. M., 132

Achievement: and ability, 131–132; aptitude compared with, 72; and assessment, 63; and careers, 210; and curriculum issues, 167; and cutoff scores, 73; and the development/endowment controversy, 34–35; and goals, 12; and group intelligence tests, 68–72; and identification, 6, 61–62, 63, 72–78, 95, 101–102; and individual differences, 72; and inferiority feelings, 12; and labeling, 34–35, 73; and morals/values, 220; as a need, 30–31; and norms/percentiles of tests, 72–73, 74; objectivity/subjectivity of, 73; and parents, 24, 131; and persistence, 12; purpose of tests for, 72; and self-confidence, 12; and states of mind, 28–29; and teachers' observations, 131. *See also* Academic achievement/aptitude; Underachievement; *name of specific assessment instrument*

Administrative program models, 143–149

Affective domain, 80, 157, 172–173, 174

Aloneness/solitariness, 33, 56–57, 154, 210

Alpha Biographical Inventory, 119

Aptitude, 64, 65, 68–72, 112, 178. *See also* Academic achievement/aptitude

Art, 4–5, 63, 80, 155. *See also name of specific assessment instrument or program*

Arthur Point Scale of Performance Tests, 119

Artists-in-Schools Program, 213

Assessment: of academic achievement, 72–78; of creativity, 47–48, 78–82; of gifted behaviors, 84–86; needs, 198–201. *See also* Assessment instruments; Evaluation; *name of specific instrument or type of evaluation*

Assessment instruments, 62, 63–68, 79, 94, 100, 102, 199. *See also name of specific instrument or characteristic being assessed*

Association of Black Psychologists, 118–119

Attitudes, 29–33, 43–44, 49–50

"Back to basics" movement, 216–217

Baker, Robert, 216

Baldwin, A. Y., 121

Barron, F., 56–57

Barstow, D., 120

Beggs, D., 70–71

Behavior, 10, 45–47, 55, 64, 153–155. *See also* Gifted behavior

Behavioral checklists, 154–155

"Beyond Theory: Math and Science Related to Industry and Community" [program], 136

Bilingual education, 120, 121–122, 123–124

Binet, Alfred, 6–7, 14, 22

BITCH [Black Intelligence Test of Cultural Homogeneity], 119

Bloom, Benjamin S.: and the characteristics of gifted people, 12, 23; and creativity, 44, 106; as a developmentalist, 11, 23, 24–25, 35; and gifted behavior, 174, 177; and higher-level thinking, 174; and identification, 106, and IQ, 23, 153; and the nature/nurture controversy, 11, 23, 24–25, 35; and self-awareness, 111; taxonomy of, 44, 71, 170–171, 174, 177; and teaching styles, 24–25

Brain growth, 19, 26, 27–28

Burt, Cyril, 21

California Achievement Test [CAT], 76

Callahan, C., 86

Careers, 207–215. *See also name of specific assessment instrument*

Carson, R., 42

Renzulli (cont.)
    46; and the compacting curricu-
    lum, 167; and creativity, 12, 46;
    and the definition of giftedness,
    12, 85, 97, 104, 106; and the En-
    richment Triad, 12, 118–179, 182,
    183; and gifted behavior, 12, 14,
    86, 177; and identification, 95–96,
    97, 104, 106, 107; and Revolving
    Door Identification, 14, 95–96,
    104, 106, 183; and Summer Gifted
    Confratute, 195–196; and talent
    characteristics, 120; and work
    samples, 177
Resnick, Lauren, 174
Resolution of Conflict Strategy
    [Taba], 218
Restak, R., 26
Results-oriented evaluation, 191–192
Retesting, 65, 77
Revolving Door Identification Model
    [Renzulli], 14, 95–96, 104, 106,
    183
Rewards, 30–31, 47, 50, 218, 219
Richardson [Sid W.] Foundation/
    Study, 5–6, 35, 143–144, 148, 166,
    181–183
Rimm, Sylvia, 34, 50, 79, 80, 131
Risk taking, 46, 78, 79, 80
Ritter, Margaret Hill, 212
Rockford, Illinois, 159–160
Roe, A., 12
Rogers, C., 42, 47
Role models/mentors, 136, 215
Roodey, Thomas J., 80
Ross Test of Higher Cognitive Proc-
    esses, 71

Sactucit, Joseph, 78
Sadker, Myra and David, 134
Samuda, R. J., 119
Sandberg, Kate, 173–174
Saturday learning experiences, 145,
    149–152
Scales for Rating Behavioral Charac-
    teristics of Gifted Children, 86
Scholastic Aptitude Tests, 167
School Ability Index, 69
Schools, 49–54, 133, 216
Science, 75, 130–138, 211, 212. See
    also name of specific assessment
    instrument or program
Science Research Associates Achieve-
    ment Test [SRA], 75
Screening Assessment for Gifted Ele-
    mentary Students [SAGES], 82–
    83
Scriven, Michael, 189–190, 192, 195,
    201
Scruggs, T. E., 122

Seashore Measure of Musical Tal-
    ents, 78
Self-actualization, 31, 41–42
Self-concept/acceptance, 31–33, 42–
    43, 208
Self-confidence, 12, 29–33, 42–43, 80
Self-directed learning, 179
Self-direction, 80
Self-evaluation, 46–47, 111, 112, 179
Sense of humor, 80, 154
SEOE [California], 125
Sequential Tests of Educational
    Progress [STEP], 75
Shakeshaft, Carol, 133
Sisk, Dorothy, 120
Situational problems/tests, 105–107
Skill/technique, 42–43
Slosson Intelligence Test, 67
Smith, J., 70–71
Smith, L., 86
Smutny, Joan: and careers, 211–212,
    213–214; and creativity, 50–51,
    53; and gifted behavior, 96, 183;
    and minority students, 120–121,
    125; and program evaluation, 196;
    and stereotyping, 135–136. See
    also Project '86, '87, and '88
Social studies. See name of specific
    assessment instrument
SOI Gifted Screening Form, 83
SOI-LA [Structure of the Intellect—
    Learning Abilities], 69, 119
Solitariness. See Aloneness
SOMPA [the System of Multicultural
    Pluralistic Assessment], 119
Spearman, Charles, 21, 22
Special class model, 6, 147–148, 158
Special school model, 148–149
Specific Academic Aptitudes, 95,
    101, 109
Spelling. See name of specific assess-
    ment instrument
Spontaneity, 42–43
Staff meetings, 196
Stakeholders. See Program evalua-
    tion
Standardized tests. See Assessment
    instruments; Testing; name of
    specific type of test or program
Stanford Achievement Test, 76
Stanford-Binet Intelligence Test, 7, 8,
    9, 21, 64, 65–66, 67, 154
Stanley, Julian, 166, 167
State government, 5, 94, 199, 201,
    220
Stein, Morris I., 8, 47–48
Stereotyping, 130, 133, 135–136, 137,
    208, 209, 211, 212
Sternberg, Robert, 9, 10–11, 14, 100
Stockard, J., 132

Structure of the Intellect theory
    [Guilford], 9, 44, 69, 112, 119
Students and program evaluation,
    154, 189–190
Study of Mathematically Talented
    Youth, 166
Study of Verbally Gifted Youth, 166
Success, 96–97, 206–207, 208
Summer Gifted Confratute [Ren-
    zulli], 195–196
Summer programs, 149–152, 195–196
Superbaby syndrome, 158
Swartz, Robert, 173

Taba, Hilda, 218
Talent, 95, 119
Taxonomy: Bloom's, 44, 71, 170–
    171, 174, 177
Taylor, Calvin, 104
Teachers: and academic achievement,
    72; and attitudes, 49–50; and ca-
    reers, 215; and creativity, 49–54;
    and the definition of giftedness,
    104; and early childhood gifted ed-
    ucation, 154, 155; and gifted be-
    havior, 112; importance of, 35, 49;
    as master teachers, 25, 35; and mi-
    nority students, 120, 121; as nur-
    turers, 24, 35; observations/rec-
    ommendations of, 6, 72, 84–85,
    94–95, 104, 112, 120, 121, 131,
    154, 155; and program design, 142;
    selection/training of, 143, 153; as
    specialists, 24–25, 35; and team
    teaching, 153. See also Teaching
    styles; name of specific assessment
    instrument, program, or program
    design
Teaching styles, 24–25, 35
Technique and creativity, 42–43
Terman, Lewis M., 7, 8–9, 12, 14, 21,
    111, 118, 132–133. See also Stan-
    ford-Binet Intelligence Test
Test of Cognitive Skills [TCS], 69–70
Test of Creative Potential [TCP], 81
Test of General Ability, 119
Testing: as a biased system, 118, 119;
    and curriculum issues, 167; and
    early childhood gifted education,
    153–155; emphasis on, 117–118;
    and identification, 101, 121, 153–
    155; and minority students, 22,
    117, 118–119, 121; and the validity
    of tests, 8, 104, 117–118. See also
    Assessment instruments; name of
    specific type of test or program
Tests in Print [Mitchell], 62, 63
Test of Standard Written English,
    167
Thinking Creatively in Action and
    Movement [TCAM], 78, 81, 154